GULLS: A GUIDE TO IDENTIFICATION

GULLS

A Guide to Identification

by P. J. GRANT

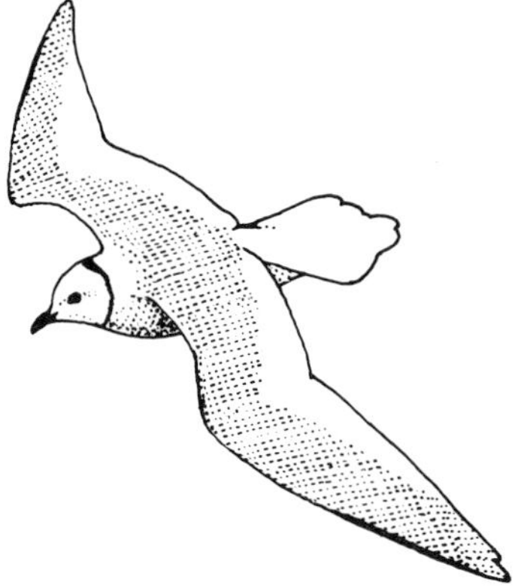

Illustrated by the author

SECOND EDITION

T & A D POYSER
London

ISBN 0 85661 044 5

Published by T & A D Poyser Ltd
24-28 Oval Road, London NW1 7DX

First edition 1982
Second Edition 1986
Reprinted 1989, 1997

A catalogue record for this book is available from the British Library

Text set in 9/10½pt Linotron 202 Plantin, printed and bound at The Bath Press

This book is printed on acid-free paper

Contents

Photographs

Introduction to the first edition

Gulls are widely abundant; they are relatively large, comparatively approachable, and are often slow-flying. They thus provide ample opportunity for close study, unequalled by other groups of birds. It is possible to observe the timing and progress of their moults, the effects of wear and fading on their plumage, and the changes in appearance brought about by these factors. The topography of their plumage can be closely studied, and the various groups of feathers and their arrangement in different postures can be distinguished. Distance and changed light conditions affect their colour tones, and partly subjective criteria such as size, structure and flight action are important in their identification. They are prone to hybridity and plumage abnormalities such as leucism and albinism. In fact, they demonstrate an almost complete range of factors which, with proper interpretation, are relevant to the identification of most other birds. Competence in identifying and ageing gulls can provide an invaluable foundation for competence in bird identification generally. I recommend gull-watching to beginner and expert birdwatcher alike: gulls provide a test-bed for identification skills at all levels of experience.

However, standard field guides do not adequately cover the complexities of identifying and ageing gulls. This situation prompted the publication of a series of five papers dealing with the field identification of west Palearctic gulls in the monthly journal *British Birds* (71: 145–176; 72: 142–182; 73: 113–158; 74: 111–142 and 74: 363–394). This book is an enlarged and much revised version of those papers, with many new and additional photographs: it deals with the 23 species of gulls (about half the world total) which occur in Europe, the Middle East, and eastern North America.

The ability to recognise the age of an individual immature is just as important as specific identification. It is a challenge in its own right to the serious bird-identifier, but it is also of value in studies of population, distribution and migration. Indeed, identification and ageing go hand-in-hand, for it is only by practising his skills on common species—of all ages—that an observer will acquire the degree of familiarity necessary for the confident identification of the occasional rarity.

Introduction to the second edition

Interest in gull identification continues to increase. This has led to a great deal of new information, which I have tried to incorporate in this second edition. Hardly a page of the original text remains unchanged, and most of the species drawings and nearly all of the distribution maps have been improved. The amendments in some cases involve small refinements or add extra minor detail to the text or illustrations, but most of them are substantial and important. Also, the General Information section has been expanded, the texts for Ring-billed Gull and Audouin's Gull in particular have been extensively rewritten, an expanded treatment and revised discussion of the geographical variation of Herring Gull is included, as well as completely new sections dealing with the subspecies of Common Gull and with the distinctive subspecies of Iceland Gull which breeds in northeast Canada *L. g. kumlieni* (Kumlien's Iceland Gull).

The major new feature of this second edition, however, is the addition of Group Seven, dealing with eight extra species which occur on the west coast of Canada and the USA: this means that all species and distinctive subspecies which occur regularly in the whole of North America are now covered. The number of photographs of species in Groups One to Six has been increased from 376 to 465, including 207 new ones, with an additional 79 photographs of the new Group Seven species, giving a total of 544.

Suggested amendments to the text, illustrations or maps, or new photographs which improve upon or add to those already included, would be welcomed for possible inclusion in future editions of this book. They should be sent to P. J. Grant, 14 Heathfield Road, Ashford, Kent TN24 8QD, England, or c/o T. & A. D. Poyser Ltd.

Acknowledgements to the first edition

The large and enthusiastic response to appeals for information and photographs for this project has made this book much more complete than would otherwise have been the case, and I am greatly indebted to all those who have contributed.

The photographs published here are a selected fraction of those received, which in total have provided an invaluable source of reference. I am particularly grateful to Dr Richard Chandler, M. D. Gallagher, Peter M. Harris, Dr Pamela Harrison, E. J. Mackrill and Norman van Swelm, who provided an exceptional number of photographs, taken mostly with this project especially in mind: EJM's expertly analysed field notes and priceless portraits of Franklin's Gull from breeding and wintering areas prompted extensive revisions of the original text for that species, and provided confirmation of its atypical moults which have previously not been fully described. Jeffery Boswall, R. A. Hume and Bernard King have been regular correspondents, supplying many useful leads and much literature and information. Gull skins at the British Museum (Natural History), Tring, have been an essential reference: I thank the staff for their ready assistance during my frequent visits. Descriptions of rare gulls on the files of the *British Birds* Rarities Committee have been a most useful reference: I thank the observers who submitted them and Michael J. Rogers, the Committee's secretary, for making them available to me.

I thank I. J. Ferguson-Lees, P. F. Bonham and the other members of the *British Birds* editorial board for much constructive criticism and advice during the initial planning of the series of papers in that journal, especially the present managing editor Dr J. T. R Sharrock for his substantial encouragement and assistance during its preparation and publication. I am especially grateful to H. A. R. Cawkell who, by his sound advice, started my interest in gulls, and to R. E Scott from whose expertise I greatly benefited during my initial studies of gull plumages.

The enormous debt owed to Jonathan Dwight and his classic monograph *The Gulls of the World* (1925) is readily acknowledged: his work remains an essential reference for gull enthusiasts after more than half a century.

For their provision of photographs, information, advice, opinions, criticisms and various assistance, I sincerely thank the following:

F. G. H. Allen, R. Allison, T. B. Ardamatskaya, Keith Atkin, S. Baines, D. Banks, R. Barber, John Barlee, Bengt Bengtsson, Arnoud B. van den Berg, R. Bijlsma, T. E. Bond, J. B. & S. Bottomley, Dr W. R. P. Bourne, T. E. Bowley, Alan Brady, E. A. Bragin, D. J. Britton, P. L. Britton, A. Brown, R. Burridge, G. P. Catley, P. Chadder, M. L. Chalmers, S. Chapman, John W. Chardine, J. Charman, R. A. Cheke, C. Clark, William S. Clark, J. R. Clarkson, B. M. Clarkson, J. Chardine, R. H. Charlwood, P. Clement, D. L. Clugston, M. Coath, R. K. Coles, S. G. D. Cook, R. Coomber, D. M. Cottridge, Dennis Coutts, Stanley Cramp, J. G. Cranfield, A. J. Croucher, L. J. Davenport, M. Davenport, M. Davies, N. R. Davies, G. Davis, Tom Davis, A. R. Dean, I. Dawson, M. Densley, Dr P. Devillers, Wendy Dickson, F. Dixon, P. A. Doherty, G. van Duin, Jon Dunn, P. J. Dunn, J. N. Dymond, J. Elmelid, F. Erhardt, D. Emley, Davis Finch, Crispin Fisher, G. H. Fisher, P. R. Flint, A. Forsyth, T. Francis, R. Frankum, R. A. Frost, R. Frost, J. R. Furse, E. F. J. Garcia, Frank B. Gill, Dr Peter Gloe, P. D. Goriup, M. Gosselin, P. Grandjean, P. J. Greenhalf, A. J. Greenland, P. Gregory, Harold E. Grenfell, J. Haapala, S. Hahn, D. M. Hanford, M.

Hario, Dr M. P. Harris, S. Harris, W. G. Harvey, D. M. Hawker, Brian Hawkes, P. de Heer, Stellan Hedgren, P. Helo, R. Higson, W. R. Hirst, R. N. Hobbs, R. H. Hogg, A. J. Holcombe, M. A. Hollingworth, S. Holohan, R. A. Hughes, B. Hulbert, D. B. Hunt, E. J. van IJzendoorn, V. Iljashenko, T. P. Inskipp, H. Insley, Eric Isakson, F. H. Jansen, J. V. Jenson, E. de Juana, T. Källqvist, A. Keppler, Jan Kihlman, P. K. Kinnear, J. Kist, A. A. Kistchinski, Alan Kitson, P. de Knijff, A. J. Knystautas, Dr Brigitte Königstedt, Dr D. Königstedt, A. F. Kovshaz, J. van der Laan, Lars Larsson, L. A. Laidler, Lasse J. Laine, C. S. Lawson, Paul Lehman, C. R. Linfoot, L. Lippens, S. C. Madge, W. & I. Makatsch, P. Maker, K. K. Malmström, E. L. Marchant, B. A. Marsh, E. Maugham, N. V. McCanch, A. McGeehan, B. S. Meadows, Piet Meeth, H. Meltofte, Kauri Mikkola, T. Milbled, J. Miller, Richard T. Mills, F. de Miranda, D. Moerbeek, Dr P. Monaghan, S. Moon, C. C. Moore, S. Mori, J. Moss, Killian Mullarney, Wim C. Mullié, Dr Irene Neufeldt, Gerry Nicholls, J. C. Nicholls, P. F. Nichols, P. Nicolau-Guillaumet, D. M. Norman, P. Oliver, Gerald J. Oreel, G. L. Ouweneel, M. J. Palmer, J. Palmgren, E. N. Panov, M. Parker, T. Parmenter, K. Pellow, P. Perry, T. Pettay, U. Pfaendler, Jeff Pick, René Pop, Richard Porter, Peter W. Post, A. J. Prater, E. S. & S. R. D. da Prato, J. G. Prins, P. Puhjo, Dr M. N. Rankin, V. Ree, G. H. Rees, J. F. Reynolds, P. Richardson, J. De Ridder, A. H. Rider, Don Roberson, A. Roberts, N. Rogers, S. Rooke, Will Russell, J. Seeviour, T. Shiota, J. C. Sinclair, M. Sinden, V. D. Siokhin, H. B. Skjelstad, D. Smallshire, Donald A. Smith, P. William Smith, R. Smith, J. B. Steeves, P. Steyn, E. Stirling, Ralph Stokoe, P. J. Strangeman, M. P. Sutherland, Lars Svensson, M. E. Taylor, Jean Terschuren, D. Thomas, P. Tomkovitch, Gerald Tuck, N. Tucker, Laurel A. Tucker, V. Tucker, Bobby Tulloch, R. E. Turley, David & Katie Urry, J. van Impe, J. M. Varela, Richard Vaughan, P. Vines, K. E. Vinicombe, E. de Visser, J. Visser, M. A. Voinstvensky, Prof. Dr K. H. Voous, D. I. M. Wallace, F. E. Warr, A. Wassink, C. E. Wheeler, A. Williams, Ian Willis, M. B. Withers, P. Yésou, B. Zonfrillo, V. A. Zubakin and L. Zykova.

Acknowledgements to the second edition

I am indebted to many people for their contributions towards this second edition. I am especially grateful to Per Alström, Raymond Henson, W. (Ted) Hoogendoorn and Killian Mullarney for their extensive and very useful comments on various parts of the first edition, which have resulted in many improvements and much new information. WH also assisted greatly with revisions to the section dealing with subspecies of Herring Gull, with the result that the published version is much more thorough than would have been the case without his help. The photographs are a vital part of this book, and I thank all the photographers who have contributed their work. Dr Richard Chandler and E. J. Mackrill have once again provided a very large number of pictures, as also have Arnoud B. van den Berg, Paul Doherty, Urban Olsson, David W. Sonneborn and Richard E. Webster, and I am especially indebted to them. Jon Dunn, Ronald E. Goetz, Paul Lehman, Guy McCaskie and Phoebe Snetsinger have commented extensively on parts or all of the first draft of the text for Group Seven, dealing with the west coast North American species: the published version has benefited greatly from their expertise, for which I am most grateful. JD also arranged the collection of many of the photographs of Group Seven species, and I sincerely thank him and the photographers for their assistance. Will Russell's expertise has assisted this project, and he has helped in several other ways, not least by providing travel opportunities (as a tour leader for Wings Inc) which have indirectly enabled me to study such species as Red-legged Kittiwake and Slaty-backed Gull in the field: I am especially grateful to him.

For their provision of photographs, information, advice, opinions, criticisms and various assistance, I also sincerely thank the following:

S. Asker, Keith Atkin, Takao Baba, Louis R. Bevier, Rick Blom, Alan & Juliet Bloss, Jeffery Boswall, J. B. & S. Bottomley, Alan Brady, Jean Brandt, H. Bruns, Graham Bundy, Martin Cade, I. Castle, B. Cave, Carl-H. Christiansson, Erik Christopherson, William S. Clark, T. R. Cleeves, Dr D. B. Collinge, David M. Cottridge, Dennis Coutts, C. Cummings, W. H. Dady, H. Darrow, R. H. Day, A. H. Davis, M. Densley, Pierre Devillers, Philippe J. Dubois, P. J. Dunn, J. N. Dymond, K. J. Eigenhuis, G. Ekström, M. J. Everett, M. Forsberg, D. Forsman, I. Forsyth, M. D. Gallagher, Kimball L. Garrett, J. Gaskell, Paul Géroudet, Dr Peter Gloe, J. F. Graham, P. J. Greenhalf, B. J. M. Haase, Peter M. Harris, Stanley W. Harris, A. H. J. Harrop, P. C. Heathcote, K. W. Horton, R. A. Hume, H. Huneker, Dustin Huntington, S. C. Hutchings, F. H. Jansen, J. K. Jensen, E. de Juana, B. Kemp, Bernard King, Frank King, G. G. Koerkamp, Dr A. J. Kondratiev, Kenn Kaufman, P. G. Lansdown, H. J. Lehto, Tim Loseby, A. McGeehan, S. C. Madge, Gerald & Laurette Maisel, E. Meek, H. & M-L. Meeus, John Miller, E. Mills, Dirk Moerbeek, Jan Mogren, A. V. Moon, Colin Moore, Jan Mulder, D. Oelkers, K. M. Olsen, J. Palmgren, Knud Pedersen, P. Potts, S. R. D. da Prato, J. G. Prins, Raphael Vidal Quintana, D. Radford, T. Randla, Phil Ranson, A. Rider, Don Roberson, P. Rönnberg, E. F. Sangster, L. Schack-Nielsen, G. R. Shannon, James Smith, Rich Stallcup, P. Steyn, P. Strangeman, Lars Svensson, P. B. & C. A. Taylor, Brian Thomas, Stuart Tingley, J. Varela, B. Vercruysse, Phil Vines, K. E. Vinicombe, A. Wassink, F. J. Watson, Claudia Wilds, John F. Will, J. Wilson, Tom Wurster, D. Young and Steve Young.

General Information

A thorough understanding of the following general aspects of gull plumage will greatly clarify the seemingly complex field situation, and will provide the essential foundation for expertise in identifying and ageing gulls.

LENGTH OF IMMATURITY

The length of time taken for a gull to reach adult plumage is generally related to the size of the species—the smaller the gull, the shorter its period of immaturity. Most small species (eg Black-headed Gull or Bonaparte's Gull) become indistinguishable from the adult with the full acquisition of second-winter plumage (about 13–16 months after hatching), most medium-sized species (eg Common Gull or Ring-billed Gull) with third-winter plumage (about 25–28 months after hatching), and most large species (eg Herring Gull) with fourth-winter plumage (about 37–40 months after hatching. Fig. 1 shows the timing of moults and the sequence of plumages, from juvenile to adult, of typical small, medium-sized and large gulls. There are exceptions to this general rule; probably the majority of Little Gulls, for example, have readily distinguishable second-year plumages, and do not become fully adult until third-winter plumage is acquired (instead of second-winter as might be expected in view of the species' very small size). This and other exceptions and variations are fully described in the respective species accounts.

AGE TERMINOLOGY

The age terminology used in Fig. 1 is recommended for describing the age of an individual gull. It avoids the imprecision of such terms as 'immature' or 'sub-adult', which are unhelpfully used to describe individual gulls in many field guides and in records submitted to local bird reports. Even 'first-*year*' (instead of the more precise 'first-winter' or 'first-summer'), 'second-*year*' and so on are inadequate in late summer or autumn, since they do not indicate whether the individual has undertaken its autumn moult and, therefore, do not indicate whether it is at the beginning or end of its 'year'. When a gull is in a transitional stage of moult, it is useful to record this fact, eg 'first-summer moulting to second-winter'. In some cases, especially with immatures of the large species (as explained more fully in the introduction to Group Three on p. 78) it may not be possible to age individuals more precisely than, for example, 'second- or third-summer': in cases where the differences between winter and summer plumage are not well-marked, it may not even be possible to get closer than 'second- or third-year' or 'first-winter or -summer', although whether it is a summer or winter plumage will often be obvious, of course, from the month of observation.

The more general terms 'first-year' (referring to juvenile, first-winter and first-summer plumages together), 'second-year' (second-winter and second-summer), 'third-year' (third-winter and third-summer) and so on, may be used when referring to the general age groups of gulls.

This 'plumage-year' terminology should not be confused with 'calendar-year' terminology ie 'first calendar-year' (referring to individuals from fledging to 31st December of their hatching year), 'second calendar-year' (1st January to 31st December of the year after hatching) and so on. Use of calendar-year terminology is useful whenever precise plumage definition is unnecessary or not determinable.

Euring codes, used by ringers, are 3J (juvenile), 3 (first calendar-year, not juvenile), 5 (second calendar-year), 7 (third calendar-year) and so on (thus odd numbers for individuals of known age); and 2 (age unknown), 4 (at least second calendar-year), 6 (at least third calendar-year) and so on (thus even numbers for individuals for which the hatching year cannot be determined).

The term 'immature' refers to individuals in any plumage other than adult. Gulls occasionally breed in the immature summer plumage of the year prior to that in which they first acquire full adult summer plumage.

MOULT

The first moult of all gulls is the post-juvenile moult to first-winter plumage, which commences at or shortly after fledging. It is a partial moult, replacing the juvenile head and body feathers, and also an individually variable amount of coverts of the inner wing, reducing the extent of the dark carpal-bar of many small and medium-sized species. Subsequently, there is a regular sequence at all ages of two moults a year—a partial one in spring, and a complete one in autumn, apart from the two species which are exceptions to this rule, as noted later.

Spring moult: this is a partial moult replacing the head and body feathers, resulting in immature or adult summer plumage. On small and medium-sized species, this moult often also includes some or, rarely, most of the coverts of the inner wing (further reducing the extent of the carpal-bar), sometimes the tertials, and (especially on Little Gull, but also occasionally on some other small species) one or more pairs of central tail feathers (rarely the whole tail), causing a white gap in the otherwise complete dark tail band of first-summers.

Autumn moult: this is a complete moult, resulting in immature or adult winter plumage. Adults usually start the moult near the end of breeding activity; immatures begin the moult earlier. Large species can take as long as four or five months to complete this moult, whereas small species take four to six weeks, but there is much individual variation both in the duration of the moult and in the starting time. Some immature large gulls may start the moult as early as April, while some adults may not complete it until December or January. The moult dates given in the species accounts refer to the extreme dates between which active moult can be expected: most individuals will start and complete their moult within this period.

Broadly speaking, the moult of the primaries provides the yardstick by which the progress of the autumn moult is measured. The moult commences with the shedding of the innermost (10th) primary, and progresses outwards. The moult of the rest of the plumage takes place mainly within the period when the primaries are being renewed, so that the full growth of the outermost (1st) primary comes at or near the end of the moult. The rate of renewal of the primaries is slow, with usually only two or three adjacent feathers growing at any one time.

The secondaries and tail feathers are moulted in a much less regular pattern, and large gaps are often visible where groups of feathers have been shed simultaneously.

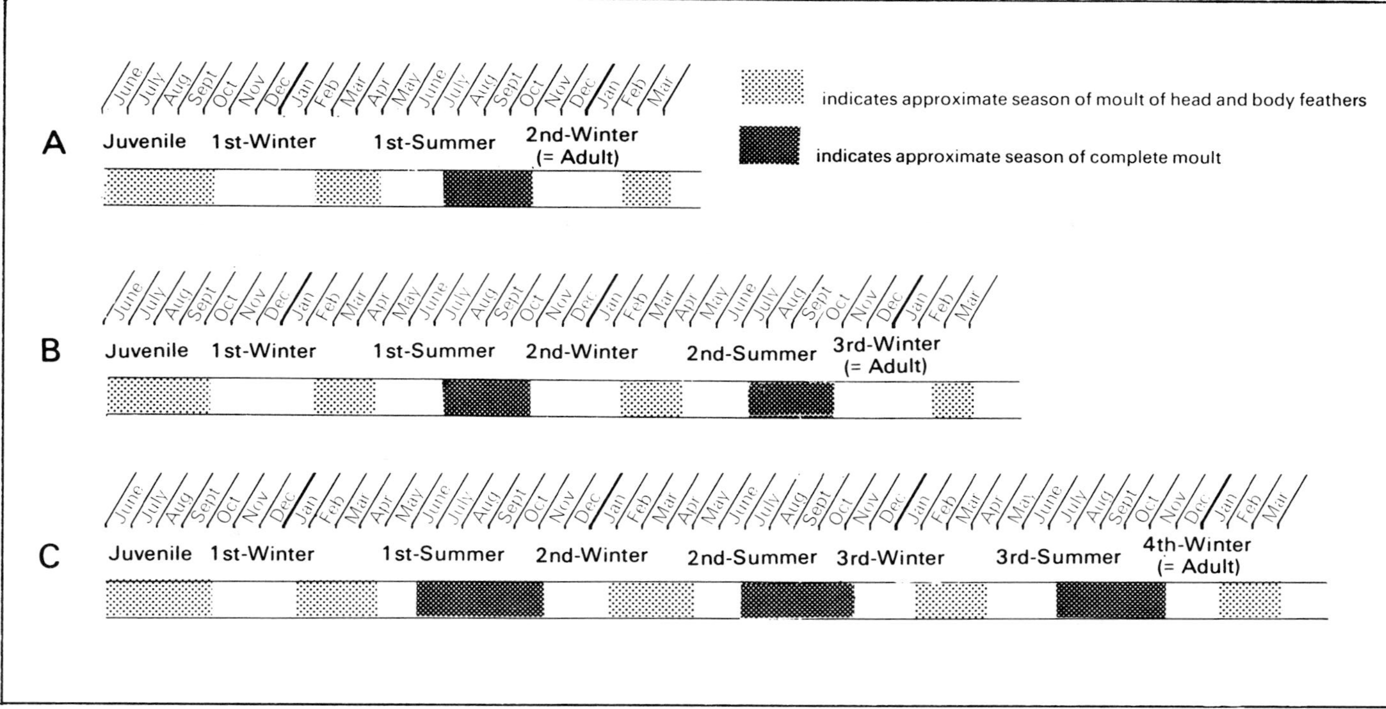

Fig. 1. Sequence of plumages and moults from juvenile to adult of typical small (A), medium (B) and large (C) gulls.

Wing coverts are shed in groups, revealing the whitish bases of the underlying feathers, producing whitish patches and lines on the upperwing in late summer and autumn, which are especially obvious on adults or near adults of species with a dark grey or blackish upperwing (eg as shown by the moulting Great Black-backed Gull in Photo 311).

Exceptions: two species covered in this book are exceptions to these general rules about the timing and extent of the spring and autumn moults. Sabine's Gull has a complete moult in spring, and a partial one in autumn (the reverse of the moult timing in other gulls), and juvenile plumage is retained throughout the first autumn, the post-juvenile moult not beginning until arrival on or near the wintering areas. Franklin's Gull has the usual post-juvenile moult, but subsequently has a complete moult in spring and another in autumn. The timing and extent of the moults of these two species are more fully discussed in the respective species accounts.

Miscellaneous: the outer primaries and tail feathers of juvenile gulls, which are retained throughout the first year, are rather pointed and rounded respectively. At subsequent ages (second-winter onwards), the outer primaries have more rounded tips and the tail feathers are rather square-ended. Although these differences are rarely discernible in the field, they are sometimes a useful clue to age in sharp photographs.

When a feather is lost accidentally, its replacement usually resembles that which would normally have grown at the next moult. Immatures with one or more replacement tail feathers are quite frequent, showing as a white break in the otherwise complete tail band.

Moult may be delayed or inhibited by sickness or injury. For no obvious reason, adult Black-headed Gull (and presumably also other hooded species) very rarely may have a full hood in mid-winter, or winter head pattern in mid-summer. There are also apparently very rare cases (eg for a Common Gull, *Brit. Birds* 75: 578–579) in which, for no obvious reason, the post-juvenile moult (presumably also other partial moults) does not take place: it seems best to regard such instances as extreme examples of the usual variable extent of these moults. Some large species (certainly Herring Gull and Great Black-backed Gull, and perhaps other large gulls), however, not infrequently retain a large part or all of their juvenile upperparts plumage well into or throughout their first winter. There are apparently no known cases (for gulls or any other species) where vagrancy alone has been the cause of aberrant moults, although a moult may well be delayed in cases where the end of migration (or the end of vagrant wanderings) is the trigger for a moult to commence.

WEAR AND FADING

The effects of wear and fading are always most obvious in spring and summer, when the wing and tail feathers are at their oldest, just before the complete autumn moult. White plumage is more prone to wear than dark, and the white tips and fringes may disappear completely. Brown plumage, especially the wing coverts of immatures, fades markedly with age, often to whitish; and black or blackish areas progressively fade browner. Fading of plumage is most marked on gulls which spend long periods in areas with long sunshine hours, and wear of plumage is especially marked when gulls frequent wide, sandy beaches, where their plumage is effectively sand-blasted on windy days. In areas where long sunshine hours and sand-blasting coincide, gulls—especially first-years—can show extreme wear and fading as they approach the complete autumn moult, as shown by the first-summer Ring-billed and Laughing Gulls in Photos 135 and 156, taken in Florida, USA in May.

By late summer or early autumn, when the wing and tail moult is under way, the mixture of faded and worn old feathers and complete and growing new ones often presents a most bedraggled appearance, especially on immatures, and produces wing patterns which may be unfamiliar. Further, while the outermost primaries are still growing, the wing-tip is more blunt or rounded than normal, and the wing-beat is quicker than usual until the full extent of the wing area is restored. It is impossible to illustrate the endless variations of wing pattern exhibited by gulls in wing moult, but their appearance can be visualised by comparing the wing patterns of the two adjacent ages involved. As an example, Fig. 2 shows some transitional wing patterns of a typical Mediterranean Gull moulting from first-summer to second-winter plumage.

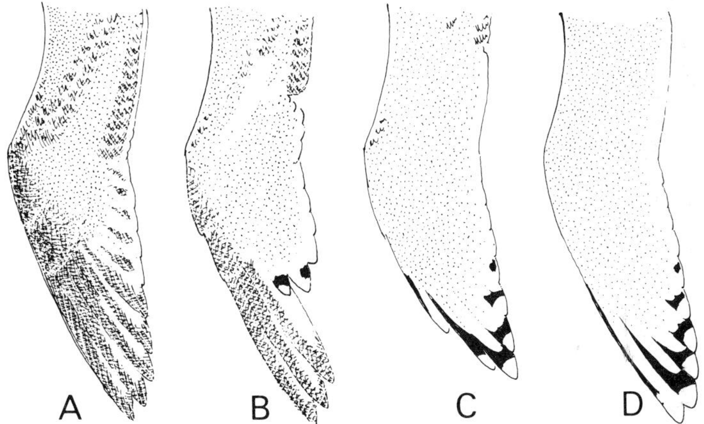

Fig. 2. Wing of **Mediterranean Gull** *Larus melanocephalus* in moult from first-summer to second-winter. (A) faded first-summer pattern immediately prior to start of moult; (B) moult half complete, inner four primaries new, 5th and 6th partially grown, 4th missing, 1st–3rd old; outer secondaries new, and white patches on inner wing indicating moult of coverts; (C) moult three-quarters complete, 1st and 2nd partially grown and held partially concealed by adjacent primaries; note that tips of outer primaries rounded in second-year (and subsequently), not pointed as in first-year; (D) fresh second-winter pattern.

COLOUR ABNORMALITIES

Albinism is not uncommon in gulls: single feathers, patches of plumage (often symmetrical on each side of the bird), or—rarely—the whole plumage, is white instead of the normal brown, grey or black. Lesser Black-backed Gulls (also more rarely Herring and Great Black-backed Gulls) with white patches of variable extent, usually symmetrical, on the wings (especially on the greater primary coverts) are of fairly regular occurrence (about one in every thousand adults). Definite examples of gulls which are true albinos (all-white plumage also with pink or pale-coloured bare parts lacking their normal pigmentation) are unknown to the author and are probably extremely rare. Rare cases of all-white albinistic gulls are therefore usually identifiable and ageable by their normal bare parts coloration as well as structure and size, although it should be noted that all-white plumage may give a false impression of shape (especially wing shape in flight) and—especially—size. All-white albinistic gulls are liable to be misidentified as Glaucous, Iceland or adult Ivory Gulls. For firm identification of the latter it is essential to note its distinctive bare parts coloration (especially its short, black legs), whilst Glaucous and Iceland Gulls (as more fully explained under 'Identification pitfalls' for those two species on p. 144) are never really all-white, although they may appear so at a distance.

Definite examples of leucistic gulls, on which the plumage colours are paler than usual giving a washed-out version of normal plumage, are rare: most claims of leucistic immature Herring Gulls, for example, are more likely to refer to Glaucous X Herring Gull hybrids. A few examples of leucistic Black-headed Gulls are known to the author. Melanism, too, is apparently very rare (no certain cases known to author), and in claimed cases of such (or other colour abnormalities) it is often difficult to certainly eliminate oil staining or contamination by other colorants as the cause.

Abnormal bare parts coloration occurs very rarely: two or three cases of adult Black-headed Gull (one also leucistic) and one of adult Laughing Gull, all with bright orange-red or bright crimson bill and legs instead of the normal dark red, are known to the author, as well as several examples of yellow, orange, pink or red leg colour on adult Kittiwakes (instead of the usual black).

PINK COLORATION

The pink coloration on some species of gulls (and terns), usually most prominent on adult summer plumage, is apparently not caused by feather pigmentation but is said to be the result of pink colorant contained in the preen-gland oil being coated onto the feathers during preening. The pink coloration may pervade all parts of the plumage, but shows up most on those areas, especially the underparts, which started out white when the feathers were newly grown. On non-hooded species, the head (which cannot be reached by the bill during preening) remains white or much less pink than the underparts. It is probable that diet and the degree of breeding condition affects the strength of the colorant in the preen-gland oil, and variation in these factors presumably results in individual variation in the strength of colour on 'pink gulls' such as Ross's and Slender-billed. Pale pink tones are often not evident at long range or in bright sunlight, and are best discerned at close range in overcast conditions. Pink coloration is usually brightest in adult summer plumage, but it is also often evident on 'pink' species in winter, suggesting that the degree of breeding condition is not the prime factor in producing the colorant in the preen-gland oil. Exceptionally, some individuals of normally non-pink or slightly pink species (such as Black-headed Gull) may be strongly pink-toned.

HOOD SHAPE

On those species which have a dark hood in summer, the shape and extent of the hood can provide useful specific differences (eg the hood of Mediterranean Gull extends much farther down the neck than on Black-headed Gull). Note, however, that the apparent shape and extent of the hood is affected by posture: when the head is hunched into the shoulders, the head feathers are compressed and the hood decreases in extent; when the neck is held erect, the hood assumes its full extent. The two extremes are well illustrated in two photographs of Mediterranean Gull—Photo 116 (hunched, with 'small' hood) and Photo 119 (neck erect, with full-extent hood).

JUDGING SIZE

Difference in size is among the important features for identifying some species, but making comparative size assessments can be much more difficult than is implied in most bird-identification literature. The difficulties are especially marked when the subject is standing (or especially when flying) on its own, with no other birds alongside for direct size comparison. There is also the potentially very misleading effect of 'size-illusion', as fully described and explained in *British Birds* 76: 327–334: size-illusion occurs whenever binoculars or telescopes are used, and makes farther objects look larger than they really are in comparison to nearer ones. Size-illusion can be easily demonstrated by looking through binoculars at two same-sized objects, one nearer than the other, on the ground a few metres away (or at any rectangular object, such as a book or paving slab): the farther object (or the far side of the rectangle) will look larger than the nearer one. The illusion is greater the nearer the object and the higher the magnification. The illusion is also evident in photographs taken with telephoto lenses (eg the close first-winter Herring Gull in Photo 295 looks much smaller than the one at the back). It is important to bear these problems in mind when making size assessments which are crucial to identification, such as when distinguishing a Ring-billed from a Common Gull, or an Iceland from a Glaucous Gull. It is advisable in such cases to rely only on side-by-side size comparison or, when this is not possible, to attach more importance to specific differences which involve structure, plumage marks or bare parts colour and pattern, rather than any apparent size difference.

ASSESSING GREY TONES

The tone or shade of grey on the wings and upperparts of adult or near-adult gulls is important in identifying some species and subspecies. Bright sunlight has the effect of reducing contrasts, so that species which have an actual marked difference in grey tones can appear similar in colour. In sunny conditions, for example, it is often difficult to distinguish even between the rather dark grey of a Common or Mew Gull and the much paler grey of a Black-headed or Ring-billed Gull. It should also be noted that the apparent shade of grey can change as a gull alters the angle of its body in relation to the observer. Cloudy conditions, without direct sunlight, are best for revealing true tones of grey, and it is important to have other species immediately alongside, and in the same body-alignment, when making assessments of grey tones which are crucial to an identification. When this is not possible, it is advisable to attach more importance to other specific differences which involve structure, plumage marks or bare parts colour and pattern.

Photographs can be very misleading in this respect, being subject not only to variation arising from lighting and viewing-angle, but also to variation which results from different exposures, films, developing processes and probably also several other more subtle factors. The resultant variation is evident in different photographs of the same species in this book, for example the Laughing Gulls in Photos 157 or 158 ('palest') and 162 or 165 ('darkest'). As a general rule, the grey tones on adult or near-adult gulls of the same species are remarkably consistent, and the 'differences' in these photographs are the result of external factors rather than actual.

SEXING

Males are generally larger than females, with larger bills. There are few, if any, reliable differences as to plumage or bare parts coloration. So sexing gulls in the field is, at least, difficult. The structural differences can often be discerned, however, in a pair standing side-by-side, or alternatively sex can be determined by behaviour in breeding areas. The size differences between sexes are generally more marked in the larger species.

TOPOGRAPHY

Topographical terminology follows that recommended by *British Birds* magazine (74: 239–242), with the addition of several terms applicable to special plumage features of gulls, marked * in the charts.

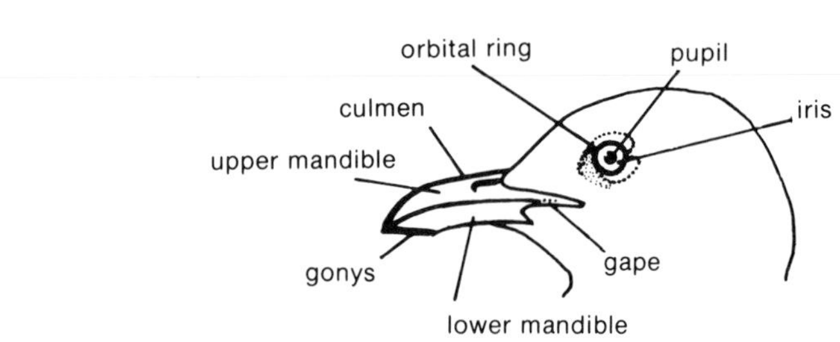

Head—bare parts
The orbital ring is the fleshy, unfeathered (and, on adult gulls, often brightly coloured) ring immediately surrounding the eye. The *mouth* is the fleshy interior of the bill.

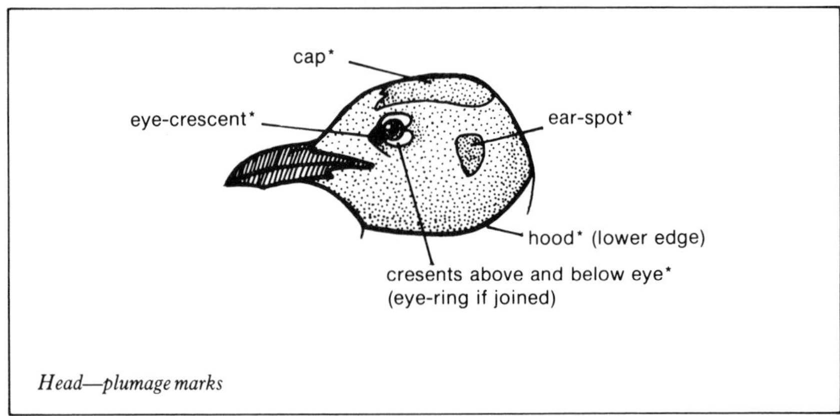

Head—plumage marks

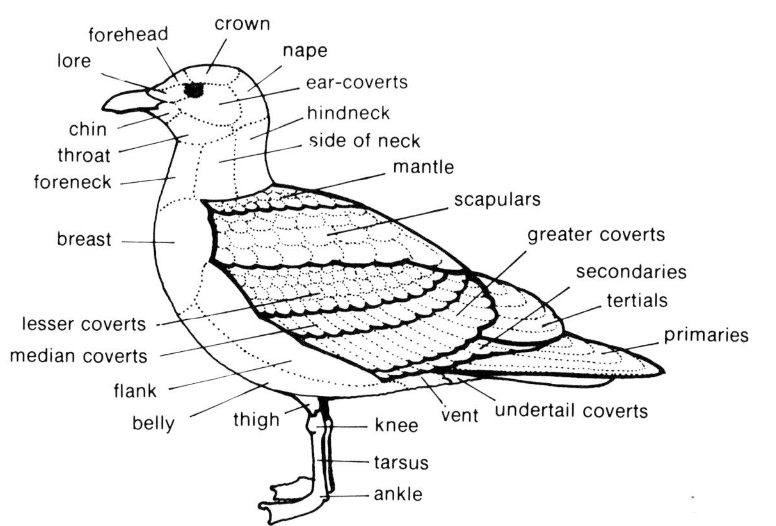

Standing gull

More or less of the coverts of the inner wing will be visible depending on the extent to which the scapulars are held bunched or spread: often, most of the coverts will be concealed by the overlapping scapulars and breast-side and flank feathers so that, for example, the carpal-bar of many first-year gulls will be totally invisible on a standing bird. The *scapular-crescent** (formed by white tips to the rearmost scapulars) and *tertial-crescent** (formed by white tips of the longest tertials) are often prominent on standing adult or near-adult gulls of some species, contrasting with the otherwise grey or blackish coloration of the remainder of their upperparts.

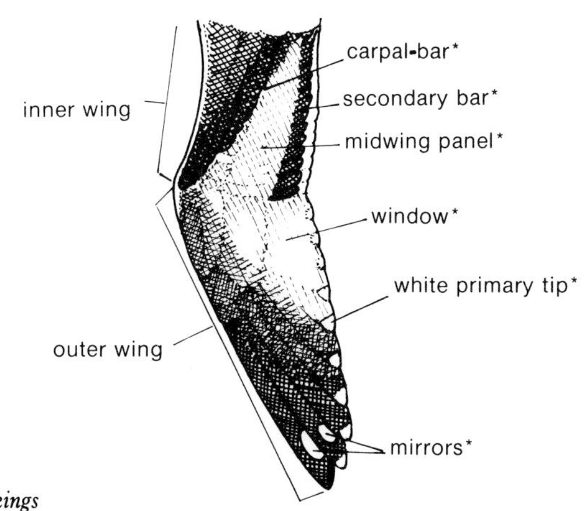

Upperwing markings

The mirrors are usually not visible on the closed wing (unless it is spread when preening, or unless the wing-tip can be viewed from below): they should not be confused with the white primary tips which, if present, are always visible on a perched gull.

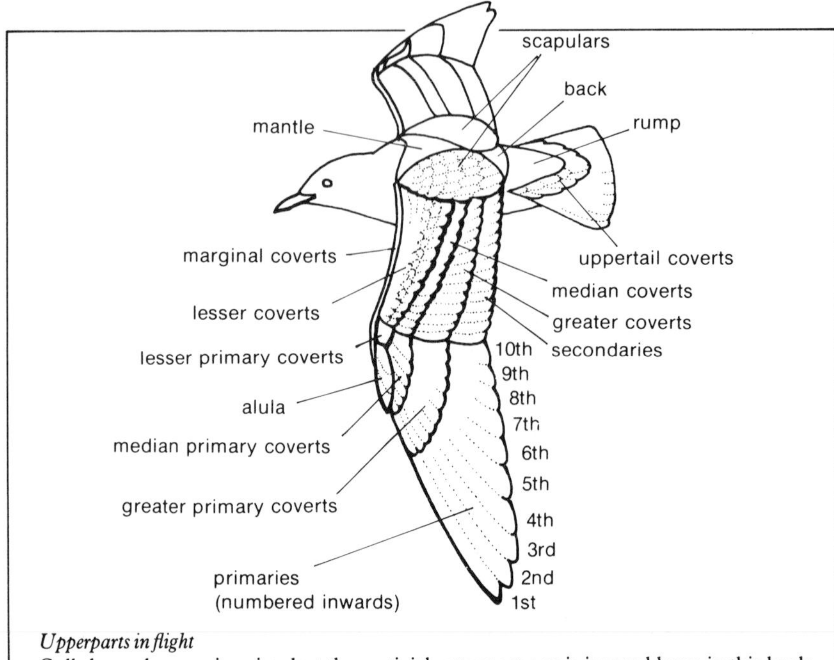

Upperparts in flight

Gulls have eleven primaries, but the vestigial outermost one is ignored here; in this book the primaries are numbered inwards from the outermost large (1st) primary to the innermost (10th). Note that the scapulars extend back as the wing is opened, covering the tertials completely in flight (the white scapular-crescent thus forms the inner part of the white trailing edge of the inner wing in flight).

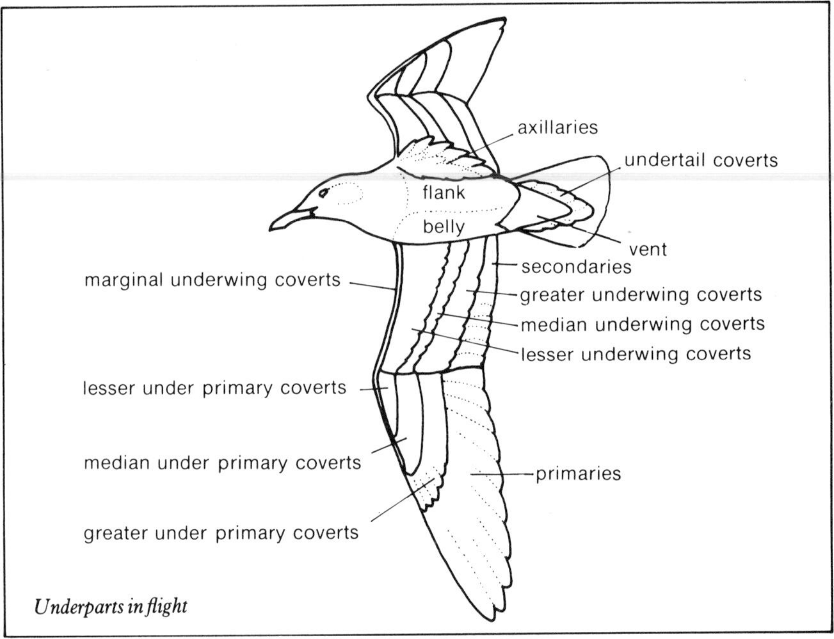

Underparts in flight

Format

Each of the first six groups brings together species which share similar characters, especially in their immature plumages where the possibility of confusion is greatest. The introduction to each group covers general points relating to the species which it includes, with a table of measurements from Dwight (1925) and a page of drawings depicting standing birds in first-winter plumage to aid size and structure comparisons. Dwight's measurements are included because they are a readily obtainable series by the same measurer and because they provide an indication of the size variation within each species, and to aid size comparisons between different species: in some cases the samples are small, and thus probably do not indicate the extremes of variation.

The wing measurements were taken with the wing in its natural position, not with primaries straightened and flattened as is the modern practice: Dwight calculated that measurements taken by the latter method would produce results on large wings averaging 2.3% greater, and on smaller wings averaging 1.9% greater. Bill measurement is from the tip to the forwardmost extension of feathering on the culmen.

For groups one to six (the west Palearctic species) the general introduction is followed by the species accounts, including flight drawings of adults and immatures of each species (in which the wing length and tail spreads have been slightly exaggerated to enable the flight patterns to be more clearly shown), a map showing approximate breeding and winter distribution, an identification summary, an ageing summary (intended as a quick reference to the main age characters of each species), detailed descriptions of each plumage from juvenile to adult, and (where appropriate) a section on geographical variation in which the differences between subspecies are described.

Group Seven (p. 163) deals separately with species occurring regularly on the west coast of North America.

The photographs have been selected to illustrate the identification features of as many different plumages as possible for each species.

GROUP ONE

Black-headed, Slender-billed, Bonaparte's and Grey-headed Gulls

These four small- to medium-sized species form a distinct group. Their most striking common feature is the extensive white on the leading edge of the outer wing in flight. This is more extensive on adults than on immatures, but is readily visible at all ages. It is least extensive on Grey-headed Gull, which also has mirrors on the outer two primaries when adult, giving a diagnostic wing pattern; on this species—unlike the other three—the white leading edge is not visible from below.

Immatures of all four have dusky head markings of varying strength, wing patterns of brownish carpal-bar and blackish secondary bar, as well as the white on the leading edge, and white tails with a thin, clear cut, blackish subterminal band.

All except Slender-billed have dark hoods in adult summer plumage, but—surprisingly—even that species usually has an ear-spot in winter and immature plumages, although it is much more faint than on the others.

Black-headed, Slender-billed and Bonaparte's normally reach adult plumage in their second winter; some Grey-headeds probably do so as well, but others have identifiable second-year plumages and do not become fully adult until their third winter. The proportion of Grey-headed Gulls having this longer immaturity is not known, but it is clearly much greater than for the others in this group, for which it is rarely possible to distinguish between second-years and adults.

Throughout most of its range, the Black-headed is the commonest and most familiar small gull (map, Fig. 4). Slender-billed is rare anywhere north of its localised Mediterranean and southwest Asian breeding areas (map, Fig. 6). Bonaparte's is an American species (map, Fig. 8), with only one or two records annually in Britain. Grey-headed is the typical gull of some African coasts and inland lakes (map, Fig. 10), and has been recorded only once in Europe (Ree 1973).

Table 1: Measurements (mm) of four gulls Larus *(from Dwight 1925)*

	sample	*wing*	*tail*	*bill*	*tarsus*
Black-headed Gull *L. ridibundus*	12	280–315	104–124	30–37	42–47
Slender-billed Gull *L. genei*	24	278–320	110–125	35–46	46–54
Bonaparte's Gull *L. philadelphia*	27	246–271	99–108	27–32	33–37
Grey-headed Gull *L. cirrocephalus*	22	305–338	120–134	35–42	48–60

Fig. 3. First-winter **Black-headed** *Larus ridibundus*, **Slender-billed** *L. genei*, **Bonaparte's** *L. philadelphia* and **Grey-headed Gulls** *L. cirrocephalus*, showing comparative sizes, shapes and stances.

For European observers, the abundance of the Black-headed Gull makes it the key species for identifying the others in this group. Complete familiarity with its appearance, especially in immature plumages, from different angles and in varying light conditions, will greatly aid recognition of the others, and avoid the dismissal of one of them as an odd-looking Black-headed.

Black-headed Gull

Larus ridibundus

(Figs 3A and 5, Photographs 1–24)

Adult winter

IDENTIFICATION

This is the smallest of the abundant western Palearctic gulls. It is noticeably smaller than the European race of the Common Gull *L. c. canus*, and this is accentuated in flight, when the slimmer, more pointed wings and quicker wingbeats are discernible. It is easily separable from all gulls except the other three species in this group, the best point being the white along the leading edge of the outer wing in flight—more extensive on adults than immatures—visible at long range from both above and below. The brown hood of summer adults and some first-summer birds is diagnostic among western Palearctic gulls (the others having black or grey hoods), but it invariably looks blackish at a distance. In winter, the head is mainly white, with a neat blackish ear-spot and eye-crescent; the bill is maroon-red in breeding plumage, red or bright red with dark tip in winter, and dull flesh or yellowish-flesh with dark tip on first-years. The legs are the same colour as the bill.

The separation of Black-headed from the other three species in this group is less straightforward: the brown hood colour of summer adults is the only wholly diagnostic character, so a combination of factors involving size, structure and plumage must be used. With practice, a quick scan through flocks of Black-headed Gulls—checking characters of size, head pattern and shape, and wing pattern—is sufficient to eliminate the possible presence of one of the other species: Bonaparte's is smaller, with a neat blackish bill and translucent white primaries; Slender-billed has a diagnostically elongated forehead and bill, and head all white or with a very pale grey ear-spot; Grey-headed is larger and more heavily built, with a wholly dusky underwing and a distinctive wing pattern.

Fig. 4. World distribution of **Black-headed Gull** *Larus ridibundus*, showing approximate breeding range (solid black) and approximate southern limit of winter/non-breeding range (black line). Has bred Newfoundland, and records in North America increasing.

AGEING SUMMARY

Juvenile: extensive ginger-brown on head, mantle, scapulars and sides of breast (summer to late September).

First-winter: grey mantle and scapulars, brown carpal-bar, blackish secondary bar and tail band, winter head pattern (July to April).

First-summer: faded pale brown carpal-bar, blackish secondary bar and tail band, hood developed to variable extent (March to October).

Second-winter and second-summer: a very few can be aged as second-years (see detailed description under second-winter), but vast majority inseparable from adults.

Adult winter/second-winter: adult wing pattern, all-white tail, winter head pattern (August to March).

Adult summer/second-summer: adult wing pattern, all-white tail, fully developed hood (January to September).

DETAILED DESCRIPTIONS

Juvenile (Fig. 5A; underwing and tail similar to first-winter 5F)

HEAD Chin, throat and collar on upper hindneck white, remainder washed buff when recently-fledged, with dark markings forming partial hood, separated from mantle by white collar on hindneck.

BODY Underparts and rump mainly white, breast and sometimes whole underparts washed buff when recently-fledged. Mantle, scapulars, lower hindneck and breast-sides mainly rich ginger-brown, with pale feather-fringes giving scaly pattern especially on scapulars.

WINGS Brown carpal-bar; tertials brown, broadly fringed paler. Secondaries blackish-brown with pale fringes, forming dark subterminal secondary bar. Outer greater coverts mainly pale grey, forming pale midwing panel. Typical outer wing patterns shown in 5A and 5B: blackish-brown on outer primaries sometimes more extensive, reducing white to two elongated mirrors as in 5C and Photo 9. Inner primaries have usually small white tips from 4th or 5th (occasionally 3rd) inwards. From below, secondaries and outer primaries appear mainly blackish-grey, with narrow translucent white leading edge to outer wing.

TAIL White, with clear-cut, narrow blackish-brown subterminal band, broadest in centre, outer pair of feathers sometimes all-white.

BARE PARTS Iris and orbital ring dark brown, basal two-thirds of bill dull flesh or yellowish-flesh, tip blackish; legs flesh or yellowish-flesh.

First-winter (Figs 3A, 5B and 5F) Acquired by post-juvenile head and body moult, which starts at fledging and is usually complete by late September.

HEAD White, with dusky eye-crescent, prominent blackish ear-spot (often with faint grey extension over rear crown) and faint grey band above eye extending over crown.

BODY Mantle and scapulars uniform pale grey, sometimes a few brown juvenile feathers retained. Very pale grey wash extending from mantle to lower hindneck and breast-sides. Rump and underparts white.

WINGS As juvenile, but brown and blackish-brown areas faded paler, and white tips on primaries reduced or lacking. Variable number of median and lesser coverts usually included in post-juvenile moult, new feathers mainly grey like outer greater coverts, with whitish tips.

TAIL As juvenile, but band faded, and terminal whitish fringe reduced.

BARE PARTS Much as juvenile.

First-summer (Fig. 5C, underwing and tail similar to first-winter, 5F. When standing, similar to first-winter, 3A, but hood usually more extensive) Acquired by head and body moult, February to April. *As first-winter except:*

HEAD Dark blackish-brown hood (fading to pale brown by mid-summer) of variable extent. Sample of 90 in May in southeast England showed 7% full hood; 58% white-flecked full hood; 24% more white than brown; 11% winter head pattern. Acquired later than on adult.

BODY Hindneck and breast-sides off-white or grey-washed on individuals with winter head pattern.

WINGS AND TAIL Becoming extremely worn and brown areas much faded on some by mid-summer. Central tail feathers (very rarely whole tail) sometimes included in moult, new feathers white.

BARE PARTS Legs and base of bill more orange, less flesh-coloured; prominent dark tip to bill.

Adult winter/second-winter (Fig. 5E, upperwing and tail patterns similar to adult summer, 5D) Acquired by complete moult June to October.

HEAD AND BODY Usually as first-winter, but exceptionally with extensive dark markings or even full summer hood in mid-winter. Exceptionally, underparts have pink flush of varying strength, rarely intense.

WINGS Primaries and primary coverts with more white than in first-year plumages, black restricted to outer web of 1st primary and primary tips inwards as far as 6th to 8th: pale grey tips to primaries usually from the 5th inwards. Remainder of wing pale grey, with thin white leading and trailing edges. Diffuse white tertial-crescents usually obvious. From above and below, white leading edge to outer wing more extensive than in first-year plumages, and dark area on underside blacker and restricted to outer primaries, not extending onto secondaries. Underwing coverts white or very pale grey.

TAIL All white.

BARE PARTS Bill red or bright red, with dark tip; legs usually dark reddish.

A few fail to acquire full adult plumage in their second winter, showing dark markings, especially on the greater primary coverts and alula, usually undetectable in the field. Obvious black lines or fringes on the outer webs of the 2nd and 3rd primaries are probably an indication of second-year plumage (see Photo 19). Individuals with orange-yellow bill with dark tip, and orange-flesh legs, may be confidently aged as second-years which have yet to acquire the adult bare parts colour. Variation in the number of primaries with black and the number and extent of the pale grey tips does not seem to be connected with age. Individuals with normal adult summer plumage except for white flecks in the brown hood and paler bare parts are probably in second-summer plumage.

Adult summer/second-summer (Fig. 5D, underwing and tail similar to adult winter, 5E) Acquired by head and body moult, December to April. *As adult winter except:*

HEAD Blackish-brown hood (looking blackish at a distance when fresh, but often

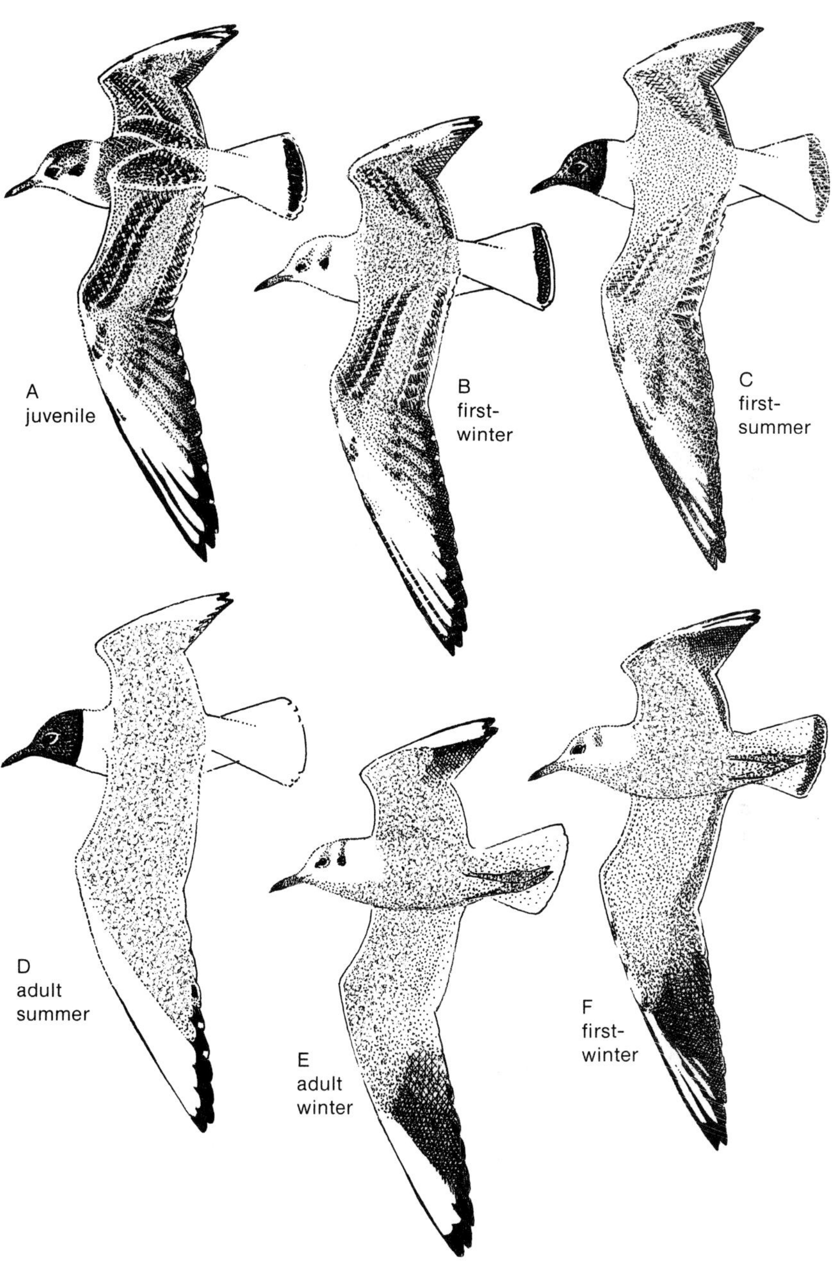

Fig. 5. **Black-headed Gulls** *Larus ridibundus* in flight.

fading to pale brown by mid-summer) fully developed, darker around rear margin, with prominent white crescents posteriorly above and below eye, usually joining at rear.

BODY Some show pink flush of variable strength on underparts, rarely intense.

WINGS Pale grey tips to inner primaries reduced or lacking.

BARE PARTS Iris brown. Orbital ring maroon-red. Bill dark maroon-red, sometimes tipped blackish, only slightly paler in tone than brown of head; mouth and gape bright red. Legs dark red.

Slender-billed Gull

Larus genei

(Figs. 3B and 7, Photographs 25–26)

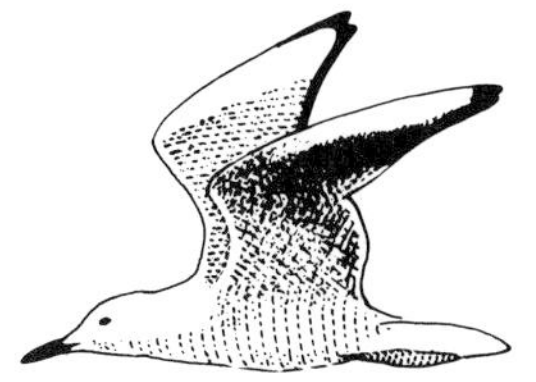

Adult summer

IDENTIFICATION

Marginally longer-legged and larger than Black-headed Gull, noticeable only when the two species are together. In flight, the tail looks slightly longer and fuller, as if to counterbalance the elongated head and neck: the tail is not wedge-shaped, contrary to some statements in the literature. The peculiar shape of head, neck and bill is perhaps the most important field mark at all ages: Black-headeds can look long-necked at times, but they never have the almost grotesque, 'giraffe-necked' look of Slender-billed with its neck fully extended when alert or alarmed. The distance from the eye to the forwardmost extension of feathering on the upper mandible is greater than on Black-headed, and the forehead is strikingly elongated, producing a peculiar 'snout' effect, which is further exaggerated by the longer bill: Black-headed rarely even suggests this appearance, having a more rounded head profile and shorter bill. Watson (*Brit. Birds* 76: 137–138) points out that the feathering on the upper mandible projects farther beyond the feathering on the lower mandible than on Black-headed Gull. P. Alström (*in litt.*) suggests that on average the wings project less far beyond the tail-tip than on Black-headed Gull, that the extension of the primaries beyond the tertials averages shorter, and that (when swimming) the wings are held flatter than on Black-headed Gull.

The first-year wing pattern differs from Black-headed by usually having a paler brown carpal-bar and less extensive black. The eye-crescent and ear-spot are much paler (both may be lacking on some), and the paler bill (with dark tip much smaller or completely lacking) and legs are further differences. Throughout the year the adult is separable from Black-headed by the all-white head (occasionally with a faint grey

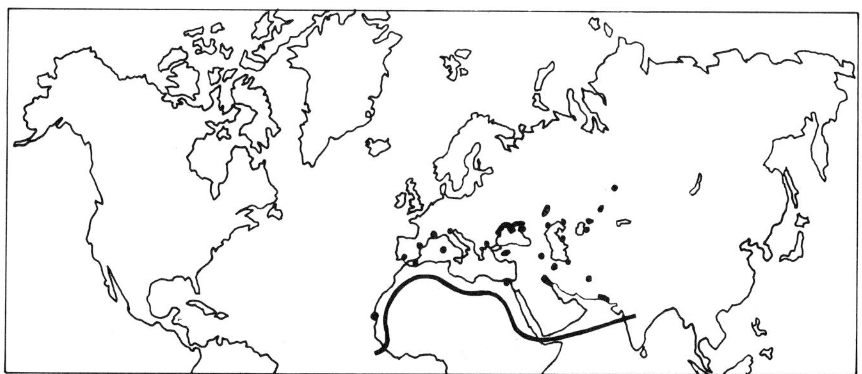

Fig. 6. World distribution of **Slender-billed Gull** *Larus genei*, showing areas of proved breeding (solid black) and approximate southern limit of winter/non-breeding range (black line). Rare vagrant anywhere north of breeding range; up to end 1984, three records in Britain and Ireland, all in coastal southeast England, in 1960, 1963 and 1971.

ear-spot in winter), the pale eye (although breeding adults often look black-eyed, especially at long range), and by the usually strongly pink-flushed underparts (although this coloration may not be obvious at long range in bright sunlight).

Grey-headed Gull has a head shape intermediate between Black-headed and Slender-billed, and, like the latter, has a long neck when alert, pale eyes when adult and pale head markings in winter; but its larger size, extensive black on the outer primaries at all ages, mainly dusky underwing without white, and the darker grey tone of the wings are the most obvious differences.

AGEING SUMMARY

Juvenile: extensive grey-brown on head, mantle and scapulars (summer to late September).

First-winter: pale grey mantle and scapulars, pale brown carpal-bar, blackish secondary bar and tail band, pale grey ear-spot, pale bill and legs (July to April).

First-summer: faded, very pale brown carpal-bar, faded blackish secondary bar and tail band, pale bill and legs (March to October).

Adult winter/second-winter: adult wing and tail pattern, pale grey ear-spot usually present, faintly pink-flushed underparts, pale iris, dark bill and legs (August to March).

Adult summer/second-summer: adult wing and tail pattern, all-white head, pink-flushed underparts, pale iris, dark bill and legs (March to October).

DETAILED DESCRIPTIONS

Juvenile (Not illustrated, but wing and tail pattern similar to first-winter Figs 3B, 7A and 7C: head, body and bare parts as described below) *Basic pattern of plumage similar to juvenile Black-headed except:*

HEAD White, with pale buff and grey markings. Ear-spot and partial hood effect much less defined or lacking.

BODY Mantle, scapulars and sides of breast grey-brown, lacking rich ginger-brown coloration of Black-headed.

WINGS Carpal-bar probably slightly paler brown, and blackish areas at tips of inner primaries less extensive, hence dark trailing edge to middle wing less prominent. White on outer primaries, primary coverts and alula usually more extensive and black never so extensive as on some Black-headeds (cf. Fig. 5C). An isolated black mark on the alula may be typical.

BARE PARTS Iris dark brown perhaps quickly becoming pale (it is possible that some individuals never have a dark iris); orbital ring dark. Bill mainly pale orange-flesh, with dark tip small or lacking. Legs pale orange-flesh.

First-winter (Figs 3B, 7A and 7C) Acquired by post-juvenile head and body moult, which starts at fledging and is usually complete by late September. *Basic pattern of plumage similar to first-winter Black-headed except:*

HEAD Dark eye-crescent and ear-spot of variable strength, but averaging much

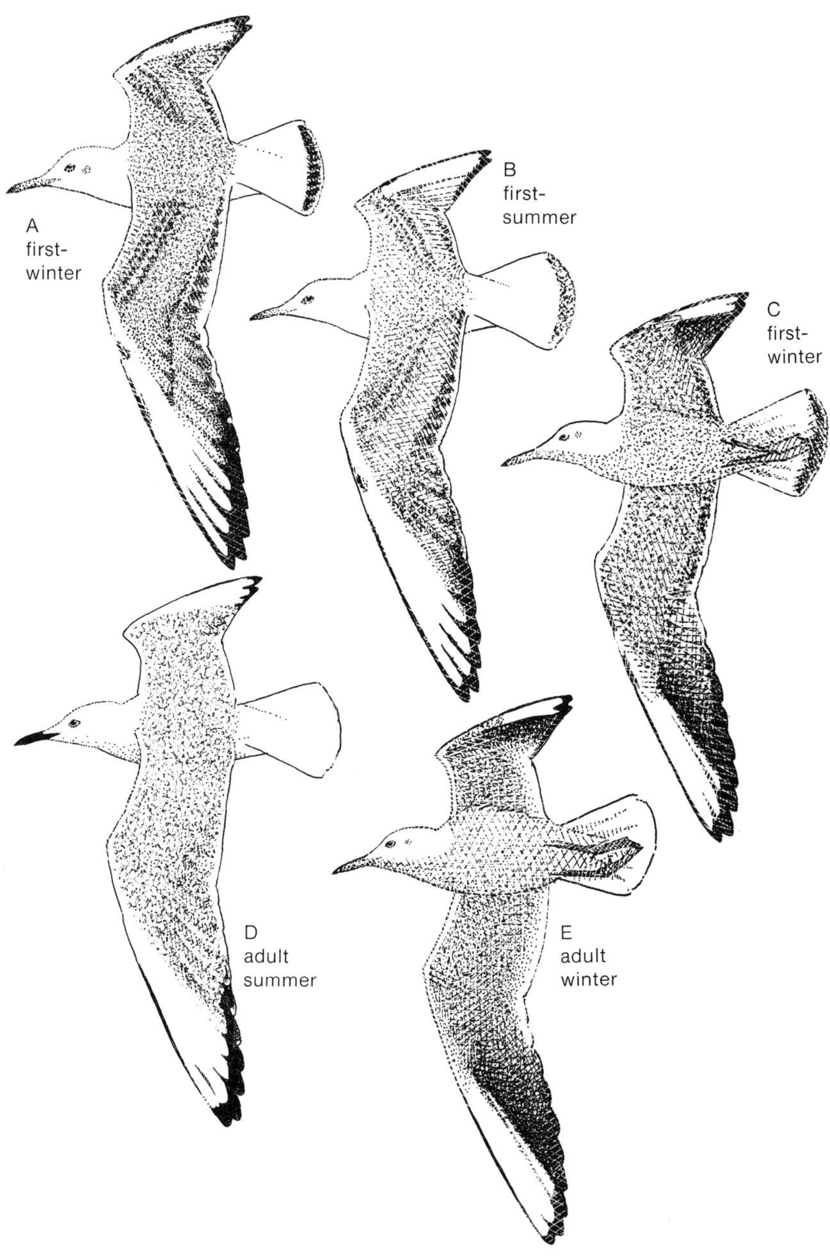

Fig. 7. **Slender-billed Gulls** *Larus genei* in flight.

paler than Black-headed Gull and sometimes lacking.

BODY Underparts white, sometimes faintly tinged pink.

WINGS As juvenile, but brown and blackish areas faded paler.

BARE PARTS As juvenile, except iris pale (often visible only at close range), and some may show reddish bill and orbital ring. (See summary at end of first-summer description.)

First-summer (Fig. 7B, underwing and tail similar to first-winter, 7C. When standing, similar to first-winter, 3B, but carpal-bar and ear-spot usually lacking.) Acquired by head and body moult, February to April. *Appearance as first-winter except:*

HEAD Pale grey ear-spot usually lacking.

WINGS AND TAIL Invariably becoming very worn and faded, so that pale brown carpal-bar (and sometimes even dark secondaries) appear hardly darker than grey of upperparts and rest of wings. Central tail feathers often new, all-white.

BARE PARTS Iris pale; orbital ring usually reddish. Bill and legs orange-flesh or pale orange, and some may acquire hint of adult coloration by late summer.

Because of their general paleness, some distant perched first-year birds are separable from adults only by paler bill and legs, and (in summer) by lack of strongly pink-flushed underparts; in flight, first-year wing pattern and banded tail are obvious.

Adult winter/second-winter (Fig. 7E, wing and tail pattern similar to adult summer, 7D) Acquired by complete moult, June to October.

HEAD AND BODY As first-winter, except eye-crescent and ear-spot often lacking, and underparts pink-flushed to variable extent and strength.

WINGS AND TAIL As adult Black-headed, but white on outer primaries slightly more extensive, giving more prominent white leading edge to outer wing, and tertial-crescents much less obvious, often lacking.

BARE PARTS Iris white, pale yellow or greenish. Bill dark red or orange-red, looking black at distance. Legs not so dark as bill, with more orange tone.

Adult summer/second-summer (Fig. 7D, underwing and tail as adult winter, 7E) Acquired by head and body moult, February to April. *As adult winter except:*

HEAD All white, sometimes with pale pink flush.

BODY Whole underparts with usually strong pink flush, strongest on breast and belly.

WINGS AND TAIL White areas often suffused with pink.

BARE PARTS Iris white, pale yellow, greenish or greenish-grey: breeding individuals often look black-eyed, especially at long range; orbital ring red. Bill dark blood-red with blackish tip, darker than adult summer Black-headed and looking black at distance. Legs slightly less dark than bill.

Bonaparte's Gull
Larus philadelphia

(Figs. 3c and 9, Photographs 37–49)

Adult summer

IDENTIFICATION

This attractive small gull is a miniature version of Black-headed, between Black-headed and Little Gull in size. Size and the combination of quicker wingbeat, whiter underwing, neat blackish bill and surface-picking feeding suggest a rather tern-like appearance. The legs are proportionately shorter than on Black-headed Gull (W. Hoogendoorn *in litt.*). The small size and the neatly black-bordered, white underwing with translucent outer primaries are among the best distinctions from the others in this group at all ages. Some worn and faded first-summer Black-headeds can seem to have a translucent underwing at times, but this impression is usually fleeting.

In first-year plumages, there are several other differences from Black-headed. The smaller bill is black, sometimes with a reddish base (pale with dark tip in the case of Black-headed). The carpal-bar is darker brown and looks blackish at a distance. Compared with Black-headed, the primaries usually have more prominent white terminal spots (although these are subject to wear), and the subterminal black on the inner primaries forms a thinner, neater black rear border to the middle wing. The outer greater primary coverts are mainly blackish, while the inner ones are mainly plain grey (on Black-headed Gull the outer greater primary coverts are mainly or wholly white, whereas the inner ones are mainly dark). The grey mantle and scapulars are a shade darker (obviously so in dull light), and, on first-winters, this colour extends onto the hindneck and breast-sides much more strongly than on Black-headed Gull.

Adults, as well as having the size and underwing differences, are further dis-

Fig. 8. World distribution of **Bonaparte's Gull** *Larus philadelphia*, showing approximate breeding range (solid black) and approximate southern limit of winter/non-breeding range (black line). Vagrant to western coastal Europe, with average of one or two records annually in Britain and Ireland.

tinguished from Black-headed by all-black bill, blackish-grey hood in summer, with more prominent white crescents above and below the eye, usually strong pink flush on the underparts (rarely so on Black-headed), darker grey upperparts (difference most obvious in dull light, approaching Common Gull *L. canus* in shade of grey), and (in winter) grey hindneck and breast-sides.

First-year Little Gull (p. 119) is smaller than Bonaparte's. The carpal-bar is blackish and the outer upperwing lacks the extensive white on the leading edge, although, when the wing is fully spread, the white inner webs of the outer primaries give a lined black-and-white appearance. The underwing is mainly white, lacking the translucent area on the outer primaries. Little Gull has a neat dark cap in winter and first-summer plumages, which Bonaparte's lacks.

AGEING SUMMARY

Juvenile: extensive blackish head markings and rich brown on mantle, scapulars, back and breast-sides (summer to late September).

First-winter: pale grey mantle and scapulars, dark brown carpal-bar, black secondary bar and tail band, winter head pattern (July to April).

First-summer: faded brown carpal-bar, blackish secondary bar and tail band, hood developed to variable extent (March to October).

Adult winter/second-winter: adult wing pattern, all-white tail, winter head pattern (August to March).

Adult summer/second-summer: adult wing pattern, all-white tail, fully developed hood (February to October).

DETAILED DESCRIPTIONS

Juvenile (Fig. 9A shows an individual in moult from juvenile to first-winter. Underwing and tail similar to first-winter, 9F). *Basic pattern of plumage similar to juvenile Black-headed except:*

HEAD Markings blacker with less brown. Ear-spot darker and more defined, and often with clear-cut cap.

BODY Mantle, scapulars, back and breast-sides brown, without ginger tone.

WINGS Carpal-bar darker brown, looking blackish at distance. From above, pattern of primaries and secondaries is similar, but primaries from 3rd inwards usually more prominently tipped white, and less black on 4th inwards, giving thinner, neater, dark trailing edge. Figs. 9A (with most black) and 9B (with least black) show extent of normal variation. Inner web of all primaries white (except for black near tip), and lacks complete broad dusky border, this difference visible on upperwing as cleaner grey inner primaries, and on underwing as neat, thin black border; area of translucent white in triangle along leading edge; and lack of dusky on inner primaries. Outer primary coverts mainly blackish, inner ones mainly grey. Very rare variant (one example known to author) has more extensive black on upperwing, so that no white visible on outer upperwing, and carpal-bar extending to almost all coverts.

BARE PARTS Iris dark brown. Bill black, or with usually small pale area at base. Mouth flesh. Legs pale flesh.

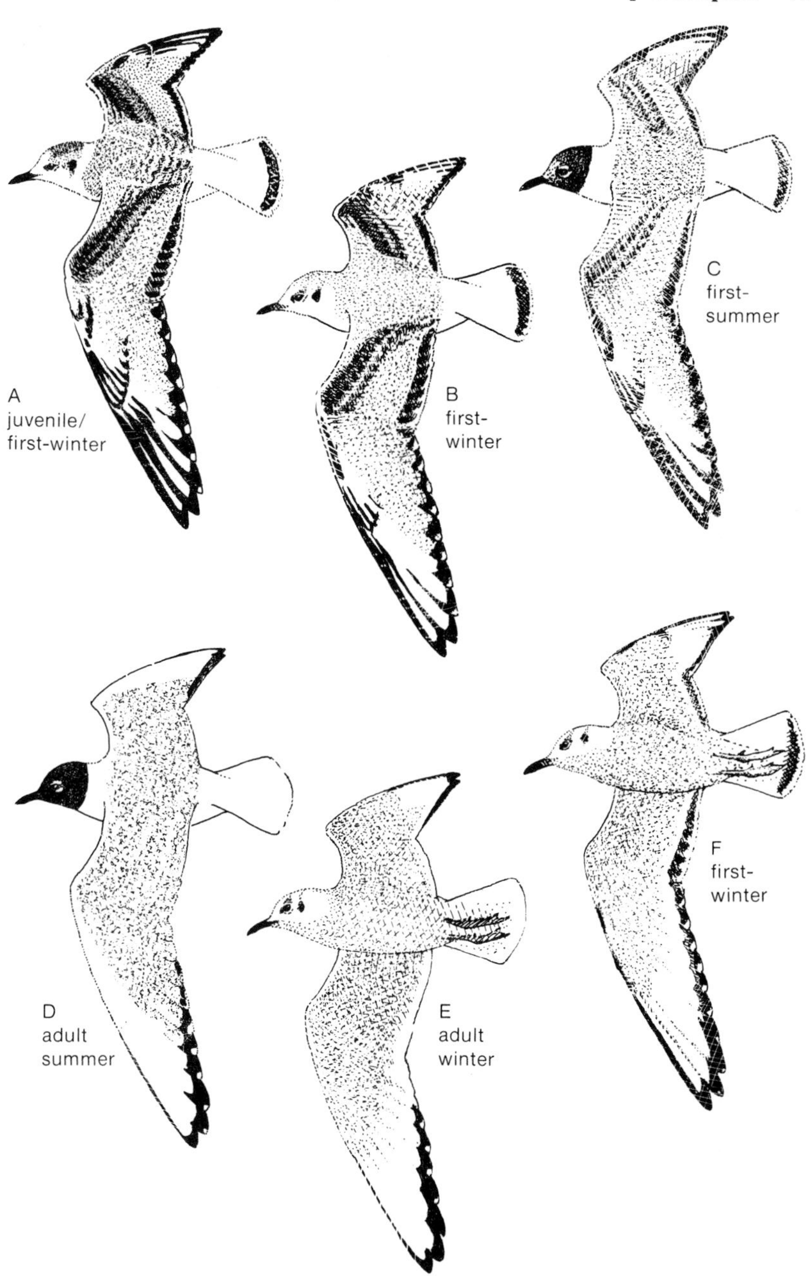

Fig. 9. **Bonaparte's Gulls** *Larus philadelphia* in flight.

First-winter (Figs 3C, 9B and 9F) Acquired by post-juvenile head and body moult, which starts at fledging and is usually complete by late September. *Basic pattern of plumage similar to first-winter Black-headed except:*

HEAD Ear-spot usually blacker and more defined. Hindneck (and sometimes nape and crown) obviously grey, (extension of mantle colour), not very pale grey or white as Black-headed.

BODY Mantle, scapulars and back uniform grey, slightly darker than Black-headed, sometimes with a few retained brown juvenile feathers. Grey of upperparts usually extends strongly to breast-sides, unlike Black-headed Gull on which breast-sides white or faintly grey-washed.

WINGS As juvenile, but white primary tips reduced.

BARE PARTS Much as juvenile, but bill often with some red at base.

First-summer (Fig. 9C, underwing and tail similar to first-winter, 9F. On the ground, similar to first-winter 3C, but hood usually more extensive) Acquired by head and body moult, February to April. *As first-winter except:*

HEAD AND BODY Black usually more extensive, and a few may acquire full hood and lose grey hindneck and breast-sides.

WINGS Becoming worn and faded by late summer, white primary tips may disappear.

TAIL Central feathers sometimes included in spring moult, thus white, breaking tail band. White tail fringes may disappear through wear.

BARE PARTS Much as juvenile.

Adult winter/second-winter (Fig. 9E, wing and tail pattern as adult summer, 9D) Acquired by complete moult, July to October.

HEAD AND BODY As first-winter but underparts may be slightly flushed pink.

WINGS Upperwing similar to adult Black-headed, but, from below, primaries lack extensive blackish: instead they are white with translucent triangle along leading edge, bordered along rear edge by thin black line formed by tips to outer six to nine primaries. Grey of upperwing slightly darker than on Black-headed Gull (like mantle, scapulars and back).

TAIL White.

BARE PARTS Iris dark brown. Bill black, sometimes with some red at base. Legs usually flesh-pink.

A few second-winters fail to acquire full adult plumage, showing dark markings especially among greater primary coverts and rarely on tail: these usually faint marks rarely visible in field.

Adult summer/second-summer (Fig. 9D, underwing and tail as adult winter, 9E) Acquired by head and body moult, January to April. *As adult winter except:*

HEAD Full blackish-grey hood with prominent white crescents above and below eye, thickest at rear. Neck white.

BODY Variable pink flush on underparts, usually obvious.

WINGS As adult winter, but whitish tips to primaries reduced or lacking.

BARE PARTS Orbital ring black. Bill black. Mouth orange-red. Legs orange-red.

Grey-headed Gull

Larus cirrocephalus

(Figs 3D and 11, Photographs 50–62)

Adult summer

IDENTIFICATION

The Grey-headed Gull is unfamiliar to most European observers, yet the record of one in Spain (Ree 1973) shows that it may occur elsewhere in southern Europe or even Britain.

It is the largest member of this group, between Common Gull *L. c. canus* and Black-headed in size. Compared with Black-headed, it is broader-winged and, when gliding, the wings are held flatter and less angled, giving a 'sail-plane' appearance. On the ground, it has a more upright carriage, with longer legs, and, when alert, has a 'head up, tail down' posture. It is longer-necked than Black-headed, with a sloping forehead and heavier and longer bill, recalling Slender-billed Gull. These size and structural differences are among its best field marks at all ages.

In first-year plumages, other differences from Black-headed are the darker grey of the wings, mantle and scapulars, all-black outer primaries, less extensive white on the leading edge of the outer upperwing, wholly dusky underwing, thinner black tail band and usually less well-defined head markings.

Grey-headed is the only one in this group which regularly takes an extra year to reach adult plumage, as might be expected in view of its larger size: second-years are fairly readily distinguishable in the field, as described in the detailed descriptions of second-winter and second-summer.

To some European eyes, adults may recall Common Gull rather than Black-headed because of the larger size, broader wings, darker grey upperparts and the prominent mirrors on the outer two primaries. The combination of extensive white on the leading

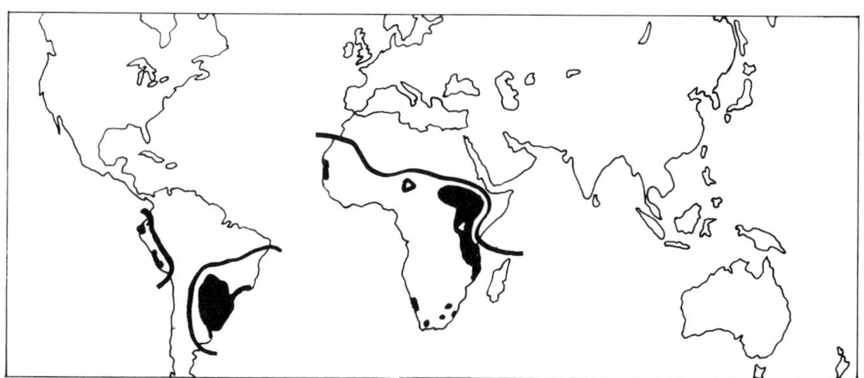

Fig. 10. World distribution of **Grey-headed Gull** *Larus cirrocephalus*, showing approximate breeding range (solid black) and approximate limits of winter/non-breeding range (black line). One European record: adult at Las Marismas, Spain, 20th June to 15th August 1971 (Ree 1973).

edge of the upperwing and prominent mirrors gives a pattern diagnostic among western Palearctic gulls: this and the wholly blackish underwing, pale iris, and (in summer at least) pale dove-grey hood, as well as the size and structural differences, give a strikingly distinctive appearance.

AGEING SUMMARY

Juvenile: extensive grey-brown on head, mantle, scapulars and breast-sides. (See comments under detailed description of first-winter about timing of moults.)

First-winter: brown carpal-bar, blackish secondary bar and tail band, head mainly white with grey markings and ear-spot.

First-summer: brown carpal-bar, blackish secondary bar and tail band, hood developed to variable extent.

Second-winter: as adult, except dusky markings on secondaries and tertials forming darker trailing edge to inner wing. More black than white on outer upperwing, and white primary tips and mirrors small or lacking. Iris darker than adult and bare parts dull flesh. Head pattern as first-winter, or pale, ill-defined hood.

Second-summer: as second-winter, but bare parts nearer or matching colour of summer adult. Hood usually fully developed.

Adult winter/third-summer: adult wing pattern; head pattern as first-winter, or pale, ill-defined hood; obvious white iris; bare parts duller than adult summer.

Adult summer/third-summer: adult wing pattern, full hood, dark red bill, red legs.

DETAILED DESCRIPTIONS

Juvenile (Not illustrated, but wing and tail pattern similar to first-winter, Figs 3D, 11A and 11C: head, body and bare parts as described below)

HEAD White, with extensive grey-brown clouding, darker ear-spot and eye-crescent, forming partial hood, separated from mantle by whitish collar on upper hindneck. Thin white crescents above and below eye.

BODY Underparts white, with grey-brown breast-sides extending from mantle. Mantle and scapulars brown, with pale feather fringes giving obvious scaly pattern on scapulars. Rump pale grey.

WINGS Pattern similar to juvenile Black-headed, but grey areas on inner upperwing slightly darker: outer wing has less white, outer two or three primaries wholly black. White on outer webs at base of 3rd or 4th to 5th or 6th primaries form patch in middle of outer wing which extends onto outer greater primary coverts. Inner four or five primaries and their coverts mainly grey, with blackish areas at tips which join with blackish secondary bar to form dark trailing edge. All but outer two or three primaries have tiny white spots at tips, increasing in size inwards. Inner web of all primaries blackish, and underwing coverts grey, so that, from below, underwing appears wholly dusky (but not so dark as adult's), except for two or three translucent spots which correspond with white area on upperwing.

TAIL White with neat black subterminal band, usually thinner than Black-

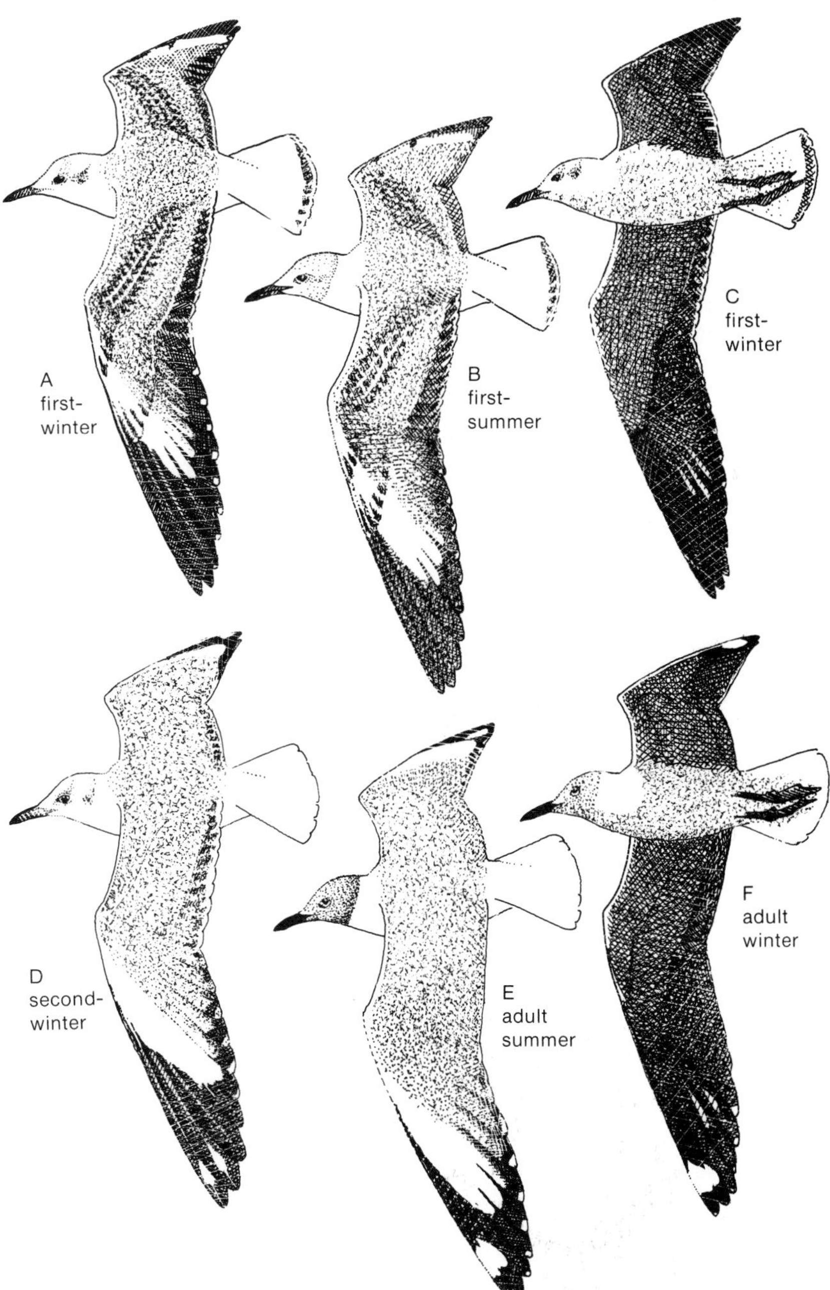

Fig. 11. **Grey-headed Gulls** *Larus cirrocephalus* in flight.

headed's and often not extending to outer feathers: when tail spread, black may appear as separate spots.

BARE PARTS Iris brown. Bill pale flesh or yellowish-flesh, with extensive dark tip. Legs dull flesh or yellowish-flesh.

First-winter (Figs 3D, 11A and 11C) Acquired by post-juvenile head and body moult, which starts at fledging and is usually complete within about two months. Published breeding records from Africa refer to the period April to September, but breeding may take place outside this period. The timing of the post-juvenile and later moults is fixed by the fledging date, so temporal limits cannot be fixed for the moults of this or other equatorial breeding species which have a variable season.

HEAD White, with pattern of dark markings similar to Black-headed Gull, but usually paler, more diffuse. Lower hindneck pale grey.

BODY Underparts and rump white. Mantle and scapulars uniform grey, without white scapular-crescent, and darker than Black-headed, sometimes with a few brown feathers retained from juvenile plumage.

WINGS As juvenile, but brown and blackish areas faded, and white primary tips and secondary fringes reduced.

TAIL As juvenile, but band faded and whitish terminal fringe reduced or lacking.

BARE PARTS Much as juvenile.

First-summer (Fig. 11B, underwing and tail similar to first-winter 11C. When standing, similar to first-winter, 3D, but carpal-bar paler and hood usually more extensive) Acquired by head and body moult, which starts about six months after fledging. *As first-winter except:*

HEAD Grey usually more extensive, and some may acquire adult hood and lose pale grey on lower hindneck.

WINGS AND TAIL Dark areas become much faded (especially brown carpal-bar) and white primary tips and terminal fringes on secondaries and tail often disappear.

Second-winter (Fig. 11D) Acquired by a complete moult, which starts about 12 months after fledging. Some may reach adult plumage at this age, but probably the majority take an extra year. *As adult winter except:*

WINGS Black usually more extensive than white on outer primaries, and white primary tips usually small or lacking. Mirrors, if present at all, usually smaller than on adults, or confined to outer primary. Tertials and secondaries with dusky centres, forming darker trailing edge to inner wing. Sometimes a few brown feathers among greater primary, median and lesser coverts.

BARE PARTS Iris usually becoming pale, but lacking full adult colour and looking dark at distance. Bill and legs dull flesh.

Second-summer (Wing and tail patterns similar to second-winter, Fig. 11D) Acquired by head and body moult, which begins about 18 months after fledging. *As second-winter except:*

HEAD Full adult hood usually acquired.

BARE PARTS Much as adult summer, but iris may remain darker.

Adult winter/third-winter (Fig. 11F, wings and tail as adult summer, 11E) Acquired by complete moult, which starts towards the end of breeding activity. Some, probably a minority, may acquire adult plumage in their second winter.

HEAD As first-winter or with pale version of adult summer hood.

BODY Mantle and scapulars uniform grey, without prominent scapular- or tertial-crescents, a shade darker than Black-headed Gull.

WINGS Inner wing uniform grey, darker than Black-headed. White more extensive than black on outer primaries, with prominent pear-shaped white mirrors on outer two. White tips, usually prominent, on 3rd or 4th to 7th or 8th primaries. Inner webs of primaries (except mirrors) wholly blackish and underwing coverts grey, whole underwing thus appearing dark, apart from the mirrors and a few translucent spots showing through fully spread wing, corresponding to white on upperside.

TAIL White.

BARE PARTS Iris pale yellow or whitish. Orbital ring red or orange red. Bill dull red or orange-red with variable amount of dark at tip. Legs dull red or orange-red, usually paler than bill.

Adult summer/third-summer (Fig. 11E, underwing and tail as adult winter, 11F) Acquired by head and body moult, which starts before the beginning of breeding activity. *As adult winter except:*

HEAD Hood fully developed, extending farther down throat and nape than on Black-headed Gull, pale dove-grey shading to whitish around bill and with usually complete darker grey rear border. White crescents above and below eye or complete diffuse whitish eye-ring contrasting with red orbital ring. Hindneck white.

BODY Sometimes with faint pink flush on underparts.

WINGS Whitish tips on primaries reduced or lacking.

BARE PARTS Bill red, sometimes with dark tip: bill much darker in tone than hood and looking black at distance. Legs red, brighter than bill.

GROUP TWO

Common, Mediterranean, Ring-billed, Laughing and Franklin's Gulls

The five species in this group are small or medium-sized gulls sharing a first-year plumage pattern of blackish outer primaries and secondary bar, extensive brownish carpal-bar, more or less defined tail band, and mainly white or lightly marked underparts. The species in Group Three (Herring *Larus argentatus*, Lesser Black-backed *L. fuscus*, Great Black-backed *L. marinus*, Audouin's *L. audouinii* and Great Black-headed Gulls *L. ichthyaetus*) have some rather similar immature patterns, but at least their greater size should be obvious and avoid confusion between the two groups, except perhaps in the case of Ring-billed Gull *L. delawarensis* and Herring Gull. Adult Mediterranean *L. melanocephalus*, Laughing *L. atricilla* and Franklin's Gulls *L. pipixcan* are hooded in summer, and Ring-billed Gull is the only one with pale eyes when adult.

All normally reach adult plumage in their third winter: second-years are normally readily aged, mainly by the pattern of the outer wing, and, in the cases of Ring-billed and Laughing Gulls, often also by traces of a dark secondary bar and tail band. Franklin's Gull has a *complete* moult in both spring and autumn, unlike any other gull, and normally reaches adult plumage in its second summer, a shorter period of immaturity, which might be expected in view of its small size.

While the Common Gull *L. canus* is abundant in most of the western Palearctic (map, Fig. 13), the Mediterranean Gull is uncommon in much of the area (map, Fig. 15), and Ring-billed, Laughing and Franklin's Gulls are rare vagrants from America (maps, Figs 17, 19 & 21).

Table 2: Measurements (mm) of five gulls Larus *(from Dwight 1925)*

	sample	*wing*	*tail*	*bill*	*tarsus*
Common Gull *L. canus canus*	16	320–385	124–148	30–38	48–58
Mediterranean Gull *L. melanocephalus*	21	282–311	113–127	31–38	47–53
Ring-billed Gull *L. delawarensis*	23	335–392	134–162	36–46	52–62
Laughing Gull *L. atricilla*	26	295–330	113–133	35–44	46–55
Franklin's Gull *L. pipixcan*	26	262–286	97–111	27–34	39–45

Fig. 12. First-winter **Ring-billed** *Larus delawarensis*, **Mediterranean** *L. melanocephalus*, **Common** *L. canus*, **Franklin's** *L. pipixcan* and **Laughing Gulls** *L. atricilla*, showing comparative sizes, shapes and stances.

Familiarity with the appearance of Common Gull at all ages will greatly aid the recognition of the others in this group, especially Mediterranean and Ring-billed Gulls which it particularly resembles in first-year plumages. In second-year and adult plumages, all five are much more distinctive, although the differences between Common and Ring-billed Gulls are sometimes obvious only at close range.

Common Gull
Larus canus

(Figs 12c; 14 and 14 (a), Photographs 63–97)

Adult summer

IDENTIFICATION

This is one of the most familiar and abundant gulls in much of the western Palearctic. It resembles adult and some immature plumages of the much larger and generally more abundant Herring Gull: at a distance (when the otherwise obvious size and bare parts colour differences may be difficult to judge) it is best told by its proportionately much smaller, neater bill, thinner-winged, unlaboured flight, and much larger mirrors when adult. At long range at all ages, it is best told from Black-headed Gull by its lack of white leading edge to the outer wing, its less pointed wings and lack of a hood or dark ear-spot; at close range, the larger size, darker grey upperparts and lack of reddish on the bill and legs are further differences.

On the ground it often has a characteristically elegant look, caused by the compound effect of rather small and often very slim-looking bill, rounded head with 'gentle' expression, rather long wings and somewhat dainty gait. The first-year flight pattern is not shared by any other *common* medium-sized gull. Second-years and adults are best identified by the medium size, rather dark blue-grey upperparts, prominent white tertial-crescent when perched, and yellowish or greyish bare part colour.

The others in this group are told from Common Gull by a combination of characters as described in the respective species accounts. It is always worth checking the obvious characters of Common Gull—size, bill shape, head pattern and tone of grey on the upper parts—to eliminate the possible presence of one of the others; Ring-billed is slightly larger with thicker bill and paler grey upperparts, and perched second-years

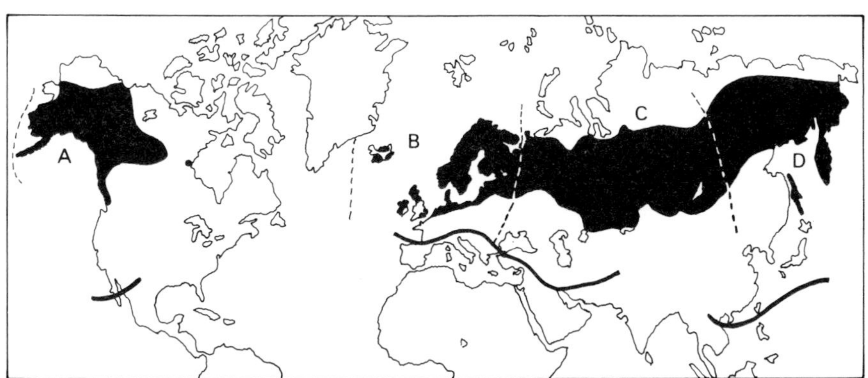

Fig. 13. World distribution of **Common Gull** *Larus canus*, showing approximate breeding range (solid black) and approximate southern limit of winter/non-breeding range (black line). The dotted lines indicate the approximate breeding ranges of the subspecies. (A) *L. c. brachyrhynchus*; (B) *L. c. canus*; (C) *L. c. heinei*; (D) *L. c. kamtschatschensis*. The geographical variation of Common Gulls is described on pages 55–57.

and adults lack the prominent white tertial-crescent. Mediterranean Gull is slightly smaller, usually with an obviously rather heavier bill; first-years have a clear-cut black streak behind the eye, much paler grey upperparts, more contrasting upperwing pattern, and whiter underwing. Second-year and adult Mediterranean and all ages of Laughing and Franklin's Gull have a distinctive appearance and are unlikely to be mistaken for Common Gulls.

AGEING SUMMARY

Juvenile: scaly brown mantle and scapulars, and extensive dusky markings on head and underparts (summer to September).

First-winter: dusky head and body markings, uniform grey mantle and scapulars, blackish outer primaries, secondary bar and tail band, brown carpal-bar, and black-tipped bill (July to April).

First-summer: as first-winter, but head and body whiter and wing pattern faded paler and contrasting with blue-grey mantle and scapulars (March to October).

Second-winter: wings uniform grey, with black tip not confined to primaries, but extending along leading edge of the outer wing, small mirrors, white primary tips tiny or lacking, and much dusky head streaking (July to April).

Second-summer: as second-winter, but head white or lightly marked (March to October).

Adult winter/third-winter: black of wing tip confined to primaries, large mirrors, prominent white primary tips (obvious when perched), dusky head markings, and bill pale, with thin dark subterminal mark or band. (August to March).

Adult summer/third summer: as adult winter, but head white and bill yellowish-green (March to October).

DETAILED DESCRIPTIONS (These refer top the European race *L. c. canus*: for difference of other races see 'Geographical variation' on pp. 55–57)

Juvenile (Fig. 14A. Underwing and tail similar to first-winter, 14D)

HEAD Forehead white, throat and nape whitish. Ear-coverts and crown densely streaked grey-brown, sometimes forming ill-defined partial hood. Thin white crescents above and below eye and dusky eye-crescent.

BODY Lower hindneck, flanks and often defined broad breast band uniform or mottled grey-brown. Belly and vent white. Mantle and scapulars buff, with neat pale feather fringes giving scaly pattern most prominent on scapulars. Rump and uppertail- and undertail-coverts white, with dark arrowhead markings or bars.

WINGS Carpal-bar brown, with rounded brown feather-centres and pale fringes, and tertials with broad whitish fringe and pointed dark centre. Greater coverts (except three or four innermost) uniform pale grey-brown, forming pale midwing panel. Outer greater primary coverts and outer three to five primaries wholly blackish-brown except for pale fringes at tips: dull grey on outer webs increasing in extent (and subterminal

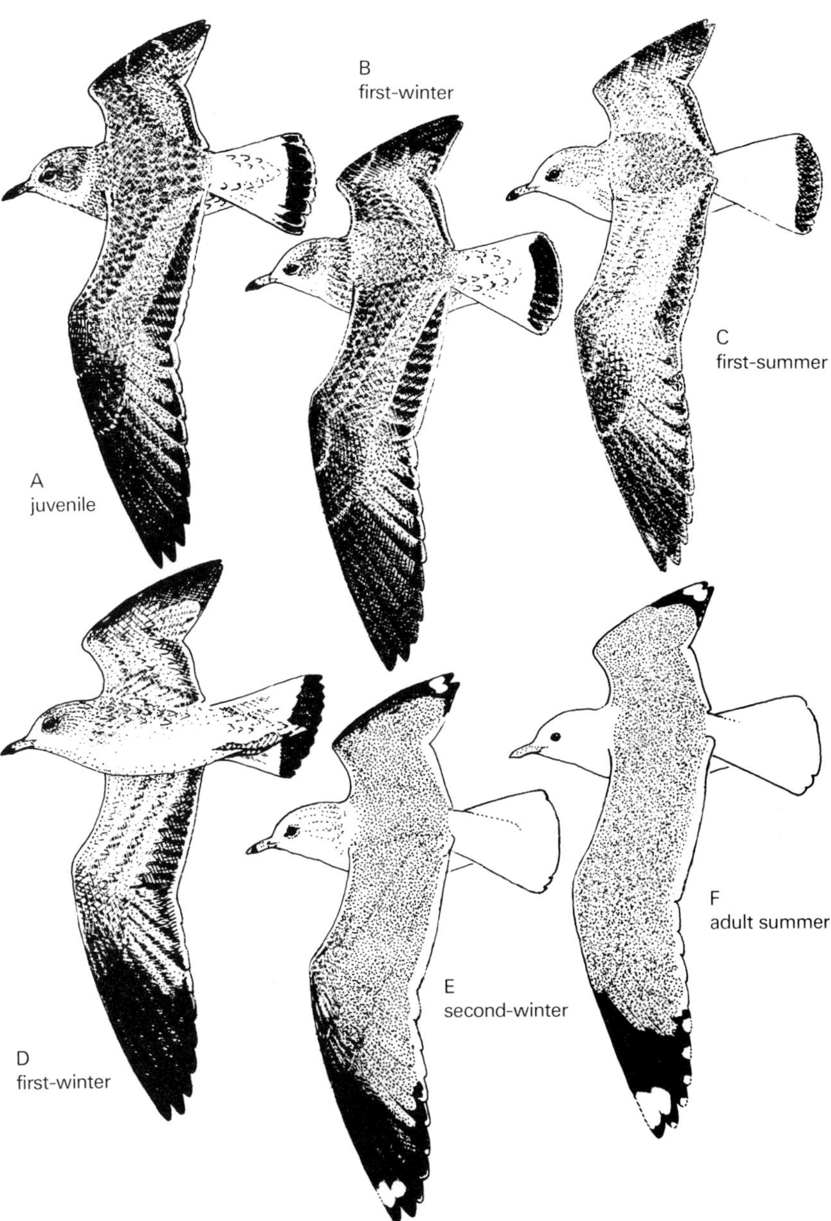

Fig. 14. **Common Gulls** *Larus canus* in flight.

blackish areas decreasing) from base of 5th or 6th primary inwards, forming pale division between outer primaries and secondary bar. Underwing whitish, axillaries and most coverts with dark tips, forming lines.

TAIL White, typically with clear-cut, broad, solidly blackish-brown subterminal band: outer pair of feathers often with dark only on inner webs or occasionally all-white. Sometimes, blackish-brown, occasionally greyish, extends up the side of each feather, giving a notched or diffuse leading edge to the tail band.

BARE PARTS Iris dark brown. Bill blackish with diffuse dull flesh, flesh-pink or greyish-flesh base sometimes confined to lower mandible. Leg colour as bill-base.

First-winter (Figs 12C, 14B and 14D) Acquired by post-juvenile head and body moult, which starts at fledging and is usually complete by late September.

HEAD As juvenile, but whiter.

BODY Lower hindneck, breast or breast-sides and flanks with variable grey-brown mottling, streaks or spots, most dense on lower hindneck and breast-sides; underparts otherwise white. Mantle, back and scapulars uniform blue-grey, latter rarely with faint brownish subterminal marks. Dark marks on rump and uppertail- and undertail-coverts less prominent than on juvenile or lacking.

WINGS AND TAIL As juvenile, but brown and blackish areas faded. Occasionally, fading produces pale subterminal spot on 1st primary, forming sometimes well-marked mirror as in Photo 72.

BARE PARTS As juvenile, but bill with clear-cut black tip. Legs and base of bill usually greyish.

First-summer (Fig. 14C. Underwing and tail similar to first-winter, 14D) Acquired by head and body moult, February to April. *As first-winter except:*

HEAD AND BODY Often whiter, less streaked: often wholly white.

WINGS AND TAIL Brown and grey areas becoming very faded, often almost uniform whitish, and black areas browner, often bleached light brown, especially primary tips. Wings, therefore, pale and contrasting with fresh blue-grey mantle and scapulars, giving saddle effect.

BARE PARTS Base of bill typically yellowish-flesh, but also greenish or greyish. Extreme tip of bill may begin to pale from May onwards (or, rarely, as early as February). Legs blue-grey or greyish-flesh.

Second-winter (Fig. 14E) Acquired by complete moult, June to October.

HEAD AND BODY As first-winter, but dark markings usually less extensive, especially on breast-sides and flanks. Rump and uppertail- and undertail-coverts white.

WINGS As adult, but black extending to 6th to 8th primary and along leading edge of forewing onto greater and median primary coverts and alula; primaries lack prominent white tips (which, if present, usually wear off quickly so that by mid-winter most have all-black wing-tip when perched), and mirrors on outer two are smaller. Some have a few brown-centred outer lesser coverts (rarely also outer median coverts) and small blackish marks centrally on the tertials. Individuals showing prominent traces of secondary bar are rare.

TAIL White, occasionally with a few dark subterminal marks.

BARE PARTS Iris brown. Bill typically blue-grey or grey-green, occasionally yellowish, with dark tip or subterminal band. Legs blue-grey or greyish flesh.

Second-summer (wing and tail pattern similar to second-winter, Fig. 14E) Acquired by head and body moult, February to April. *As second-winter except:*

HEAD AND BODY Usually white or lightly marked.

WINGS Black areas faded browner, and tiny white primary tips usually lacking through wear.

Adult winter/third-winter (wing and tail pattern as adult summer, Fig. 14F) Acquired by complete moult, late summer to October.

HEAD White, with fine dark streaks and spots most dense on lower hindneck. Eye-crescent dusky, and thin white crescents above and below eye.

BODY Underparts and rump white, sometimes a few dark spots and streaks on breast-sides and flanks. Mantle, scapulars and back uniform blue-grey with small white scapular-crescents.

WINGS Clear-cut black above and below on wing-tip confined to primaries and extending inwards to 5th or 6th; prominent white tips to all except 1st, and large mirrors on outer two (larger on 1st than 2nd), occasionally also small mirror on 3rd. Remainder of wing uniform blue-grey, with thin white leading edge (marginal coverts) and broad white trailing edge and tertial-crescent. Underwing coverts white.

TAIL White.

BARE PARTS Iris brown, or exceptionally (two cases known to author) pale greenish-yellow (K. Mullarney and G. Koerkamp *in litt.*). Bill yellowish, with thin or faint dark subterminal mark or band and usually greyish base (Strangeman, *Brit. Birds* 75: 289–290). Legs yellowish, greenish, or greyish, often tinged flesh.

Adult summer/third-summer (Fig. 14F) Acquired by head and body moult, February to April. *As adult winter except:*

HEAD White.

BODY Underparts white.

WINGS White primary tips reduced.

BARE PARTS Orbital ring red. Bill usually wholly yellow or yellowish-green. Mouth flesh; gape orange.

GEOGRAPHICAL VARIATION

Four subspecies are generally recognised, and are described below. Marked plumage differences between *canus* and *brachyrhynchus* are, in themselves, apparently sufficient to warrant specific status for latter (thus Mew Gull *L. brachyrhynchus*), but clinal nature of plumage and size differences between the four subspecies, especially intergradation between *heinei* and *kamtschatschensis* in Siberia, and the similarities of plumage (especially first-years) between *kamtschatschensis* and *brachyrhynchus*, are strong arguments against any split.

L. c. canus: Photos 63–89. Breeds northwest Europe, winters within southern part of breeding range and south to southern Europe, uncommon in Iberia and Mediterranean (map, p. 51). Detailed descriptions and Fig. 14 refer to this subspecies. Wing 320–385 mm (Dwight 1925), 321–380 mm (*BWP* III).

L. c. heinei: Breeds central Russia and western and central Siberia, winters Black Sea, southern Caspian, Iraq and Persian Gulf, also smaller numbers probably annual in Baltic and elsewhere in western Europe, including Britain (see Osborn, *Brit. Birds* 78:

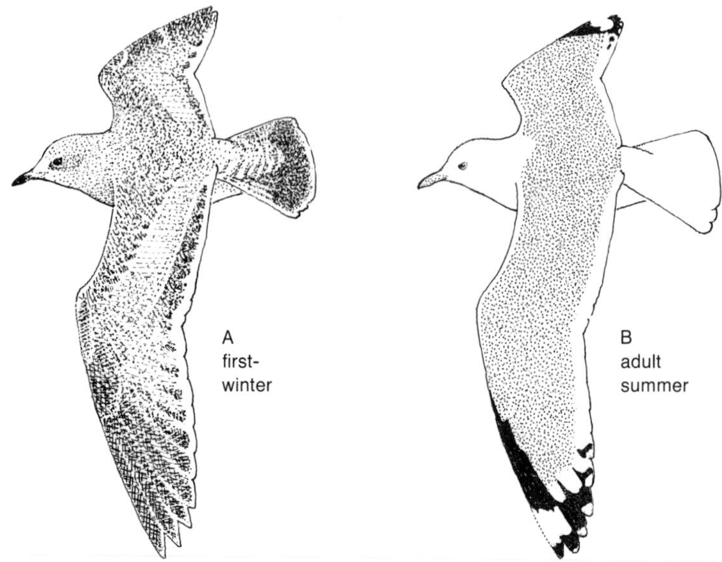

Fig. 14(a). **Common Gulls** *Larus canus brachyrhynchus* (Mew Gull) in flight.

454); also possibly China and eastern Mediterranean (map, p. 51). All plumages similar to *canus*, except adult upperparts darker (darkest of all four subspecies), especially individuals from eastern part of range. Large, averaging between *canus* and *kamtschatschensis*. Wing 351–395 mm (*BWP* III).

L. c. kamtschatschensis: photos 96, 97. Breeds northeast Siberia, winters in coastal eastern Asia (map, p. 51). The largest of the four subspecies (largest overlapping with small Herring Gull). Adults average slightly darker than *canus* and *brachyrhynchus*; first-years (and probably also second-years) similar to *brachyrhynchus*. Wing 365–412 mm (*BWP* III).

L. c. brachyrhynchus (Mew Gull): Fig. 14(a); Photos 90–95. Breeds Alaska and western Canada, rarely Manitoba; winters (mainly on coast) south to California (map, p. 51). Records on east coast of North America apparently all *L. c. canus* from Europe. Similar to *canus* in size and structure (although some individuals look decidedly small-billed), but differs in plumage at all ages. Adult has more white in wing-tip than *canus*, giving noticeably different pattern (especially white 'divide' between grey and black on 3rd to 5th primaries, from above and below); winter head markings much more diffuse, giving uniform grey-brown head (*canus* more darkly mottled and streaked, less uniform); bill usually lacks dark subterminal mark in winter; and iris often noticeably pale, greenish-yellow (iris dark, except very rarely, on *canus*). Second-years as *canus*, except for much more frequent retention of immature markings on wings and tail (like Ring-billed Gull in this respect), thus majority have variable pattern of dark markings on tail, forming partial or broken tail band; often also dark markings on secondaries and tertials; dark areas on outer primaries and their coverts often obviously brownish;

upperwing coverts often washed brownish (often much faded to whitish by second summer); and underwing- and undertail-coverts sometimes lightly marked or barred. Iris sometimes pale; winter head markings as adult. First-years look strikingly different from first-year *canus*, having paler and browner wing markings (upperwing often looking very faded and 'washed-out' especially by first-summer; extreme faded examples have wing, including outer primaries, almost wholly whitish in first summer); tail markings browner, and barred and mottled at base, from distance tail appearing wholly dark except for terminal pale fringe (not clear-cut, broad black tail band and white tail-base as on *canus*); head, underparts and rump more extensively and uniformly brownish-grey; mantle, scapulars and back often mottled pale brownish with little clear grey in first winter; and dark bill-tip often more extensive and contrasting less sharply with pale base. Wing 328–366 mm (Dwight 1925).

Mediterranean Gull

Larus melanocephalus

(Figs 12B and 16, Photographs 98–119)

IDENTIFICATION

Past comparison between Mediterranean and Black-headed Gulls is somewhat misleading. When perched, there is a rather superficial resemblance at all ages, but the distinctive appearance of Mediterranean Gull in second-year and adult plumages render it unlikely to be overlooked. In first-year plumages, especially in flight, it is much more likely to be dismissed as a Common Gull, owing to its similar flight pattern. It is, however, smaller than Common Gull (nearer to Black-headed) with a marginally stouter and shorter-looking bill which (mainly due to its often dark colour) often appears blob-ended or heavy and drooping. It appears longer-legged and has a strutting gait, often with head hunched between the shoulders. In flight it appears heavy-bodied and bull-necked, with less angled wings, stiffer wingbeats and less spread tail.

First-years differ from Common Gull in having blacker outer primaries and secondary bar, and paler grey midwing panel, giving a more contrasting upperwing pattern. The extensive white on the inner webs of the outermost primaries is sometimes visible from above when the wing is fully spread (Common Gull has all-dark outermost primaries), and the underwing is almost wholly white, with the dark outer primaries and secondary bar showing prominently through the wing. The tail band is thinner, especially at the sides. The underparts and head are white, the latter with dark markings of variable extent, in winter usually confined to a more or less well-defined dark patch

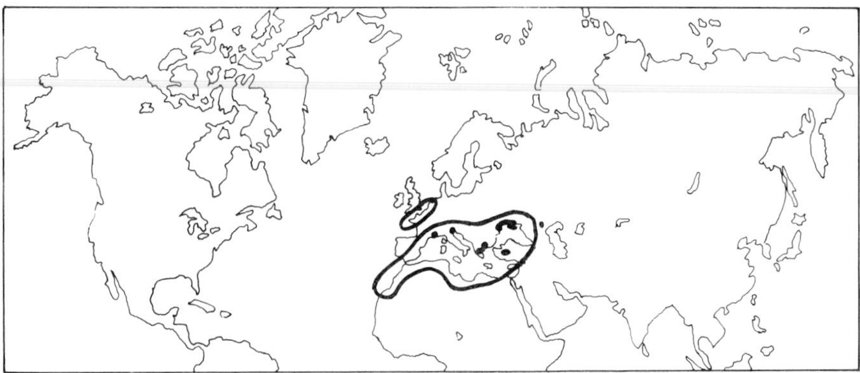

Fig. 15. World distribution of **Mediterranean Gull** *Larus melanocephalus*, showing approximate breeding range (solid black) and approximate limits of winter/non-breeding range (black line). Has bred Hungary, German Democratic Republic, Austria, Estonian SSR, Lithuanian SSR, Netherlands, Belgium, France and England. Increasing in recent years in Britain, with over 100 records annually, mainly in southern coastal areas, where present spasmodic breeding of a few pairs may eventually lead to permanent colonisation.

behind the eye which often extends diffusely across the nape. In first-winter and subsequent plumages, the grey of the upperparts is pale pearl-grey, much paler than on Common Gull. Juveniles have a neat scaly pattern on the scapulars and a surprisingly plain head (usually with no more than a hint of the first-winter pattern) and white underparts with a faintly mottled, pale grey-brown breast band and flanks: the rather plain head and underparts, lacking any obvious dark streaking, and the neat scaly upperparts, give juveniles a smart, clean appearance. Bill and leg colour is highly variable in the first year, darker than Common Gull or with striking orange or reddish coloration.

Second-years and adults have a distinctive appearance, which is unlikely to be confused with any other species of gull. Second-years are readily aged by the variable black markings on the outer primaries. Adults have a black outer web on the outermost primary (rarely two outermost), but otherwise the wings and upperparts are pale pearl-grey (looking whitish at a distance), shading to white on the secondary and primary tips. In summer, the hood is black and extends farther down the nape than on Black-headed Gull, and the bill is scarlet, strikingly paler in tone than the black hood (Black-headed Gull lacks this bill/hood contrast), often with a dark subterminal mark and yellowish tip; the legs are scarlet.

AGEING SUMMARY

Juvenile: scaly brownish mantle and scapulars (summer to September).

First-winter: uniform pale grey mantle and scapulars, blackish outer primaries, secondary bar and tail band, brown carpal-bar, winter head pattern (July to April).

First-summer: as first-winter, but hood sometimes developed to variable extent, wing pattern faded, and brown carpal-bar reduced or lacking (March to October).

Second-winter: as adult winter, except for variable amount of black on outer primaries (July to April).

Second-summer: as second-winter, but hood often fully developed (March to October).

Adult winter/third-winter: adult wing pattern (black confined to outer web of outer primary), winter head pattern (August to March).

Adult summer/third-summer: adult wing pattern, full black hood (February to October).

DETAILED DESCRIPTIONS

Juvenile (Fig. 16A. Underwing and tail similar to first-winter, 16D)

HEAD White, creamy or buff-washed. Plain, or ear-coverts and extension over rear crown greyish, giving faint trace of first-winter head-pattern. Eye-crescent blackish; thin white crescents above and below eye.

BODY Underparts and rump white, except for broad band across breast and extending onto flanks, pale grey-buff or brownish with darker mottling. Lower hindneck and mantle grey or grey-brown, uniform or with fine pale feather fringes giving frosty appearance; scapulars grey-brown, or rusty brown with darker subterminal crescent and neat pale buff or whitish fringe on each feather giving neat scaly pattern.

WINGS Carpal-bar dark grey-brown or brown with paler feather fringes; median coverts with darker shaft-streaks and subterminal crescents. Tertials dark-centred, often with darker subterminal mark and always clear-cut whitish fringes. Inner three or four greater coverts dark-centred, remainder clear pale grey, forming pale midwing panel. Secondaries black, with fine white edges and broad tips. Outer webs of outer five or six primaries and their coverts mainly black; inner primaries mainly grey, with subterminal black marks decreasing in size inwards; inner webs of primaries have extensive white, reaching nearly to tips; sometimes, outer primary (rarely outer two) all-black. Greater primary coverts tipped paler. Underwing almost all-white, with dark markings usually confined to outer primaries, secondary bar, and tips of greater under primary coverts: much whiter than Common Gull.

TAIL White, with clear-cut blackish subterminal band, narrower and often broken on outer feathers, outer pair sometimes all-white. White terminal fringe often broader than on Common Gull.

BARE PARTS Iris dark brown. Bill mainly blackish, with a usually small area of pale grey or flesh at base. Legs blackish.

First-winter (Figs 12B, 16B and 16D) Acquired by post-juvenile head and body moult, which starts at fledging and is usually complete by late September. *As juvenile except:*

HEAD White with blackish markings of variable extent, typically rather clear-cut mask or patch of fine streaks from behind eye, often extending diffusely over nape or rear crown. Sometimes an isolated dark ear-spot similar to Black-headed Gull. Eye-crescent blackish; thin white crescents above and below eye.

BODY Underparts white. Mantle, scapulars and back uniform pale pearl-grey, same shade as grey of wings.

WINGS AND TAIL Brown of carpal-bar faded (often very ginger-brown), black areas slightly faded, and white tips and fringes of inner primaries, secondaries, tertials and tail reduced.

BARE PARTS Bill sometimes wholly blackish or brownish-black, but usually with pale base of variable extent, with clear-cut or diffuse blackish tip: extreme tip sometimes reddish. Colour of base highly variable, from buff, flesh or yellowish, through orange to red. Mouth dull flesh. Legs similarly variable from blackish or grey (sometimes with olive-green tinge) through orange to red.

First-summer (Fig. 16C. Underwing and tail similar to first-winter, 16D) Acquired by head and body moult, February to April. *As first-winter except:*

HEAD Black head markings usually more extensive; a few acquire full hood.

WINGS AND TAIL Becoming very worn and faded in some, although black areas fade less than on most Common Gulls. A few replace most innerwing coverts, and thus lack brown carpal-bar.

BARE PARTS Bill and leg colour highly variable, much as first-winter, but some may acquire near-adult coloration and bill pattern.

The least advanced individuals have dull bare parts, and wing and head patterns little different from first-winter, while the most advanced have adult-like bill and legs, well-developed or complete hood, and lack a carpal-bar.

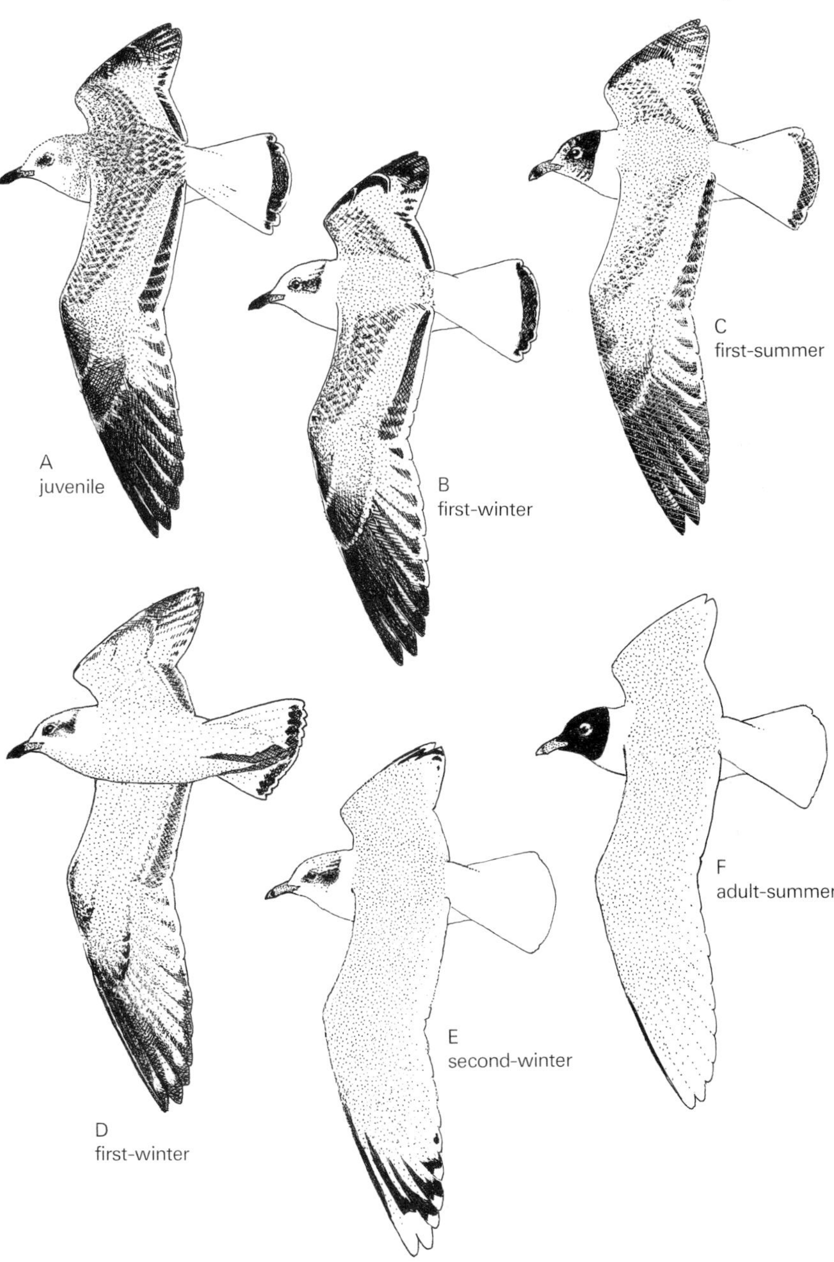

Fig. 16. **Mediterranean Gulls** *Larus melanocephalus* in flight.

Second-winter (Fig. 16E) Acquired by complete moult, May to September. *As adult winter except:*

HEAD As first-winter.

WINGS Outer three to six primaries with subterminal black marks of variable extent and pattern. Outer greater primary coverts and alula occasionally with black marks.

BARE PARTS Bill flesh to reddish, with dark tip or subterminal band. Legs as adult winter or more orange-red.

It seems likely that a few advanced individuals may be indistinguishable from adult at this age.

Second-summer (Wing and tail pattern similar to second-winter, Fig. 16E) Acquired by head and body moult, February to April. *As second-winter except:*

HEAD Hood fully developed or with white flecking.

WINGS White primary tips reduced or lacking.

BARE PARTS Bill and legs much as adult summer.

Adult winter/third-winter (Wing and tail pattern as adult summer, Fig. 16F) Acquired by complete moult late summer to October.

HEAD AND BODY As first-winter.

WINGS Pale pearly-grey shading to white on primary tips: at distance, whole outer wing appears flashing white; 1st (and rarely 2nd) with thin black line of variable extent on outer web. Secondaries and underwing white.

TAIL White.

BARE PARTS Iris brown. Orbital ring red or orange-red. Bill usually red, orange-red or orange, sometimes pink, with black subterminal mark, band or whole tip, or bill occasionally mainly blackish. Extreme tip often yellowish. Mouth and gape red. Legs usually dull reddish, red or orange-red, occasionally blackish.

Adult summer/third-summer (Fig. 16F) Acquired by head and body moult, January to April. *As adult winter except:*

HEAD Hood jet black, extending farther down nape than on Black-headed Gull. Prominent white crescent posteriorly above and below eye.

BARE PARTS Bill scarlet, with or without thin blackish subterminal smudge or band, often with yellow or orange at extreme tip. Legs scarlet.

Ring-billed Gull

Larus delawarensis

(Figs 12A and 18, Photographs 120–145)

First-winter

IDENTIFICATION

Ring-billed Gull resembles Common Gull but (compared with the European race *L. c. canus*) is usually slightly larger and heavier-bodied, with usually obviously thicker bill, slightly longer legs, and more fierce expression caused by its less rounded head, often faint dark furrow or brow over the eye, and (on second-winter or second-summer and older) pale iris. The grey of the upperparts is much paler, and perched second-years and older lack prominent white scapular- and tertial-crescents which are obvious on Common Gull. It has a plover-like gait, perhaps an effect of its slightly longer legs.

In first-year plumages, further differences from Common Gull are the more contrasting upperwing pattern (due mainly to the darker brown carpal-bar, the blacker outer primaries and secondary bar, and the paler inner primaries and greater coverts), the usually more contrasting blackish outer primaries and secondary bar from below, the usually more variegated pattern of the tail band, the usually clearly spotted (rather than mottled) lower hindneck, and the usually more defined spots or crescentic markings on the breast-sides and flanks (rather than the usually indistinct mottling on Common Gull), although these may be reduced or lacking in first-summer plumage. The brown centres of the tertials tend to be darker, with thinner whitish fringes, and the dark centres of the inner median and lesser coverts (which form the inner part of the carpal-bar) have a pointed shape at the tip, not rounded as on Common Gull, but these differences are valid only in fresh plumage because wear and fading eventually make the

Fig. 17. World distribution of **Ring-billed Gull** *Larus delawarensis*, showing approximate breeding range (solid black) and approximate southern limit of winter/non-breeding range (black line). Rare wanderer to Europe; in Britain and Ireland, first recorded in 1973 and (up to end 1984) total of 348 records, including exceptional numbers in 1981, 1982, 1983 and 1984 (55, 76, 89 and 84 respectively), mainly derived from major influx in winter of 1981/82 (Vinicombe, Brit. Birds 78: 327–337).

wing coverts uniform and whitish in both species. The inner greater coverts are usually not plain grey-brown as on Common Gull, but are marked or barred with dark. Because of the paleness of the grey upperparts, Ring-billed lacks the contrasting dark grey saddle which is obvious on first-year (especially first-summer) Common Gulls. The yellowish coloration of the bill and legs, and the black band on the bill are sometimes well-developed in first-summer plumage.

Second-years resemble adults, but are readily aged by the more extensive black on the leading edge of the outer wing, extending strongly onto the greater primary coverts and alula; unlike Common Gull, they have only one small mirror, if any, and most have prominent traces of a tail band and sometimes also a partial secondary bar which are much less often shown by second-year Common Gull (see Cade, *Brit. Birds* 75: 580). The thick, clear-cut black band on the bill is usually well developed by the second year; Common Gulls may also have a broad band on the bill in second-year plumages, but it is usually less well-defined and quickly becomes thinner than on Ring-billed Gull. Adult and most second-year Ring-billeds have a pale iris; the others in this group are dark-eyed at all ages. The wing-tip pattern of adults is close to that of Herring Gull, with mirrors much smaller than on Common Gull.

A small or small-looking immature Herring Gull with dark-tipped or dark-banded bill can rather easily be mistaken for a Ring-billed. Its actually larger size, longer and heavier bill, and longer and more sloping forehead than Ring-billed may be difficult to discern, especially on a lone bird. The main problem area is with second-year Herring, the general plumage patterns and bare parts coloration of which can closely resemble that of a first-year Ring-billed. The best differences of second-year Herring (from first-year Ring-billed) are its strongly mottled or barred tertials (dark-centred with neat pale fringe on Ring-billed), untidily barred median and lesser coverts (dark-centred with neat pale fringes on Ring-billed giving neat, scaly pattern which, however, may become worn and faded by first-summer), usually obviously pale iris (always dark on first-winter Ring-billed, and slightly—if at all—paler on first-summer), usually obvious pale bill-tip (lacking or small on first-winter Ring-billed, but may be more obvious by first-summer), extensive dusky areas on underwing coverts (neat dark tips on underwing coverts forming pattern of lines on Ring-billed), and more extensive dark markings on tail (not comparatively neater and narrower band as on Ring-billed).

AGEING SUMMARY

Juvenile: scaly brown mantle and scapulars, and extensive dark markings on head, breast and flanks (summer to September).

First-winter: dusky head and body markings, grey mantle and scapulars, blackish outer primaries, secondary bar and tail band, brown carpal-bar, and black-tipped bill (July to April).

First-summer: as first-winter, but head and body whiter, wing pattern faded paler, and band on bill usually beginning to develop (March to September).

Second-winter: wings uniform grey, with black tip extending along leading edge of outer wing, one small mirror (or none), white primary tips tiny or lacking, usually traces of tail band and sometimes secondary bar, and much dusky on head. Iris usually pale (June to April).

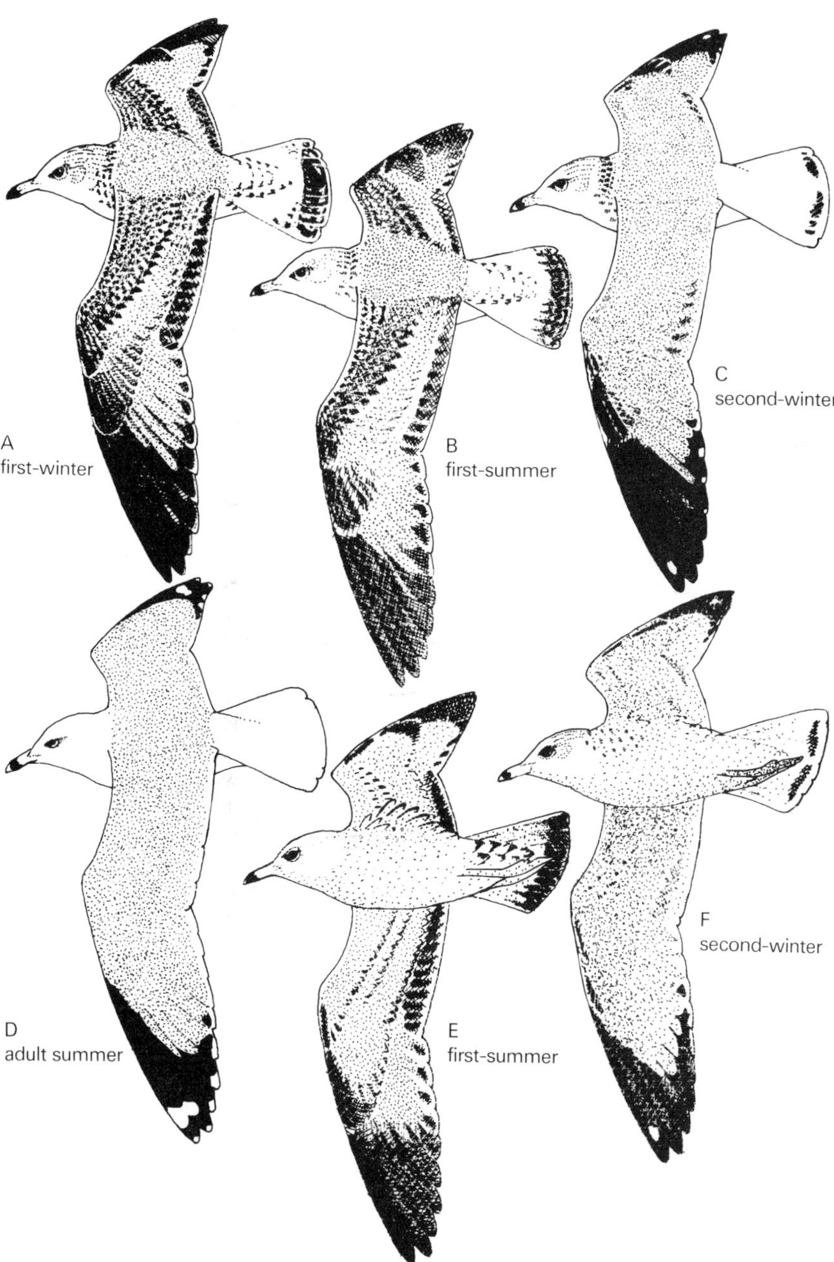

Fig. 18. **Ring-billed Gulls** *Larus delawarensis* in flight.

Second-summer: as second-winter, but head white or lightly marked. Yellow bill colour and band usually well developed (March to October).

Adult winter/third-winter: black on wing-tip confined to primaries, usually two mirrors, prominent white primary tips (obvious when perched), dusky head markings, clear-cut black band on yellowish bill, and yellowish legs (August to March).

Adult summer/third-summer: as adult winter, but head white, white primary tips may be reduced or lacking, clear-cut black band on bill, and bill and legs bright yellow (March to October).

DETAILED DESCRIPTIONS

Juvenile (not illustrated, but wing and tail pattern similar to first-winter, Figs 12A and 18A) *Resembles juvenile Common Gull except:*

BODY Lower hindneck, breast (especially breast-sides) and flanks more coarsely marked with darker grey-brown, usually with coarser pattern of distinct chevrons, crescentic markings or complex barring especially on breast-sides and flanks. Mantle and scapulars grey-brown, individual feathers with dark subterminal crescents and pale fringes forming more complex pattern than on Common Gull.

WINGS Dark areas on outer wing generally blacker, and more defined and less extensive on inner primaries: inner primaries and midwing panel basically paler grey, giving more contrasting upperwing pattern than on Common Gull. Greater coverts pale grey with usually obvious neat dark markings or bars, expecially on innermost, not uniform grey-brown as on Common Gull. Carpal-bar darker, less brown, and tip of dark central area of individual median and lesser coverts (especially innermost) pointed, not rounded as on Common Gull. Tertials and adjacent greater coverts darker than Common Gull, with thinner pale fringes on average. Pattern on underwing coverts similar, but markings perhaps darker on average, but some only faintly marked.

TAIL Subterminal band rarely solid black and clear-cut as on Common Gull, but usually broken by pale mottling of highly variable pattern: remainder of tail often shaded with grey of variable pattern. Tail pattern of Ring-billed Gulls highly variable, with any two individuals rarely identical, unlike comparatively standard pattern of Common Gull. Uppertail- and undertail-coverts more strongly barred on average.

BARE PARTS Iris dark brown. Bill blackish, often with flesh-pink base and sometimes tiny whitish mark at extreme tip. Legs flesh-pink.

First-winter (Figs 12A and 18A. Underwing and tail similar to first-summer, 18E) Acquired by post-juvenile head and body moult which starts at fledging and is usually complete by late September. *As juvenile except:*

HEAD AND BODY Head and underparts usually generally whiter, with distinct blackish spots on lower hindneck, and defined spots and crescentic markings on breast-sides and flanks. Mantle, scapulars and back pale grey, some individual feathers often with dark subterminal crescents and pale fringes: mantle and scapulars thus paler grey and often with obvious faint barring or mottling, not uniform as on typical Common Gull. A few brown juvenile scapulars are sometimes retained.

WINGS AND TAIL Brown and blackish areas becoming faded, and white tips and fringes often reduced by wear, so losing covert pattern differences from Common Gull.

BARE PARTS Bill pink, yellowish, or greenish-yellow with clear-cut black tip: extreme tip occasionally develops small pale area towards end of first winter, rarely as early as February.

First-summer (Figs 18B and 18E) Acquired by head and body moult, February to April. *As first-winter except:*

HEAD AND BODY Dark markings reduced or completely lacking. Mantle and scapulars uniform pale grey.

WINGS AND TAIL Brown and grey areas often faded to whitish, and black areas faded browner, but contrast with pale grey saddle much less marked than on Common Gull. White tips and fringes reduced or lacking.

BARE PARTS Band on bill and yellowish coloration of bill and legs often well developed.

Second-winter (Figs 18C and 18F) Acquired by complete moult, May to September. *Similar to second-winter Common Gull except:*

HEAD AND BODY Dark markings on hindneck and (if present at all) on breastsides and flanks, more distinctly spotted. Mantle, scapulars and inner wing pale grey, paler than Common Gull.

WINGS Only one mirror, if any, on 1st primary, often visible only from below. Some have dark marks on secondaries and tertials, forming partial secondary bar. White tertial fringes (and trailing edge to inner wing) thinner and shaded into pale grey remainder, thus lacking prominent tertial-crescent which is obvious on perched Common Gull. Underwing coverts sometimes faintly marked with dark.

TAIL Most have prominent dark marks of highly variable (and often asymmetrical) pattern on tail, forming partial or broken tail band.

BARE PARTS Iris usually pale. Thick black band on bill. Legs and base of bill usually greenish-yellow, sometimes yellowish, greenish-grey or grey.

Second-summer (wing and tail pattern similar to second-winter, Figs 18C and 18F) Acquired by head and body moult, February to April. *As second-winter except:*

HEAD AND BODY White, or with a few light spots on hindneck.

WINGS Black areas faded paler, and tiny white primary tips usually lacking through wear.

BARE PARTS Iris pale. Legs and black-banded bill obviously yellowish or as adult.

Adult winter/third-winter (wing and tail pattern as adult summer, Fig. 18D) Acquired by complete moult late summer to October. *Similar to adult winter Common Gull except:*

HEAD Dark markings more distinctly spotted.

BODY Mantle and scapulars (and inner wing) much paler grey.

WINGS White mirrors on 1st and 2nd primaries usually much smaller, and tertial-crescent and white trailing edge as second-winter.

BARE PARTS Pale yellowish iris, obvious at close range. Orbital ring blackish, gape orange, mouth orange-flesh. Bill with broad, clear-cut black subterminal band, yellow or greenish-yellow base; tip yellow. Legs yellow or greenish-yellow.

Adult summer/third-summer (Fig. 18D) Acquired by head and body moult, February to April. *As adult winter except:*

HEAD White.

WINGS White primary tips reduced or lacking.

BARE PARTS Orbital ring and gape orange-red. Legs and black-banded bill bright yellow or orange-yellow.

Laughing Gull

Larus atricilla

(Figs 12E and 20, Photographs 146–168)

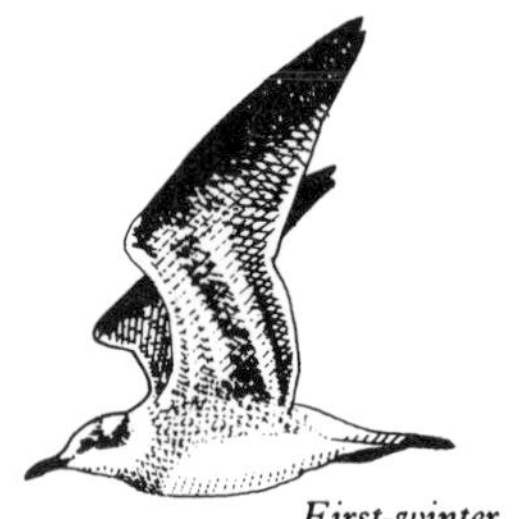

First-winter

IDENTIFICATION

Laughing Gull has a distinctive appearance at all ages, and is unlikely to be confused with any other gull except Franklin's (p. 73, which see for comparison).

Laughing is on average only slightly larger in body-size than Black-headed Gull, but because of its proportionately longer wings appears closer to Common Gull, especially in flight. It averages obviously smaller than the European race of Common Gull *L. c. canus* (but probably overlaps more in size with the west coast North American *L. c. brachyrhynchus*), but with proportionately longer wings (which give an attenuated look when perched and a rakish, long-winged silhouette in flight), longer bill (which often looks heavy and drooping) and longer legs. The grey of the upperparts is darker than on Common Gull, close in tone to that of the palest of British Lesser Black-backed Gulls *L. f. graellsii*.

In first-winter plumage, the head, hindneck, breast, and flanks are extensively dark grey, shading to whitish on the chin, throat (often extending below and behind the dark ear-coverts to form a distinctive half-collar), forehead and belly. The coverts of the inner wing are mainly brown, contrasting with the uniform grey mantle and scapulars and the mainly black outer wing and secondary bar. The underwing coverts are pale with dark tips, with a usually prominent diagonal dark bar extending from the axillaries. The tail is grey, with a broad black subterminal band, and the rump is white. First-summer plumage is similar, but often with a partial or full hood, and the wing coverts are often faded to patchy pale brown.

Second-years closely resemble adults, but are readily aged by the more extensive

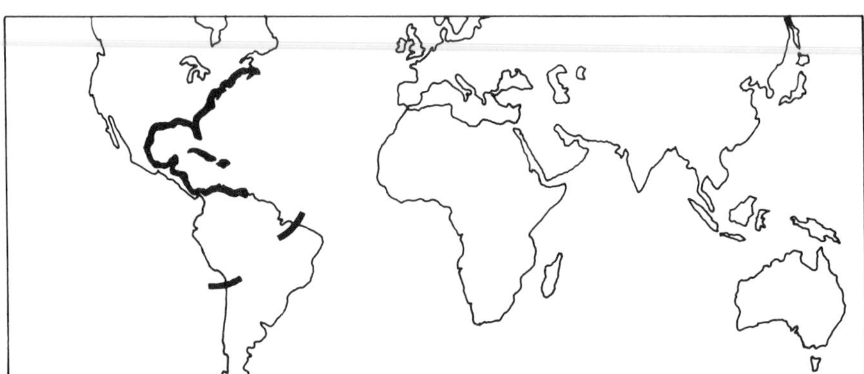

Fig. 19. World distribution of **Laughing Gull** *Larus atricilla*, showing approximate breeding range (solid black) and approximate southern limits of winter/non-breeding range (black line). Rare vagrant to Europe; in Britain and Ireland averaging two or three records annually.

black on the wing (extending strongly on to the greater primary coverts and alula), and most have traces of a secondary bar or tail band.

Adults have uniform dark grey upperparts and wings, the latter with a broad white trailing edge, and black tip (*without* mirrors) confined to the outer primaries. In summer, the bill and legs are dull red, and the extensive black hood has prominent white crescents above and below the eye. In winter, the bill and legs are blackish, and the head has dusky markings of variable extent, usually confined to the eye-coverts and extending over rear crown.

AGEING SUMMARY

Juvenile: scaly brown mantle and scapulars (summer to September).

First-winter: uniform grey mantle and scapulars, extensive grey on hindneck, breast and flanks, brown innerwing coverts, blackish outer primaries and secondary bar, and white rump contrasting with grey tail, which has broad black subterminal band (July to April).

First-summer: as first-winter, but less grey on hindneck and head, coverts of inner wing faded pale brown, and contrasting dark grey mantle and scapulars (March to October).

Second-winter: wings uniform grey, with black tip extending along leading edge of outer wing; white tips on primaries small or lacking; usually traces of secondary bar and tail band; winter head pattern; obvious grey wash on hindneck, breast-sides and flanks; and blackish bill and legs (July to April).

Second-summer: as second-winter, but hood partially or fully developed, underparts white and bill and legs usually dull reddish (March to October).

Adult winter/third-winter: black of wing-tip mainly confined to primaries, which have obvious white tips; winter head pattern with white neck and underparts; bill blackish, with red line near tip of culmen; and legs blackish (August to March).

Adult summer/third-summer: as adult winter, but full black hood, white primary tips reduced or lacking, and dull red bill and legs (February to October).

DETAILED DESCRIPTIONS

Juvenile (not illustrated, but wing and tail pattern similar to first-winter, Figs 12E, 20A and 20C)

HEAD Mainly grey-brown, paler on forehead, lores, chin and throat, and often darker on rear ear-coverts, rear crown, and nape. Eye-crescent blackish, and thin whitish crescents above and below eye (not joining at rear), less prominent than on subsequent plumages.

BODY Hindneck, broad breast-band, and flanks uniform grey-brown. Belly, vent and rump dull white. Mantle and scapulars brown, with pale buff feather fringes giving scaly appearance, most prominent on scapulars. Back uniform greyish.

WINGS Lesser and median coverts and tertials mainly brown like scapulars, with fine pale buff fringes; greater coverts grey-brown with whitish fringes. Secondaries black with fine white edges and broad white tips. Outer primaries and coverts wholly blackish, with thin white fringes at tips from 3rd to 5th inwards, and dull grey on outer and inner webs increasing from 4th to 6th inwards. Underwing coverts mainly dull white, with dusky markings especially on tips of axillaries forming prominent dark diagonal bar which often extends across median and lesser underwing coverts.

TAIL Outer webs dull grey, inner webs whitish, with broad black subterminal band always extending to the outer pair of feathers; thin white terminal fringe.

BARE PARTS Iris dark. Bill black, often with some dull brown at base. Legs blackish or dull brown.

First-winter (Figs 12E, 20A and 20C) Acquired by post-juvenile moult of head, body and variable number of coverts on inner wing, which starts at fledging and is usually complete by October. *As juvenile except:*

HEAD Mainly grey, with whitish forehead, lores, chin and throat, and darker patch on rear ear-coverts which often extends over rear crown and over crown above eye. White on throat often extends below and behind ear-coverts to form half-collar. White cresents above and below eye more prominent.

BODY Mantle and scapulars uniform dark grey.

WINGS Variable amount of new coverts on inner wing, especially median coverts, plain grey.

First-summer (Fig. 20B. Underwing and tail similar to first-winter, 20A) Acquired by head and body moult, February to April. *As first-winter except:*

HEAD Grey sometimes less extensive or with hood of variable extent.

BODY Grey on hindneck, breast and flanks may be less extensive.

WINGS AND TAIL Brown coverts of inner wing often much faded to patchy pale brown, and white terminal fringes to primaries, secondaries and tail reduced or lacking.

BARE PARTS Bill occasionally with reddish at tip of culmen.

Second-winter (Fig. 20D) Acquired by complete moult, June to late September.

HEAD White, with greyish patch of variable extent and strength on ear-coverts, usually extending over rear crown. Eye-crescent blackish. Crescents above and below eye white, not joining at rear.

BODY Underparts and neck white, except for obvious grey wash on hindneck, breast-sides and flanks. Mantle and scapulars uniform dark grey, with prominent white tertial- and small white scapular-crescent when perched. Rump white.

WINGS Uniform dark grey, with prominent white trailing edge on secondaries and inner primaries. Small white tips on primaries from about 4th inwards. Usually, variable number of secondaries with blackish on outer webs, forming indistinct secondary bar. Outer four or five primaries black, extending along leading edge of outer wing onto coverts and alula. Subterminal black from 5th or 6th to 8th. Underwing coverts white or grey-washed.

TAIL White, or with grey at base, often with black or grey subterminal spots of varying extent and pattern forming partial or broken tail band. Outer and central feathers white.

BARE PARTS As juvenile. Sometimes, hint of red on bill-tip.

Second-summer (wing and tail pattern similar to second-winter, Fig. 20D) Acquired by head and body moult, February to April. *As second-winter except:*

Fig. 20. **Laughing Gulls** *Larus atricilla* in flight.

HEAD Black usually more extensive, and most acquire full hood as adult summer.

BODY Grey clouding on breast-sides and flanks usually lacking.

BARE PARTS Bill usually dull red, or with blackish near tip, or red tip. Legs dull red or blackish-brown.

Adult winter/third-winter (wing and tail pattern as adult summer, Fig. 20E) Acquired by complete moult, late summer to October. *As second-winter except:*

BODY Very pale grey clouding confined to lower hindneck and breast-sides, much paler than on second-winter.

WINGS Clear-cut black wing-tip (in some lights showing little contrast with rest of wing) extending to 5th or 6th primary; obvious white tips from 3rd or 4th increasing in size inwards. Outer one or two greater primary coverts sometimes with some black. Underwing coverts white contrasting with blackish outer primaries and grey subterminal bar across secondaries and inner primaries.

TAIL White.

BARE PARTS Bill black or blackish-brown, usually with small red line near tip of culmen and sometimes also near tip of gonys. Legs blackish or grey.

Adult summer/third-summer (Fig. 20E) Acquired by head and body moult, February to April. *As adult winter except:*

HEAD Slaty-black hood fully developed. Prominent white crescents above and posteriorly below eye, not joining at rear.

BODY Neck and underparts white.

WINGS White primary tips reduced or lacking.

BARE PARTS Iris dark brown. Orbital ring, mouth and gape red. Bill dull red or clouded with blackish subterminally, often with bright orange-red or scarlet tip. Legs dull red or blackish-brown.

Franklin's Gull

Larus pipixcan

(Figs 12D and 22, Photographs 169–196)

Adult summer

IDENTIFICATION

This highly migratory and distinctive small gull is unlikely to be confused with any other species except Laughing Gull.

Franklin's is, on average, slightly smaller than Black-headed and Laughing Gull. On the ground and in flight its outline is reminiscent of the smaller Little Gull, lacking the long-winged silhouette of Laughing Gull. The bill can look rather stout, but it lacks the long, drooping shape which is usually striking on Laughing Gull. Its length (from the forwardmost extension of feathering on the upper mandible to the tip) is the same or slightly less than the loral distance (which is the distance from the forwardmost extension of feathering on the upper mandible to the front edge of the eye): Laughing's bill is slightly longer than the loral distance. It is also proportionately shorter-legged than Laughing. Like Laughing Gull, the grey on the upperparts is rather dark, close to that on the palest of British Lesser Black-backed Gulls *L. f. graellsii*. In winter and first-year plumages, Franklin's has a diagnostic blackish 'half-hood', covering the ear-coverts, rear crown and nape (thus much more extensive than on other hooded gulls in winter plumage which, however, often show a similar pattern at transitional stages of moult to or from summer plumage), with strikingly thick, white crescents above and below the eye which usually join at the rear.

As well as the size and structural differences, first-winters differ from Laughing Gulls of the same age in having the half-hood, almost wholly white underparts without the extensive grey breast-band and flanks, small white tips to most of the primaries in fresh plumage, mainly grey inner primaries, mainly whitish underwing coverts, and thinner black tail band which does not extend to the all-white outer pair of feathers. First-

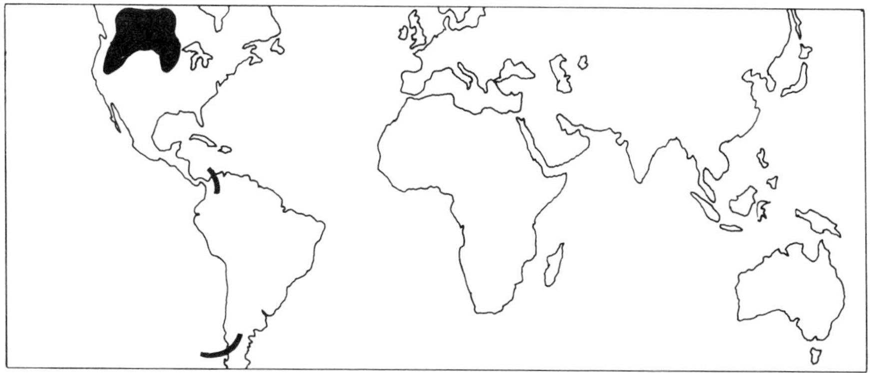

Fig. 21. World distribution of **Franklin's Gull** *Larus pipixcan*, showing approximate breeding range (solid black) and approximate limits of winter/non-breeding range (black line). Rare vagrant to Europe; in Britain (up to end 1984), ten records since first in 1970.

summers and second-years are less readily separable from second-year and adult Laughing Gulls, but the half-hood in winter, the thicker white crescents above and below the eye which usually join at the rear, the prominently white-tipped primaries (obvious when perched), and the grey-centred tail, as well as the size and structural differences, are the best distinctions. When fully adult, further differences are the distinctive wing pattern, usually pink-flushed underparts, and the diagnostic grey-centred tail, the latter unique among adult gulls.

Unlike any other gull, Franklin's has a complete moult in both spring and autumn. As with other gulls, however, the post-juvenile moult (from fledging to October) to first-winter plumage involves only the head and body feathers, and usually also some coverts of the inner wing which reduces the extent of the brown carpal-bar. The first complete moult takes place in winter quarters in January to April, from first-winter to first-summer plumage, and subsequent moults are always complete, in autumn prior to the southward migration (from July to October) to winter plumage, and in 'spring' prior to the northward migration (from November to April) to summer plumage. A very few first-winters do not have a complete moult to first-summer, instead having an arrested moult in which only a variable number of inner primaries are renewed and juvenile outer primaries are retained.

Fig. 22 shows the typical appearance of the various ages, but there is much individual variation, and winter observations in South America show that it is difficult to age with certainty the majority of second-winter/adult winter individuals in the field. Individuals showing a wing pattern similar or close to that of Fig. 22D are certain second-winters, and those with wing patterns like 22E or 22F are adult, but there is every intergradation between these extremes, and it would seem safest to assign such intermediate examples as 'second-winter or adult winter'.

I am indebted to E. J. Mackrill, whose expert analysis of the field situation which he has observed in North and South America, and whose extensive series of superb photographs of Franklin's Gulls, have been a major contribution to this summary and to the detailed descriptions.

AGEING SUMMARY

Juvenile: scaly brown mantle and scapulars (summer to October).

First-winter: half-hood, uniform grey mantle and scapulars, brown on coverts of inner wing, and blackish primaries, secondary bar and tail band (August to February).

First-summer: half-hood as first-winter (or hood partially developed); grey mantle, scapulars, and inner wing; no complete white division between grey of primaries and black wing-tip; black extensive on outer two or three primaries, often extending strongly onto greater primary coverts and alula; and sometimes an indistinct partial secondary bar or tail band (February to September).

Second-winter: as adult winter, but black on outer primaries extending up outer webs, with little or no white division from grey of primary bases. Many probably inseparable from adult winter in the field, but those with this wing-tip pattern are certain second-winters (August to February).

Adult summer/second-summer: as adult winter, but full black hood (February to September).

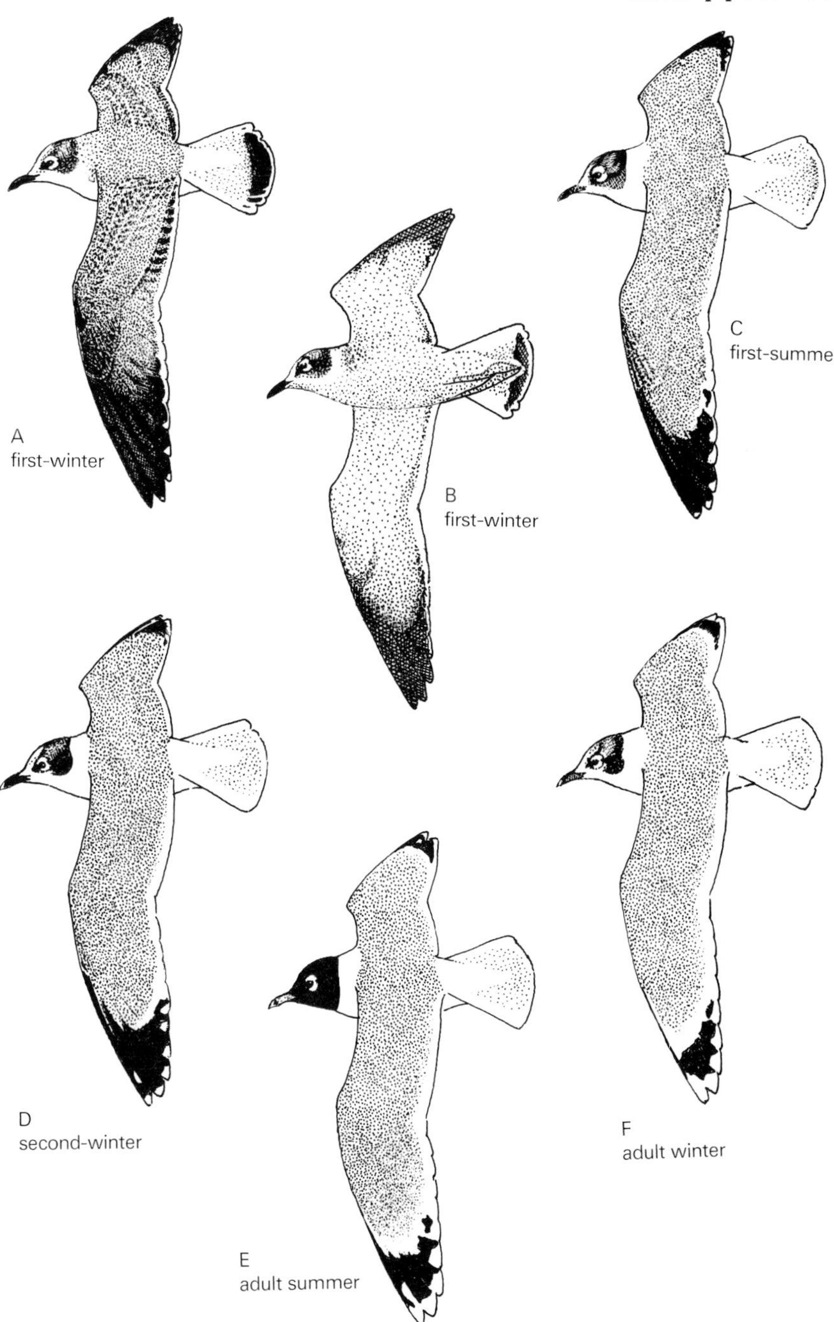

Fig. 22. **Franklin's Gulls** *Larus pipixcan* in flight

Adult winter/third-winter: half-hood; uniform grey upperparts and inner wing; obvious white division between grey of primaries and black on wing-tip; black on wing-tip less extensive than on typical second-winter, with large mirror on first primary and very large white tips to all outer primaries. Many probably inseparable from second-winter in the field, but those with this wing-tip pattern are certain adults (August to February).

DETAILED DESCRIPTIONS

Juvenile (not illustrated, but wing and tail pattern similar to first-winter, Figs 12D, 22A and 22B)

HEAD Forehead, lores, chin, throat and crescents above and below eye whitish. Eye-crescent, ear-coverts, rear crown and nape mainly uniform dark grey-brown, more streaked on crown and nape, forming clear-cut half-hood.

BODY Underparts and rump white, breast-sides faintly washed brown. Hindneck, mantle, scapulars and back brownish; scapulars fringed pale giving indistinct scaly pattern.

WING Carpal-bar brownish with pale fringes. Greater coverts mainly uniform brownish-grey. Secondaries grey-brown with blackish centres (forming secondary bar) and prominent white tips forming white trailing edge to inner wing. Outer primaries, their coverts, and alula mainly black, with grey on outer webs increasing inwards from 3rd or 4th, and black decreasing to subterminal band on 6th or 7th. Small white tips on outer primaries increasing in size inwards to 5th or 6th, remainder with prominent white fringes at tips. Greater under primary coverts prominently marked with dusky, remainder of underwing coverts mainly white.

TAIL Mainly pale grey, with black subterminal band of even width or slightly broader in centre, not extending to outer pair of feathers, which are all-white.

BARE PARTS Bill blackish, sometimes shade paler at base. Legs blackish.

First-winter (Fig 12D, 22A and 22B) Acquired by post-juvenile head and body moult, which often also includes more or less of the coverts of the inner wing, summer to October. *As juvenile except:*

HEAD Half-hood blackish-brown, with thick white crescents above and below eyes, usually joining at rear.

BODY Breast-sides faintly washed grey. Underparts sometimes pink-flushed. Back brownish. Hindneck, mantle and scapulars clear dark grey; scapulars occasionally with fine brown shaft-streaks.

WINGS Brown areas becoming faded paler, and pale tertial fringes and small white tips on outer primaries reduced or lacking.

BARE PARTS Bill black, often brownish at base. Legs black to reddish-brown.

First-summer (Fig. 22C) Acquired by complete moult, January to April.

HEAD Pattern at first-winter, but often blackish, or hood sometimes partially developed by mid-summer, but never full hood. Thick white crescents above and below eye, meeting at rear.

BODY Mantle, back and scapulars uniform dark grey, remainder white; underparts sometimes with pale pink flush.

WINGS Dark grey, with broad white trailing edge on secondaries and inner primaries. Outer five or six primaries with small but obvious white tips increasing in size inwards. Black on outer five or six primaries decreasing in extent inwards to subterminal mark on 5th or 6th, extensive on outer webs of outer two or three. Outer greater primary coverts brownish with dark centres, and alula often blackish: these dark markings form dusky extension of black wing-tip up leading edge of outer wing, which may be difficult to discern in field. Variable number of secondaries have dark centres, sometimes forming indistinct, partial secondary bar.

TAIL As second-winter/adult winter, or grey central feathers shading darker towards tip and with dark shafts: occasionally also with dark subterminal spots forming indistinct partial tail band.

BARE PARTS Bill and legs blackish, or bill reddish at base.

A very few individuals have only partial or arrested moult to first-summer plumage, in which variable number of juvenile outer primaries and their coverts (and also other juvenile wing feathers) retained.

Second-winter (Fig. 22D) Acquired by complete moult, July to October. *As first-summer except:*

HEAD Half-hood blackish.

BODY Underparts often pink-flushed.

WINGS Black on primaries less extensive, with complete black outer web only on 1st, and subterminal black bands on 3rd to 5th, and sometimes subterminal black spot on 6th. Small area of white divides black on 3rd to 6th from grey bases. Outer primaries usually with obvious white tips increasing in size inwards to 5th or 6th, and 1st often with small mirror on inner web near tip. Outer greater primary coverts grey, sometimes with indistinct dusky centres or shaft streaks. No secondary bar.

TAIL White terminal fringe and sides, grey centrally.

BARE PARTS Bill blackish or brownish, with red or orange at tip. Legs blackish or dull red. Eye and orbital ring dark.

Adult summer/second-summer (Fig. 22E) Acquired by complete moult, November to April.

HEAD Full slaty-black hood, with thick white crescents or oval patches posteriorly above and below eye, joining at rear.

BODY As first-summer, with pink flush on underparts.

WINGS Full adult has much less black than second-winter, sometimes barely extending to 5th primary and divided from grey remainder by broad band of white across all primaries. White primary tips much larger than second-winter, and large mirror often merging with white tip to form wholly white end to 1st primary. On closed wing, white primary tips merge so that black is entirely surrounded by white. Typical full adult thus has pattern like 22F, or with even less black, while other adults (perhaps second-summers), have full adult summer plumage and bare parts, but wing-tip pattern little different from second-winter 22D with similar small white primary tips (forming separate spots on closed wing) but less black.

TAIL As second-winter.

BARE PARTS Bill red, usually with dark subterminal marks or thin band. Mouth and gape scarlet. Legs red. Orbital ring rich pink.

Adult winter/third-winter (Fig. 22F) Acquired by complete moult, about beginning of July to October. As second-winter except wing pattern as adult summer, and bare parts often generally redder, and bill usually with red or orange at extreme tip, or reddish with black subterminal mark.

GROUP THREE

Audouin's, Herring, Lesser Black-backed, Great Black-backed and Great Black-headed Gulls

The five species covered here are grouped because of their large size and similar wing and tail patterns, especially in juvenile and first-year plumages. Glaucous *Larus hyperboreus* and Iceland Gulls *L. glaucoides* (Group 5) are the only other western Palearctic species of similar size, but are readily separated from this group by the lack of black or brown on wings and tail at all ages.

The identification of juveniles and first-years is often difficult, requiring reasonable views and practice. Some adult coloration is usually acquired on the mantle and scapulars during the second year, making identification easier, but in these and even in third-year and adult plumages the separation of the two similar pairs (Herring *L. argentatus*/Audouin's *L. audouinii*, and Lesser Black-backed *L. fuscus*/Great Black-backed *L. marinus*) remains difficult at long range.

The ageing of large gulls is less straightforward than is generally the case for smaller species: the longer period of immaturity gives, with each successive moult, an increasing potential for individual plumage variation. Juveniles, first-winters and first-summers can generally be aged with certainty, mainly because their first-year wings and tail have a relatively standard pattern. There is, however, an overlap in the appearance of a few advanced second-years and retarded third-years, and a much greater overlap between advanced third-years and retarded fourth-years and older. The transition from the mainly dull-coloured juvenile bill to full adult coloration is similarly

Table 3: Measurements (mm) of five gulls Larus *(from Dwight 1925)*

	sample	*wing*	*tail*	*bill*	*tarsus*
Audouin's Gull *L. audouinii*	8	370–402	138–158	43–53	52–60
Herring Gull *L. argentatus argentatus/argenteus*	18	375–447	152–189	45–58	55–70
Lesser Black-backed Gull *L. fuscus*	36	382–438	142–169	44–56	57–69
Great Black-backed Gull *L. marinus*	15	454–498	181–211	57–72	72–85
Great Black-headed Gull *L. ichthyaetus*	17	422–500	171–203	50–65	65–83

Fig. 23. First-winter **Herring** *Larus argentatus*, **Great Black-backed** *L. marinus*, **Lesser Black-backed** *L. fuscus*, **Great Black-headed** *L. ichthyaetus* and **Audouin's Gulls** *L. audouinii*, showing comparative sizes, shapes and stances.

variable: first-years have a relatively standard bill colour and pattern, but second- and third-years display great variation, generally of little help to ageing.

It is usually believed that large gulls typically acquire adult plumage in their fourth winter, but it is well known that some may still show traces of immaturity at that age or even subsequently. Monaghan & Duncan (1979) described three breeding Herring Gulls, ringed as nestlings and known to be in their fourth summer: one was adult (as would be expected at that age), but two had extensive dark markings on the outer greater primary coverts and alula, and a faint tail band, features usually considered to indicate third-year plumage. It seems likely that all large gulls—not only Herring Gulls—may be subject to similar variation. It should thus be borne in mind that the illustrations and descriptions of immatures given for this group represent what are thought to be typical examples. In practice, the ageing, at least of individuals with plumage intermediate between those described for second- and third-years, and all those with plumage resembling that described for third-years, should be tentative: use of such terms as 'second- or third-summer' and 'third-year type' is suggested to describe them.

More information based on ringed birds of known age is needed to ascertain the extent of variation in the length of immaturity and varying appearance at different ages of large gulls.

In summer, when a combination of worn, faded plumage and the start of the complete autumn moult frequently produces a generally nondescript appearance, the ageing of immature large gulls may be particular difficult, although detailed examination of the patterns of adjacent new and old primaries (on trapped birds, for example) can provide extra clues to age.

Herring, Lesser Black-backed and Great Black-backed Gulls (maps, Figs 26, 28 and 30)—in order of descending general abundance—are familiar in most of the western Palearctic. Immatures provide an identification challenge, and more attention to flocks of large gulls—and familiarisation with the identification of immatures—could lead to further European records of Audouin's (map, Fig. 24) and Great Black-headed Gulls *L. ichthyaetus* (map, Fig. 32), and a more complete knowledge of their status within their known ranges.

The subspecies of Herring and Lesser Black-backed Gulls are discussed and described under 'Geographical variation' after the detailed descriptions. While typical examples are identifiable in the field, there is a good deal of intergradation in appearance, and caution is advisable in assigning individuals to a particular subspecies outside its usual range.

Audouin's Gull

Larus audouinii

(Figs 23E and 25, Photographs 197–218)

Adult summer

IDENTIFICATION

This rare Mediterranean speciality typically frequents wave-washed rocky coasts and islands, and—especially away from the breeding areas—flat, sandy shores. Adults (mainly in winter) and immatures occur on the Atlantic coast of northwest Africa, especially Morocco (Smith 1972): it has been recorded in Portugal, and vagrants, especially immatures which are apparently less specialised in their feeding habits than adults (Garcia 1977), could occur farther north.

At all ages, differences of structure and behaviour are among the best distinctions from Herring Gull. Audouin's is obviously smaller than the Mediterranean subspecies of Herring Gull (*cachinnans/michahellis*), and is slimmer and more elegant. It is a graceful flyer, with slimmer wings than Herring Gull: it glides more, often for very long distances, on gently-arched wings, and looks slimmer-bodied, lacking Herring Gull's often bulging breast-line. It is not an aggressive scavenger like other large gulls, but feeds at sea (largely at night, often far offshore) almost exclusively on small fish, occasionally following fishing boats. It picks small fish from near the surface with a lunge of its bill and long neck, or plunges more deeply into the sea from a low-level glide. It lacks Herring Gull's fierce expression, having a smaller, slimmer head with a sloping, elongated forehead giving a marked 'snout' effect and peaking well behind the eye. When alert, the neck is long and slender, and its stance more upright than Herring Gull. The bill is shorter and looks deeper, and is often held 'drooping' downwards when perched.

Herring Gulls of the southern *cachinnans* group of subspecies (p. 95) are a potential

Fig. 24. World distribution of **Audouin's Gull** *Larus audouinii*, showing breeding areas (black spots). The winter/non-breeding range extends out of the Mediterranean, mainly to the Atlantic coast of Morocco; the black line indicates the approximate southern limit. Vagrant north to Portugal.

source of confusion to observers new to the Mediterranean, because their plumage, especially of immatures, is markedly different from that of the north European Herring Gulls. Once aware of this pitfall, however, there should be little difficulty in identifying Audouin's.

Juvenile Audouin's is described by Garcia (1977), on which this account is largely based. Compared with juvenile Herring Gull, it is generally darker, with rather smooth grey-brown head (usually without darker ear-coverts or strong patterning) and underparts, and a suffused whitish 'face' and crown. There is sometimes an obviously darker patch on the rear flanks, lacking on other juvenile large gulls. The upperwing has two uniform dark bars—a secondary bar and another across the greater coverts; the inner primaries are only slightly paler than the blackish outer ones, thus it lacks the prominent pale window which is obvious from above and below on Herring Gull. The underwing has contrasting dark and light bars on the coverts; this area is usually paler and more uniform on Herring Gull. The tail and rump patterns are quite different from Herring Gull: apart from the white terminal fringe the upperside of the tail usually looks uniformly dark (some greyish or whitish visible at the base when tail fully spread), contrasting with a usually well-marked and distinctive U-shaped white area on the lower rump and uppertail-coverts. From below, the tail has a whitish base with a broad, subterminal dark band. The legs are dark grey, whereas Herring Gull's are pinkish.

Most of the juvenile differences are also found in first-winter and first-summer plumages, although, after the autumn and spring partial moults, the head and body become generally whiter (often showing a dark half-collar on the lower hindneck, sometimes extending to the breast-sides), and the wings and tail become much worn and faded by the first summer. First-year Lesser Black-backed Gulls have a similar upperwing pattern: at long range they are probably best distinguished by their darker ear-coverts and body, rather uniformly dark underwing, more clearly banded upper side of the tail, and lack of U-shaped white pattern on rump/uppertail-coverts.

Second-years differ from Herring Gulls of the same age by having paler grey upperparts (especially compared with the rather dark grey of the *cachinnans* group of subspecies), neater, thinner tail band, more clear-cut white primary tips (visible only when perched, but liable to disappear through wear), dark legs and usually reddish-based bill.

Third-years and adults, when seen well, bear no more than a passing resemblance to Herring Gulls. At long range when perched, the very pale grey upperparts do not contrast strongly with the whitish head and underparts, so the whole head and body looks pale and contrasts sharply with the black wing-tips (the rather dark grey upperparts of *cachinnans*-group Herring Gulls contrast sharply with the white head and underparts, giving a quite different pattern of light and dark); the bill and legs are black-looking, not pale as on Herring Gull. At long range in flight, Audouin's lacks obvious mirrors in the black wing-tip, and lacks Herring Gull's prominent white leading and trailing edges to the wings. At close range, the grey upperparts coloration extends onto the upper rump and as a diagnostic faint grey suffusion on the hindneck, flanks, belly and underwing (this suffusion may be obvious in dull light or against a dark background, but it is not readily discernible in bright sunlight); the black wing-tip has only one small mirror, often lacking on third-years, difficult to see except at close range from below; when perched, the white scapular- and tertial-crescents are very faint; the bill is deep red, with an ill-defined black subterminal band and yellowish tip, the latter is often invisible, accentuating the stubby shape.

In winter, third-year and adult Audouin's apparently have a white head, lacking the

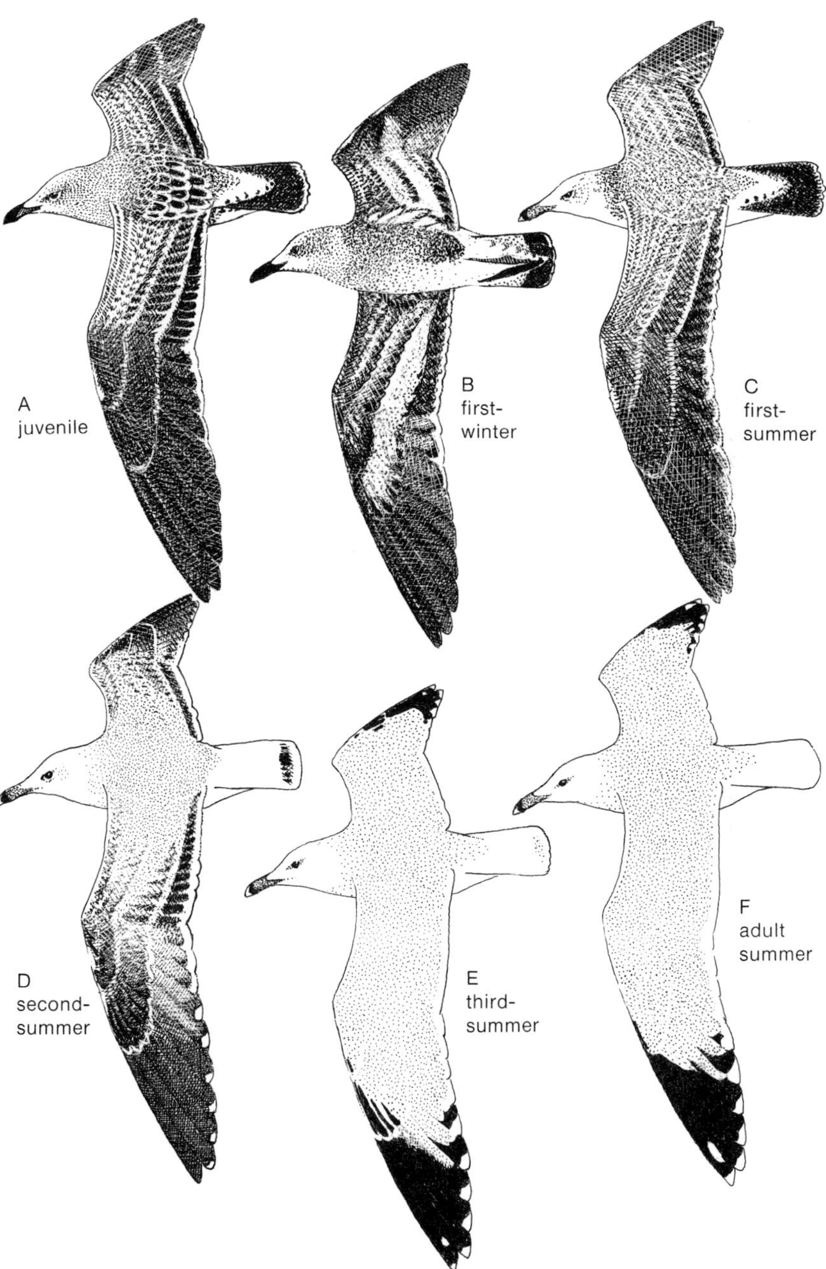

Fig. 25. **Audouin's Gull** *Larus audouinii* in flight.

dark streaking acquired by most other large gulls in winter (thus, there is apparently little difference between summer and winter plumages). Herring Gulls of the *cachinnans* group, however, have a mainly white head in winter, unlike that of north European Herring Gulls.

AGEING SUMMARY (see general discussion on ageing large gulls on pp. 78–80)

Juvenile: smooth grey-brown head and underparts, striking scaly pattern on upperparts. Primaries, secondaries and tail mainly blackish. Bill mainly black (summer to October).

First-winter: as juvenile, except head and underparts probably less smooth grey-brown, and upperparts less neatly scaled (September to April).

First-summer: as first-winter, except head and underparts mainly white, wings and tail much worn and faded. Upperparts less scaly, paler (March to October).

Second-winter: faint dusky head markings; upperparts and coverts of inner wing mainly grey. Blackish outer primaries and coverts, secondary bar and tail band. Bill base usually dark red (August to April).

Second-summer: as second-winter, except head white, and wings and tail much worn and faded (March to October).

Third-winter: as adult, except much black on outer greater primary coverts, and sometimes a trace of a tail band (August to April).

Third-summer: as third-winter, except primary tips reduced or lacking through wear (March to October).

Adult winter/fourth-winter: black on wing-tip confined to primaries (August to April).

Adult summer/fourth-summer: as adult winter, except white primary tips reduced or lacking through wear (March to October).

DETAILED DESCRIPTIONS

Juvenile (Fig. 25A. From below and when perched, similar to first-winter, 25B and 23E)

HEAD Smooth, uniform grey-brown (usually lacking darker ear-coverts) shading to whitish around bill and on crown (latter sometimes giving white-capped effect). Dusky eye-crescent and thin white crescents above and below eye.

BODY Underparts rather smooth grey-brown, often with distinctive darker patch on rear flanks; belly and vent white. Mantle grey-brown. Scapulars dark brown with neat pale fringes, forming prominent scaly pattern. Back and centre of upper rump grey-brown, finely barred with dark. Lower rump white, with mainly white uppertail-coverts forming distinctive U-shaped white area contrasting with dark tail and dark centre of upper rump.

WINGS Median and lesser coverts and tertials scaly like scapulars. Remainder of wing blackish, inner primaries only slightly paler than remainder, forming faintly paler window if any. Secondaries blackish and greater coverts blackish-brown (both with clear-cut, fine white fringes) forming double dark bar across wings in flight. Underwing coverts prominently barred with dark and light, including always prominent broad whitish central panel across bases of greater underwing coverts and inner greater under primary coverts.

TAIL From above, uniform blackish with white terminal border and sometimes fine white fringe on outer web of outer pair of feathers. Inner webs of tail feathers whitish at bases, showing from above when tail full spread and from below contrasting with broad subterminal dark band. Uppertail- and undertail-coverts white, each feather with black spot near tip, or dark with pale fringe.

BARE PARTS Iris dark brown. Bill black, often paler at base. Legs dark grey, greenish-grey or dark green.

First-winter (Figs 23E and 25B, wings and tail similar to juvenile, 25A) Acquired by post-juvenile head and body moult during autumn, probably complete by September to November.

Much as juvenile, except upperparts less scaly, appearing rather uniform dark brown, and head often whiter or with streaking on hindneck concentrated in dark half collar extending to breast-sides.

First-summer (Fig. 25C, underwing and tail similar to first-winter, 25B) Acquired by head and body moult, probably February to April.

As first-winter, except head and underparts whiter or with half collar; wings and tail becoming much worn and faded, especially median and lesser coverts which become more uniform brownish; mantle and scapulars often with much clear grey; bill paler, sometimes reddish, with blackish tip or subterminal band.

Second-winter (not illustrated, but similar to second-summer, Fig. 25D) Acquired by complete moult, probably June to October.

HEAD White, with dusky eye-crescent and often streaking or grey-brown wash on lower hindneck and breast-sides.

BODY Underparts and rump white. Mantle, back and scapulars uniform pale grey.

WINGS Blackish secondary bar; remainder of inner wing mainly clear grey, with brown markings on coverts of variable extent. Inner primaries usually clear grey, remainder of outer wing mainly blackish; all except outer one or two primaries and their coverts with neat white tips in fresh plumage. Underwing mainly white, with a few dark markings especially on coverts of outer wing.

TAIL White, with neat black subterminal band.

BARE PARTS As first-summer, except base of bill often reddish.

Second-summer (Fig. 25D) Acquired by head and body moult, probably February to April.

As second-winter, except head white; dark areas on upperwing much faded, browner; more clear grey on innerwing coverts; white primary tips often lacking through wear; base of bill usually red; orbital ring red.

Third-winter (not illustrated, but similar to third-summer, Fig. 25E) Acquired by complete moult, probably June to October. Some may acquire adult plumage at this age, but probably the majority take an extra year. *As adult winter except:*

WINGS Extensive black on outer greater primary coverts, sometimes extending onto alula, giving prominent 'headlights' effect on leading edge of outer wing in flight. Mirror on outer primary tiny or lacking.

TAIL Sometimes with faint dark subterminal marks.

Third-summer (Fig. 25E) Acquired by head and body moult, probably February to April. As third-winter, except white primary tips reduced or lacking through wear.

Adult winter/fourth-winter (not illustrated, but similar to adult summer, Fig. 25F) Acquired by complete moult, probably June to October.

HEAD White. Hindneck, nape and sometimes crown with pale grey wash extending from mantle.

BODY Underparts washed pale grey, but contrast with white head visible only in dull light at close range. Upperparts smooth, pale pearly-grey (similar in colour to upperparts of Black-headed Gull *L. ridibundus*) shading onto rump, thus no sharp division between back and rump.

WINGS Grey, as upperparts, even paler on outer wing because of diffuse whiter fringes to coverts and inner primaries. When perched indistinct white scapular- and tertial-crescents, invisible at long range. Inner wing with very thin white leading edge and diffuse, indistinct white trailing edge. Black confined to outer primaries, decreasing in extent inwards to small, isolated subterminal marks on 5th and 6th (occasionally only 5th or also 7th) forming clear-cut black wing tip above and below; remainder of underwing pale grey, secondaries and inner primaries very translucent. Some individuals have small blackish marks on outer two or three greater primary coverts, not as extensive as on typical third-years, and may be adult. Outer primaries with prominent white tips, obvious when perched but not easily discernible in flight. Small, round mirror on inner web of outer primary, usually visible only from below at close range.

TAIL White, often with grey wash at bases of central feathers.

BARE PARTS Iris brown; orbital ring, mouth and gape red. Bill deep coral-red, looking black at ranges of 100 m or more, with single or double black subterminal band and yellowish tip, the latter often invisible at long range. Legs dull greyish or olive, soles yellow.

Adult summer/fourth-summer (Fig. 25F) Acquired by head and body moult, probably February to May.

As adult winter, except white primary tips reduced or lacking through wear, and red at base of bill perhaps darker, more often appearing wholly blackish at long range.

Herring Gull

Larus argentatus

(Figs 23A and 27, Photographs 219–275)

Second-summer

IDENTIFICATION

Herring Gull is on average 20–30% smaller and proportionately less heavily built than Great Black-backed Gull. The west European subspecies *L. a. argenteus* is slightly larger than Lesser Black-backed Gull, but with heavier general build; the wings are proportionately broader and shorter, giving a heavier appearance in flight and a noticeably less attenuated rear end when perched.

In juvenile, first-winter and first-summer plumages, Herring, Lesser Black-backed and Great Black-backed Gulls have a basically similar pattern and coloration. The appearance and specific differences of juveniles are described in Table 4, and those of first-winter and first-summer plumages in the detailed descriptions. At these ages, some of the distinctions involve rather subtle comparisons of colour tones and patterns (which in themselves are subject to a good deal of individual variation), and they may not be readily discernible until after a good deal of careful study of mixed flocks containing two or all three species.

In second-year plumages, Herring Gull has generally pale upperparts (usually with extensive clear grey at least on the mantle and scapulars) reflecting the eventual adult

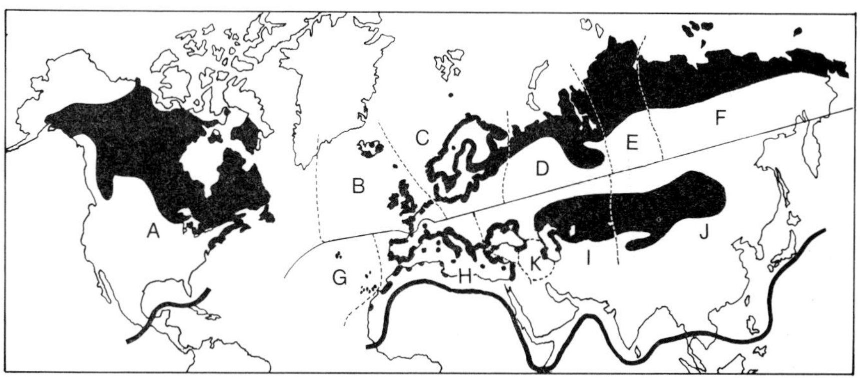

Fig. 26. World distribution of **Herring Gull** *Larus argentatus*, showing approximate breeding range (solid black) and approximate southern limit of winter/non-breeding range (thick black line). The thin line marks the division between the northern or nominate '*argentatus*' group of subspecies and the southern '*cachinnans*' group. The dotted lines mark the approximate breeding ranges of the subspecies: (A) *L. a. smithsonianus*; (B) *L. a. argenteus*; (C) *L. a. argentatus*; (D) *L. a. heuglini*; (E) *L. a. taimyrensis*; (F) *L. a. vegae*; (G) *L. a. atlantis*; (H) *L. a. michahellis*; (I) *L. a. cachinnans*; (J) *L. a. mongolicus*; (K) *L. a. armenicus*. The geographical variation of Herring Gulls is discussed on pages 92–99.

coloration, and thus is readily separable from the black-backed pair, both of which have obvious dark upperparts at these ages.

Third-years and adults are readily identifiable: Audouin's (p. 81) and Great Black-headed Gulls (p. 111) are the only other pale grey-backed large gulls with black on the primaries, and Glaucous and Iceland Gulls have all-white wing-tips. The best long range distinctions from the similar but much smaller Common Gull *L. canus* are described on page 51.

AGEING SUMMARY (see general discussion on ageing large gulls on pp. 78–80)

Juvenile: whole plumage fresh and unworn. Head and underparts rather uniformly streaked grey-brown. Neat scaly pattern on mantle and scapulars, uniformly barred wing coverts. Bill blackish, with diffuse pale base (summer to January).

First-winter: as juvenile except head and sometimes underparts generally whiter. Barred pattern on upperparts more irregular, less scaly (September to March).

First-summer: as first-winter, except head and underparts generally whitish, barred upperparts paler, wings and tail becoming much worn and faded (March to September).

Second-winter: extensive dusky streaking on head, usually some clear grey on mantle and scapulars. Outer primaries and secondary bar blackish, inner primaries and coverts of inner wing generally greyish, the latter with variable amount of brown. Blackish tail band, not as extensive as on first-years. Underwing mainly whitish. Bill extensively pale at base. Iris usually pale (September to March).

Second-summer: as second-winter, except head and underparts mainly white, mantle and scapulars uniform grey or with few brown feathers. Wings and tail becoming much worn and faded (March to September).

Third-winter: as adult winter, except much black on outer coverts of outer wing and alula, black wing-tip less clear cut and lacking prominent mirrors, usually some brown freckling on coverts of inner wing and tertials, faint tail band, black subterminal band or small mark on bill (September to April).

Third-summer: as third-winter, except head white, wings and tail faded, and white primary tips reduced or lacking through wear (February to September).

Adult winter/fourth-winter: extensive dusky head markings, upperparts and wings uniform grey, black wing-tip clear-cut and confined to outer primaries, two prominent mirrors, tail white, no black on bill (September to March).

Adult summer/fourth-summer: as adult winter, except head white, and white primary tips reduced or lacking through wear (February to September).

DETAILED DESCRIPTIONS (These refer to the west European race *L. a. argenteus*: for difference of other races see 'Geographical variation' on pp. 92–99)

Juvenile See Table 4 (pp. 90–91).

First-winter (Figs 23A and 27B, wings and tail similar to juvenile, 27A) Acquired by post-juvenile head and body moult, July to January.

As juvenile, except head (and sometimes underparts) whiter, and new mantle and scapular feathers with more complex pattern of dark bars, but scaly juvenile scapulars often retained to mid-winter or later. Generally paler than Lesser Black-backed.

First-summer (Fig. 27C, underwing and tail similar to first-winter, 27B) Acquired by head and body moult, January to May.

As juvenile, except head and underparts often extensively whitish. Dark areas on wings and tail often faded to pale brown, and pale areas faded to whitish, giving generally very pale appearance by summer, strikingly paler than first-summer Lesser Black-backed. A few clear grey scapulars may be acquired from April onwards. Bill often extensively pale at base. Iris sometimes slightly paler.

Second-winter (not illustrated, but wings and tail similar to second-summer, Fig. 27D) Acquired by complete moult, May to October.

HEAD White with usually extensive dusky streaking.

BODY Underparts and rump mainly white, with variable amount of dark streaking. Mantle and scapulars sometimes similar to first-winter, but usually with at least some clear grey.

WINGS Outer wing mainly blackish (1st primary sometimes has small mirror), but inner four primaries and their coverts mainly clear grey, thus window more clear-cut and contrasting than on first-years. Tertials barred black and white, or with extensive white internal markings, not mainly dark-centred as on first-year. Coverts of inner wing paler, sometimes with much clear grey, more uniform than on first-years, with variable amount of brown barring; greater coverts vermiculated or finely barred, not strongly barred as on first-year; prominent blackish-brown secondary bar. Underwing generally whiter than on juvenile with usually extensive areas of dark shading or barring.

TAIL Extensively whitish at base; broad, mainly solid blackish subterminal band of variable pattern.

BARE PARTS Iris usually becoming pale. Bill usually extensively flesh or yellowish-flesh, with dark subterminal area and sometimes some reddish on gonys, but pattern and colour highly variable. Legs dull flesh.

Second-summer (Fig. 27D) Acquired by head and body moult, January to April.

As second-winter, except head and underparts mainly white. Mantle and scapulars clear grey, sometimes with a few brown-barred feathers. Dark areas on wings and tail faded, and pale areas faded to whitish (often contrasting with grey mantle and scapulars to give saddle effect) by summer. Iris usually pale. Bill often developing yellowish adult coloration, and sometimes reddish spot on gonys, but usually with extensive dark subterminal mark.

Third-winter (Fig. 27E) Acquired by complete moult, June to October.

HEAD AND BODY White with extensive dusky streaking especially around eye and on crown, nape and hindneck; few streaks on breast-sides and flanks. Mantle and scapulars uniform pale grey.

WINGS As adult winter, except black area on wing-tip larger, extending onto greater primary coverts and alula, white primary tips smaller, usually only one mirror (sometimes none), and variable amount (usually much less than on second-year) of

Table 4: Detailed descriptions of juvenile **Herring** L. argentatus argenteus, **Lesser Black-backed** L. fuscus *and* **Great Black-backed Gulls** L. marinus

The specific differences are in italics: some of the distinctions involve rather subtle comparisons of colour tones and patterns (which in themselves are subject to a good deal of individual variation), and they may not be apparent until after a good deal of careful study of mixed flocks containing two or all three species

	Herring Gull (Fig. 27A. When perched—except mantle and scapulars—and from below, similar to first-winter, 23A and 27B)	*Lesser Black-backed Gull (Fig. 29A. When perched—except mantle and scapulars—and from below, similar to first-winter, 23C and 29B)*	*Great Black-backed Gull (Fig. 31A. When perched—except mantle and scapulars—and from below, similar to first-winter, 23B and 31B)*
Head and underparts	Streaked grey-brown with paler face and nape, darker ear-coverts and blackish eye-crescent. *Generally paler than Lesser Black-backed*	Streaked dark grey-brown with paler face and nape, prominent dark ear-patch and blackish eye-crescent; blackish mottling on breast-sides and flanks, belly paler. *Generally darker than Herring with coarser markings*	Streaked grey-brown with prominent blackish eye-crescent, but *head and upper breast contrastingly whiter than rest of underparts,* which are generally more coarsely marked than on Herring and Lesser Black-backed
Mantle and scapulars	Feathers grey-brown, with pale edgings forming *slightly paler, less contrasting scaly pattern than Lesser Black-backed* and lacking strongly chequered pattern of Great Black-backed	*Darker than Herring, scaly pattern more contrasting*	Feathers blackish with usually obvious pale internal markings and whitish edges, forming *more chequered and more contrasting pattern* than Herring and Lesser Black-backed
Rump	Streaked grey-brown, general tone as mantle and scapulars and base of tail, thus *contrast usually slight*	Generally whitish with darker streaking, *contrasting paler than mantle and scapulars*	Similar to Lesser Black-backed
Coverts of inner wing	General coloration as mantle and scapulars, but pattern more barred, less scaly, including *outer greater coverts which lack the uniform dark bar of Lesser Black-backed*	General coloration as mantle and scapulars; outer greater coverts mainly solid blackish-brown with fine pale fringes, forming *'extra' dark bar on inner upperwing,* lacking on Herring and Great Black-backed. Inner greater coverts barred	General coloration as mantle and scapulars, but pattern more barred, less chequered; similar to Herring in pattern, *but more contrast.* Inner greater coverts strongly marked with three dark bars, outer greater coverts less strongly barred or rather uniform greyish
Tertials	Blackish-brown, with obvious pale border and (unlike Lesser Black-backed) *obvious pale notches at sides and usually bold subterminal pale bar*	Blackish-brown with clear-cut, narrow, whitish fringe and diffuse subterminal pale area near tip, if any. *More solidly blackish-centred than Herring*	Blackish-brown with bold pale margin, often strongly notched, and often extensive pale at tips
Secondaries	Mainly blackish-brown, forming secondary bar	As Herring	As Herring

(*Table 4 cont.*)

	Herring Gull (Fig. 27A. When perched—except mantle and scapulars—and from below, similar to first-winter, 23A and 27B)	*Lesser Black-backed Gull (Fig. 29A. When perched—except mantle and scapulars—and from below, similar to first-winter, 23C and 29B)*	*Great Black-backed Gull (Fig. 31A. When perched—except mantle and scapulars—and from below, similar to first-winter, 23B and 31B)*
Outer wing	Mainly blackish-brown, but inner primaries pale (with dark subterminal marks) forming *pale window, prominent from above and below*	Almost wholly blackish; inner primaries slightly paler than remainder and secondaries, thus *lacking prominent pale window*	Pattern intermediate between Herring and Lesser Black-backed; *window effect in some lights*, not as prominent as on Herring
Underwing	*Prominent pale window, remainder rather uniform pale grey-brown*	Window effect very slight or lacking, generally dark, rather uniform blackish-brown	Slight window effect; coverts rather uniform blackish-brown, remainder grey-brown giving *rather subtle two-tone effect*
Tail	Base whitish with darker bars, generally grey-brown as rump and upperparts, thus broad, blackish-brown subterminal band less contrasting than on Lesser Black-backed, and lacking distinctive 'watered' pattern of Great Black-backed	Base typically rather whiter than on Herring, with thin black bars on outer feathers, *blackish subterminal band usually more contrasting, solidly blackish and clear-cut*	Base generally whiter than on Herring. Pattern of dark very variable, but almost always with *very distinctive, complex wavy or 'watered' barrings*, often not forming a solid dark subterminal band
Bare parts	Iris dark brown. Bill blackish with usually *prominent diffuse pale area at base*, mainly on lower mandible. Legs dull flesh	Iris dark brown. *Bill black without pale base.* Legs dull flesh	Iris dark brown. Bill wholly black except often for whitish spot at extreme tip; *larger size than Herring and Lesser Black-backed emphasised by sharp contrast with whitish head.* Legs dull flesh

brown markings on inner wing, especially on median and lesser coverts, inner greater coverts, tertials (which are mainly grey), and secondaries. Underwing as adult winter or with some brown marks on coverts.

TAIL White with subterminal markings of highly variable extent and pattern, these markings finely barred or freckled (not mainly solidly dark as second-year) or often confined to feather-centres giving tail age-distinctive dark-and-white striped pattern.

BARE PARTS Iris pale yellow. Bill colours as adult, but usually generally paler and with dark subterminal mark. Legs bright or pale flesh.

Third-summer (not illustrated, but wings and tail similar to third-winter, Fig. 27E) Acquired by head and body moult, January to April.

As third-winter, except head and underparts usually white, freckled brown areas on inner wings faded to whitish, white primary tips reduced or lacking through wear.

Adult winter/fourth-winter (Fig. 27F) Acquired by complete moult, June to November.

HEAD AND BODY As third-winter.

WINGS Uniform pale grey, black confined to outer primaries, decreasing in extent inwards, usually to small subterminal spot on 6th, forming clear-cut black wing-tip above and below; some individuals also have small blackish marks on outer greater primary coverts. Outer primaries prominently tipped white, often discernible only when perched; mirrors on two outer primaries obvious at long range. Scapular-crescent small or lacking; tertial-crescent prominent when perched. White leading edge to inner wing indistinct, but trailing edge prominent. Underwing white, with grey subterminal trailing edge and black wing-tip.

BARE PARTS Iris pale yellow. Orbital ring yellow, orange, pink or red. Bill deep or pale yellow, with orange or red spot on gonys and whitish tip; mouth and gape yellow or orange. Legs bright or pale flesh.

Adult summer/fourth-summer (not illustrated, but wings and tail similar to adult winter, Fig. 27F) Acquired by head and body moult, January to April.

As adult winter, except head and underparts white, white primary tips reduced or lacking through wear, and bill and leg colours perhaps generally brighter.

GEOGRAPHICAL VARIATION

The taxonomy of the Herring Gull is notoriously complex, and is discussed at the end of this section. The subspecies fall into three fairly distinct types: the northern or nominate '*argentatus*' group (adults mainly pink-legged except *heuglini*), the southern '*cachinnnans*' group (adults mainly yellow-legged), and the '*armenicus*' group (one subspecies). Map (p. 87) shows the approximate breeding range of each subspecies.

Northern or nominate '*argentatus*' group

L. a. smithsonianus: Photos 244–245. The only subspecies in North America (map, p. 87), except northwest Alaska where *vegae* is regular. Canadian-ringed juvenile recovered 480 km off Spain in November 1937 is only western Palearctic record (*BWP* III). Averages larger than *argenteus*, similar to *argentatus*. Adult plumage similar to *argenteus*, including very pale grey upperparts. First-years differ markedly from *argenteus*/*argentatus* in usually more uniform (less streaked) grey-brown underparts and head (although latter often whitish in first-winter and first-summer in all populations), more uniform (less barred) and browner upperparts and rump, on average more uniform (less strongly barred) blackish tertial centres, greater coverts often more finely barred or uniform (although still paler than secondary bar, unlike first-year Lesser Black-backed Gull), and almost wholly uniform dark tail (with pale terminal fringe and often some pale visible at base when tail fully spread). Second-years more similar to second-year *argenteus*/*argentatus*, but tail still almost wholly dark like first-year, contrasting with all-white rump, and greater coverts and tertials usually uniform brown or creamy-brown with pale fringes: mantle and scapulars usually extensively clear grey on second-winters, like *argentatus*/*argenteus*, contrary to some literature (eg *BWP* III) which states that second-winter *smithsonianus* more often lacks clear grey. Moult timings as *argenteus*. Wing 397–460 mm (Dwight 1925), legs pink at all ages.

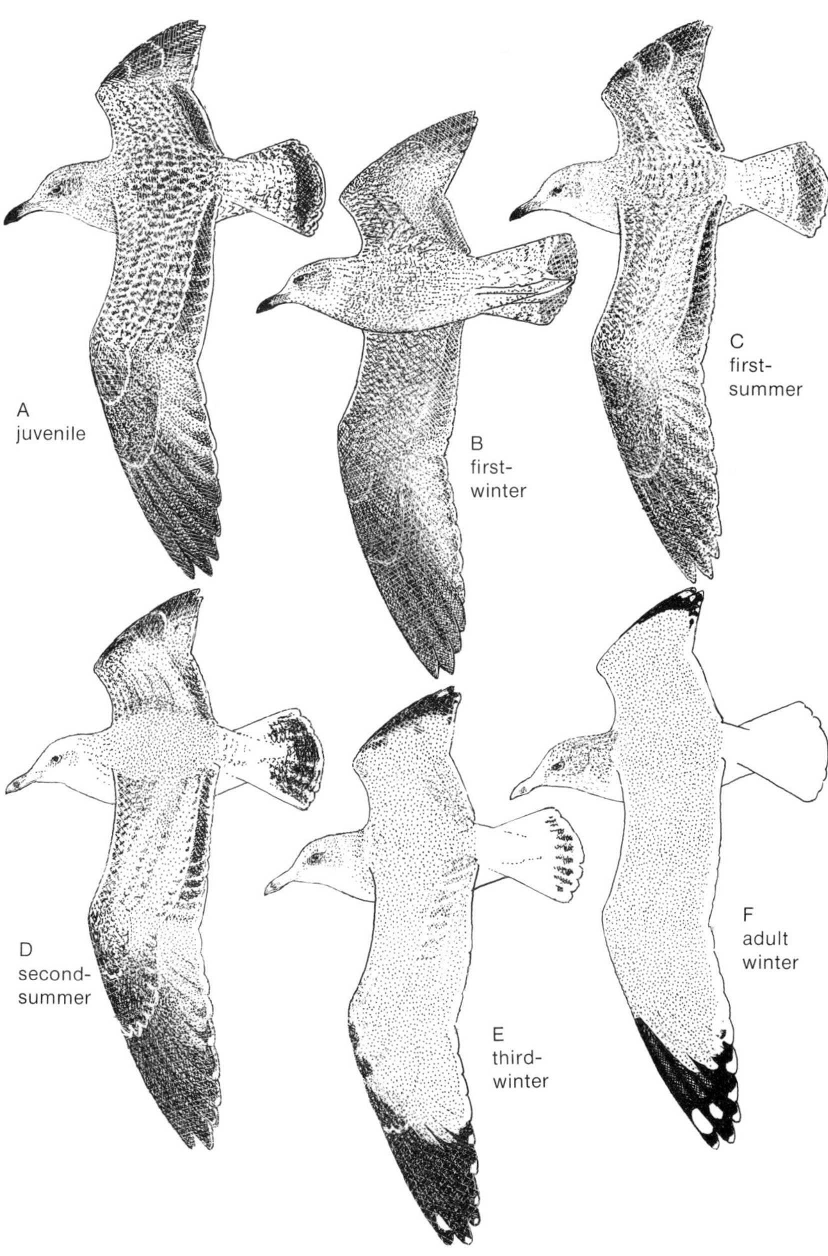

Fig. 27. **Herring Gulls** *Larus argentatus argenteus* in flight.

L. a. argenteus: Photos 219–243. Breeds western Europe and Iceland (map, p. 87). Winters in breeding range and possibly as far south as northern Iberia: in Britain and Netherlands at least, any movement fairly local dispersal, mainly less than 100 km (Stanley *et al.* 1981). Detailed descriptions (pp. 94–98) and Fig. 27 refer to this subspecies. Adult upperparts very pale grey (with *smithsonianus*, the palest of all Herring Gull subspecies), similar to or slightly darker than Black-headed or Ring-billed Gull. Wing 385–461 mm (*BWP* III), legs pink at all ages.

L. a. argentatus: Photos 246–251. Breeds Scandinavia and Baltic (map, p. 87). Winters in breeding range and south to northern Iberia; regular in sometimes large numbers in western Europe in mid-winter, eg. inland in southeast England (Stanley *et al.* 1981), mainly from northern part of breeding range. Compared with *argenteus*, averages larger (some equalling small Great Black-backed Gull), with longer, less rounded head, longer and heavier bill, longer body, and longer wing-tip extension beyond tail: often holds body and wing-tip at angle (wing-tip nearly touching ground), not horizontally as *argenteus*. Compared with *argenteus*, adults differ in slightly darker grey upperparts (some as dark or even slightly darker than west and northwest European subspecies of Common Gull *L. c. canus*, darkest examples from north of breeding range), usually paler yellow bill with usually paler spot near gonys (more orange, less red), and on average much more white and less black on wing-tip: in not infrequent extreme examples, black restricted mainly to outer webs of outer four primaries (small subterminal mark on 4th), with large all-white tip to 1st (like Great Black-backed Gull) and sometimes also 2nd; from below, wing-tip appears wholly pale except for black on 1st and subterminal marks on 2nd or 3rd to 4th. Such examples (Photos 247 and 251) thus have wing-tip similar to adult Thayer's Gull of North America (pp. 169–172), which has not been recorded in Europe, and which in any case differs from nominate *argentatus* at least in its smaller size, more rounded head, smaller bill, deeper pink legs, dark red or purple orbital ring, and dark iris. It is also possible that adult hybrid Glaucous × Herring Gull might show a similar wing-tip pattern of reduced black, but at least darkness of grey upperparts of nominate *argentatus* should preclude confusion. Adults finish the complete autumn moult later than *argenteus*, November to January. First-years average paler than *argenteus*, with whiter head and underparts, more white among narrower dark barring on upperparts, rump, wing coverts, tertials and tail, and often pale-fringed primary tips. See Photos 248 to 250 and captions for what might be extreme pale example of first-winter nominate *argentatus*. Wing 411–466 mm (*BWP* III), legs pink (sometimes greyish pink) at all ages, but yellow- or yellowish-legged adults (often also at largest and darkest extremes for this subspecies) occur in northeast of breeding range, eg inland in northern Finland ('*L. a. omissus*' of some authors). In northwest Europe yellow-legged '*omissus*' confusible with *michahellis/cachinnans*, but is infrequent and most likely to occur in mid-winter (whereas *michahellis* regular, mainly in August and September), has strong dark head-streaking in winter (when *michahellis* white-headed), less bright yellow bill and legs on average, orange spot near gonys (not bright red as on typical *michahellis/cachinnans*), and less extensive black on wing-tip.

L. a. heuglini: Photos 252, 253. Breeds northwest USSR (map, p. 87). Migrates south to winter in area bounded approximately by Black Sea, Aral Sea, northwest India, Gulf of Aden and southern Red Sea (but apparently excluding northern Red Sea and eastern Mediterranean): since about early 1970s, regular and increasing in numbers in East Africa south to Tanzania. Large and long-legged. Adults have darkest grey upperparts of all Herring Gull subspecies (many equalling west European race of Lesser Black-backed Gull *L. f. graellsii*), yellow legs, and bold but sparse head-streaking in winter, often concentrated on lower hindneck (although some are effectively white-headed). First-years resemble *michahellis/cachinnans* in all-black bill, whitish head and underparts, less obvious pale window on inner primaries than *argenteus/argentatus*, solidly dark-centred tertials, plainer (less barred) greater coverts, and general appearance recalling first-year Great Black-backed Gull. At all ages, readily separated from *L. f. fuscus* in winter range by much larger size and heavier build; proportionately longer legs; adults have dark grey not blackish upperparts, and usually bold head streaks (lacking or faint on nominate *fuscus*); first-years lack blackish bar on outer greater coverts, and show pale window on inner primaries. Adults finish complete moult late, January to March. Wing 410–453 mm (Dwight 1925), legs pink on immatures, yellow on adults.

L. a. taimyrensis: Photo 254. Breeds central northern USSR (map, p. 87). Winter range not fully known, but some adult Herring Gulls wintering in Kenya, with paler grey upperparts than *heuglini*, little head-streaking and pale or yellowish legs may be this subspecies (P. L. Britton *et al.*, *in litt.*). Devillers (*BWP* III) regards *taimyrensis* as distinctive hybrid population *heuglini* × *vegae*, supported by variable colour of adult upperparts, and intermediate plumage features and leg colour. If this is the case, winter range perhaps likely to be in eastern part of winter range of *heuglini*, and perhaps also in winter range of *vegae*. Size, structure, and plumage much like *heuglini*, but grey of adult upperparts variable between that of *heuglini* and *vegae* (thus darker than *argentatus*). Wing 410–453 mm (Dwight 1925), adult leg colour pink or yellow.

L. a. vegae: Photos 255–257. Breeds northeast USSR (map, p. 87), small numbers summer regularly in northwest Alaska. Winters Japan and coastal China. Adult upperparts darker grey than *argentatus* (thus obviously darker than *smithsonianus*), as dark as California Gull *L. californicus* or Kittiwake *Rissa tridactyla*, and slightly darker than Mew Gull *L. c. brachyrhynchus*; extensive black on wing-tip (extending to subterminal marks on 6th primary); one or two mirrors; heavy head streaking in winter; and pink legs. First-winters similar to *argenteus/argentatus* in paleness of window on inner primaries, extent and paleness of markings on greater coverts and tertials, but tail band broad and uniformly dark, contrasting with whitish base and rump. Upperparts of first-summers in Alaska (June/July, *pers. obs.*) very white with narrow subterminal dark bars on mantle and scapulars, and upperwing coverts extremely faded and whitish, giving very pale appearance compared with first-year *smithsonianus*; upperwing-coverts of second-summers also very faded and white, contrasting with grey mantle and scapulars and with dark outer primaries, secondary bar and tertials. This extreme fading matched by first- and second-summer Slaty-backed Gulls in Alaska (which, however, show obviously blackish upperparts – and other differences from *vegae* – from second-summer onwards), and may be product purely of Arctic environment (including long daylight hours in summer) rather than real subspecific difference. Wing 410–453 mm (Dwight 1925), legs pink, often bright pink, at all ages.

Southern or '*cachinnans*' group

L. a. atlantis: Photo 258. Mainly resident in breeding areas (map, p. 87); may wander to west African coast. As *michahellis*, except averages smaller, and adult upperparts darker (only slightly paler than *L. f. graellsii*) with more black on wing-tips.

Winter head-streaking as *michahellis* (C. Moore *et al.*, *in litt.*). First-year as *michahellis*, except darker inner primaries (thus window faint or lacking) and greater covert bar (thus apparently closely resembling Lesser Black-backed Gull). Wing 395–428 mm (Dwight 1925), bare parts as *michahellis*.

L. a. michahellis: Photos 259–271. Mainly resident in breeding areas (map, p. 87), but northerly post-breeding dispersal of adults and immatures in apparently increasing numbers to west European coasts and England (especially southeast coasts), with peak numbers in August and September (*Brit. Birds* 76: 191–194). Variable in size according to population (smallest from Atlantic Iberia, largest from west Mediterranean, intermediates from east Mediterranean). West Mediterranean birds are much larger than *argenteus* (about same as *argentatus*), but wings and legs proportionately longer; head flatter. All populations of *michahellis* have adult upperparts darker, more ash-grey, less blue-grey than *argenteus*; more black on wing-tip than *argenteus*/*argentatus* especially from below; yellow legs; and red orbital ring. Head of adult in winter (until November/December) very faintly streaked (sometimes concentrated around eye as grey smudge), not heavily streaked or clouded with grey as on *argenteus*/*argentatus* or *graellsii*/*intermedius*. From mid-winter onwards, most adults white-headed. Dark areas on immatures generally darker and browner than on *argenteus*/*argentatus*, often with distinctive rusty tone when faded. First-years have broad, solidly dark tail band, more defined than on *argenteus*/*argentatus* and contrasting with whiter base and rump; inner primaries less pale than on *argenteus*/*argentatus*, thus pale window less well-marked; outer greater coverts more uniformly dark, less barred than *argenteus*/*argentatus*, but not blackish as on Lesser Black-backed Gull; tertials typically dark-centred with sharply defined whitish fringe on sides and tip (not notched at sides or barred subterminally with whitish as on typical *argenteus*/*argentatus*. First-years and older immatures often have striking white head and underparts (unlike *argenteus*/*argentatus*) contrasting with darker upperparts; this and all-black bill give appearance recalling first-year Great Black-backed Gull. Second- and third-years on average have more grey on mantle, scapulars and wing coverts than *argenteus*. Wing 395–485 mm (*BWP* III). Legs pink on immatures, yellow on adults. Adult legs typically bright orange-yellow in summer, but varying (especially in winter) from bright orange-yellow through lemon-yellow to cream (always pink on *argenteus*). Bill wholly black through first year (sometimes pale at base by first-summer); on typical adults, bright yellow or orange-yellow, with bright red spot near gonys (paler yellow with orange spot on typical *argenteus*). Orbital ring red on adult (yellow or orange-yellow on *argenteus*/*argentatus*). Autumn moult May–November, averaging earlier than northern '*argentatus*' group.

L. a. cachinnans: Breeding range includes at least Black and Caspian Seas (map, p. 87); winters within breeding range or south to eastern Mediterranean, sparingly in Gulfs of Suez and Aqaba, and possibly also Persian Gulf, but apparently not Red or Arabian Seas. Two ringing recoveries show that *cachinnans* reaches west European coasts (*BWP* III), perhaps in similar dispersal to that of *michahellis*. Size and adult plumage much as *michahellis*, but upperparts on average slightly paler grey, and more white less black on wing-tip, especially from below. Immatures apparently indistinguishable from *michahellis* and *heuglini* in field. Wing 410–464 mm (*BWP* III), bare parts as *michahellis*.

L. a. mongolicus: Photos 272, 273. Breeds eastern central Asia (map, p. 87). Winter range not fully known, but includes Hong Kong (and presumably elsewhere in coastal

China at least) and, according to *BWP* III, Pakistan and India. In Hong Kong, adults wintering alongside pink-legged *vegae* have darker grey upperparts than *vegae*, usually only one large mirror, and bright orange-yellow legs (M. L. Chalmers *in litt.*). Adults in summer in Mongolia, however, are pink-legged with two large mirrors (A. R. Kitson *in litt.*), while others there had one or two mirrors, yellowish legs, and seemed to have dark iris (P. Alström *in litt.*). Wing 390–453 mm (*BWP* III).

The '*armenicus*' group

L. a. armenicus: Photos 274, 275. Breeds on Armenian lakes (map, p. 87); resident, or wandering outside breeding season to eastern Mediterranean, where sometimes large numbers regular at least on coast of Israel. Adults distinctive, differing from *cachinnans* and Mediterranean populations of *michahellis* in slightly smaller size, more rounded head, proportionately much shorter bill (which is stout and blunt-ended), extensive black on wing-tip (from above, typically appearing as solid triangle, cutting almost straight across wing from tips of greater primary coverts), prominent mirror on 1st primary, mirror on 2nd faint or lacking, thin dusky bar on underwing along bases of outer secondaries, dark grey upperparts like *michahellis* or slightly darker, white scapular crescent faint or lacking, and distinctive bare parts coloration (see below). Immatures much like *michahellis/cachinnans*, but perhaps whiter on head and underparts (in photographs of second-summers looking unmarked whitish), and underwing paler than equivalent plumages of *michahellis/cachinnans* with more defined pattern of dark markings. First-winter apparently already acquires some grey on mantle and scapulars, unlike *michahellis/cachinnans* (Dubois 1985). Wing 390–453 mm (*BWP* III), bill of adult bright orange-yellow with red spot near gonys, subterminal black band (latter unique among adult Herring Gulls), and pale yellow, yellow, or greenish-yellow tip; iris brown, paler than pupil but eye looking all-black at distance; orbital ring red; legs bright orange-yellow (at least in summer). Bare parts of immatures as *michahellis*. Autumn moult May to December, ending later than *cachinnans* group. This summary of *armenicus* based largely on Hume (*Brit. Birds* 76: 189–191), *BWP* III, and notes and photographs from P. Alström, P. Géroudet, and U. Olsson (*in litt.*).

DISCUSSION

Opinion among different authors as to the arrangement of subspecies within the Lesser Black-backed Gull *L. fuscus*/Herring Gull *L. argentatus* complex (as well as opinion on the validity or distinctiveness of some of the subspecies), is extremely inconsistent, reflecting the complexity and difficulty of the subject. In the present state of knowledge, it seems that an equally strong case could be made for several different arrangements, from combining *fuscus* and *argentatus* as one species (with *atlantis* and *heuglini* as links) at the conservative extreme, to splitting into several species, as most recently proposed, for example, by Devillers (summarised in *BWP* III) with an arrangement of five species: *L. fuscus* (Lesser Black-backed Gull) with subspecies *graellsii*, *intermedius*, nominate *fuscus*, *heuglini*, and *taimyrensis* (latter as distinctive hybrid population *heuglini* × *vegae*); *L. argentatus* (Herring Gull) with subspecies *smithsonianus*, *argenteus*, and nominate *argentatus*; *L. vegae* (Vega Gull); *L. cachinnans* (Yellow-legged Gull) with subspecies *atlantis*, *michahellis*, nominate *cachinnans*, *barabensis*, *mongolicus*, and *omissus*; and *L. armenicus* (Armenian Gull). The work of Devillers on this subject (summarised in *BWP* III) is thorough and authoritative, and is essential reading for any student of the *fuscus/argentatus* complex.

The case for specific status for the southern '*cachinnans*' group is strengthened by the separate breeding behaviour of *michahellis* and *argenteus* in the same colony on Ile d'Oléron in the Bay of Biscay in 1976 (Nicolau-Guillaumet 1977). After range expansions south (*argenteus*) and north (*michahellis*) in recent years, this is the first meeting of the northern and southern subspecific groups of Herring Gulls.

With increasing interest in recent years, many points have been clarified, and it is likely that further advances will be made in the near future. Field-based studies of plumages, series of good photographs of different populations, firmer establishment of breeding and winter ranges, and considerations such as breeding habitats of the various subspecies, are as important to the solution of the problems as museum-based studies: they go hand-in-hand. It seems that any firm conclusion as to the best arrangement of the *fuscus/argentatus* complex may still be premature, and that any proposed arrangement might best be regarded as temporary. With this in mind, the present work stays with the well-established and satisfactory arrangement of Vaurie (1965), with the addition of the now better-understood *L. f. intermedius* and *L. a. argenteus*, as well as clearer definition of *L. a. armenicus*.

The author would be especially interested in opinions, photographs or other information which helps to further clarify the following: identification of adult and immature nominate *argentatus*; the subspecific validity of *omissus*; the subspecific validity of *taimyrensis* and its distinctions from *heuglini*; field characters of *atlantis*, especially first-year plumages and their distinctions from *L. fuscus*; distinctions of the Atlantic Iberian populations of *michahellis* (which possibly merit separate subspecific status) from Mediterranean populations of *michahellis*; status of the form which breeds on the Atlantic coast of Morocco; field separation of adult and immature *cachinnans* from *michahellis*; status of the form(s) breeding in inland central and eastern Turkey; field characters of immature *armenicus* and distinctions from immatures of other subspecies of that region; the subspecific validity of *barabensis* and its winter range; and the apparently confusing variation of *mongolicus* in different parts of its range, and its winter range.

There is a good deal of intergradation between subspecies, especially where the breeding ranges adjoin, and individual variation and hybridisation (the latter with Glaucous and Lesser Black-backed Gulls in Europe, and with Glaucous, Glaucous-winged, and, rarely, Great Black-backed Gulls in North America) are factors which should be borne in mind, as they may sometimes explain the puzzling appearance of some Herring Gulls.

In an interesting study of winter Herring Gulls in central England, Hume (1978) was able to distinguish small, pale *argenteus* (about 90% of the population) and larger, darker *argentatus* (about 10% of the population), with more or less intergradation between the two types. About ten individuals were puzzling: half had extensive white and very restricted black on the wing-tip, while the remainder were small, dark-mantled and white-headed, and had extensive black on the wing-tip and yellow legs. It now seems probable that the former were extreme 'Thayer's Gull-type' *argentatus*, and the latter were *michahellis*, perhaps of the smaller, Iberian Atlantic population.

Adult Herring Gulls with yellow legs which occur in Britain and northwest Europe are likely to be '*omissus*'-type *argentatus* from northern Scandinavia, or *michahellis* or *cachinnans* from southern Europe or southwest Asia. Subspecific identification of Herring Gulls with yellow legs in Britain and northwest Europe will not always be possible, but the majority should be assignable as showing the characters of '*omissus*' or *michahellis/cachinnans* by applying the field characters summarised in the detailed descriptions of those subspecies. There are only a very few recorded cases of adult *argenteus* with yellow (actually pale yellow) legs.

Subspecific identification of Herring Gulls requires careful observation at close range, with good light (preferably not full sunlight) from behind the observer (so that colour tones can be correctly judged), and careful assessment of all the important characters. It should be noted that the apparent shade of grey can change as a bird alters the angle of its body in relation to the observer. Comparison is helped if more than one subspecies is present.

Lesser Black-backed Gull

Larus fuscus

(Figs 23c and 29, Photographs 276–293)

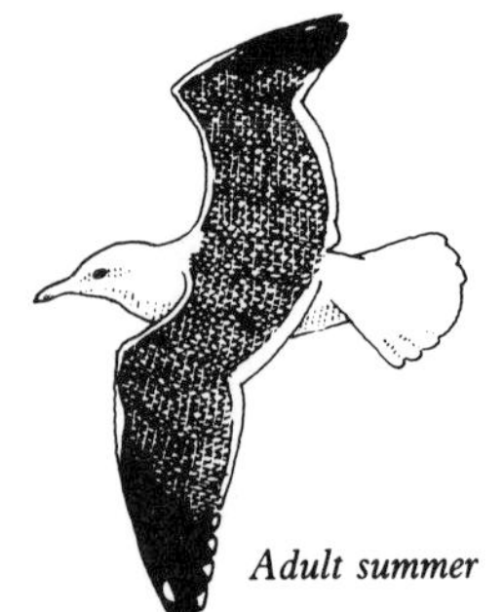

Adult summer

IDENTIFICATION

Lesser Black-backed Gull is slightly smaller than the west European race of Herring Gull *L. a argenteus*, but with lighter general build; the wings are proportionately longer, giving a slimmer-winged appearance in flight and a noticeably more attenuated rear end when perched. It is on average 20–30% smaller than Great Black-backed Gull, with proportionately much slimmer bill and smaller head, and proportionately longer wings and legs: it is generally much less bulky, and more attenuated at the rear end when perched. The size difference is very obvious when the two species are together.

The appearance of juveniles, and the differences from the similar juveniles of Herring and Great Black-backed Gulls, are described in Table 4 (pp. 90–91), and those of first-winter and first-summer plumages in the detailed descriptions.

In second-winter and second-summer plumages, the adult upperparts coloration begins to show on at least the mantle and scapulars, so there is little risk of confusion with Herring Gull. At these ages, it is best told from Great Black-backed by the generally darker and more extensive head markings in winter when Great Black-backed is rather white-headed; generally darker underwing; and in summer by the dark ash-grey rather than blackish upperparts (*L. f. graellsii* only). The size and structural differences, however, are perhaps the most reliable features at these ages.

Third-years and adults typically have extensive dark grey streaking or clouding on the head in winter (Great Black-backed has little, if any, dark streaking and remains

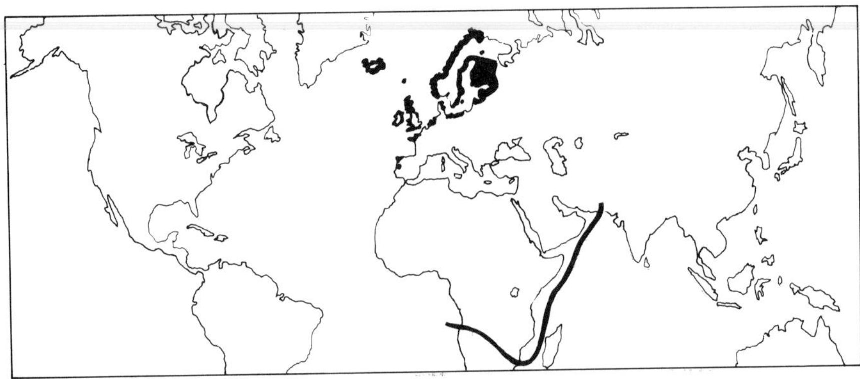

Fig. 28. World distribution of **Lesser Black-backed Gull** *Larus fuscus*, showing approximate breeding range (solid black) and approximate southern limit of winter/non-breeding range (black line). Now of regular occurrence in very small numbers in eastern coastal North America (apparently all *L. f. graellsii*).

generally white-headed in winter); dark ash-grey rather than blackish upperparts, contrasting with the black wing-tips (*L. f. graellsii* only); thinner tertial-crescent and smaller white tips to the primaries in fresh plumage, visible when perched (larger and prominent on Great Black-backed); one or two *small* white mirrors, (much more white on wing-tip on Great Black-backed); and yellowish or bright yellow legs (always flesh or creamy-flesh on Great Black-backed). A useful distinction (from Herring) of adults flying overhead is that the blackish primaries and secondaries form a complete dark trailing edge to the otherwise white underwing, whereas on adult Herring Gull only the outer primaries are dark.

First-year individuals (and to some extent, second-years), are relatively scarce in northern Europe; presumably the majority remains in the wintering/non-breeding areas during the first years of immaturity, and does not move north with the adults.

AGEING SUMMARY (see general discussion on ageing large gulls on pp. 78–80)

Juvenile: whole plumage fresh and unworn. Head and underparts rather uniformly streaked dark grey-brown. Neat scaly pattern on mantle and scapulars, uniformly barred wing-coverts. Bill black (summer to November).

First-winter: as juvenile, except dark patch on ear-coverts less well-defined, and scapulars more uniformly dark, less scaly (August to March).

First-summer: as first-winter, except head and underparts generally whiter; mantle, scapulars and upperwing more uniform and browner through fading, especially on coverts of inner wing (March to September).

Second-winter: extensive dusky head markings, variable amount of adult coloration on mantle and scapulars, and coverts of inner wing brownish, not neatly barred as on first-winter. Outer wing and secondary bar blackish, tail whiter than first-year with smaller subterminal band. Bill often extensively pale at base (September to March).

Second-summer: as second-winter, except head mainly white, mantle and scapulars acquire mainly adult coloration, wings and tail becoming much worn and faded, and bill often yellowish at base (March to September).

Third-winter: as adult winter, except black wing-tip less clear cut and often lacking mirror, much brown freckling on inner wing, faint tail band, black subterminal band on bill (September to April).

Third-summer: as third-winter, except head white, wings faded to patchy brown (not uniform grey or blackish as adult summer), and white primary tips reduced or lacking through wear (February to September).

Adult winter/fourth-winter: extensive dusky head markings, uniform dark ash-grey upperparts and wings, clear-cut black wing-tip with one or two mirrors, white tips to primaries obvious when perched, tail white, no black on bill (August to March).

Adult summer/fourth-summer: as adult winter, except head white, and white primary tips reduced or lacking through wear (February to September).

DETAILED DESCRIPTIONS (These refer to the west European race *L. f. graellsii*: for difference of other races see 'Geographical variation' on pp. 104–105)

Juvenile See Table 4 (pp. 90–91)

First-winter (Figs 23C and 29B, wings and tail similar to juvenile, 29A) Acquired by post-juvenile head and body moult, summer to November or later, sometimes after arrival in wintering areas.

As juvenile, except ear-patch sometimes less prominent and mantle and scapulars more uniformly dark, not scaly. Upperparts generally darker and more uniform than first-winter Herring and Great Black-backed. Head and underparts often becoming whiter.

First-summer (Fig. 29C, underwing and tail similar to first-winter, 29B) Acquired by head and body moult, January to April.

As juvenile, except head and underparts generally whiter, wings and tail worn and faded, old coverts (especially median and inner greater coverts) worn and often faded to pale brown, often mixed with new, plain grey feathers, and new mantle and scapular feathers plain grey-brown with pale tips: upperparts much darker than first-summer Herring and Great Black-backed. Bill usually acquires pale base. Legs sometimes yellowish-flesh.

Second-winter (not illustrated, but wings and tail similar to second-summer, Fig. 29D) Acquired by complete moult, May to October.

HEAD White with extensive dusky streaking, usually concentrated around eye and on crown and lower hindneck.

BODY Underparts white, with extensive dark streaking and blackish mottling on breast-sides and flanks. Rump mainly white. Mantle and scapulars usually with much dark grey developing.

WINGS Outer wing and secondaries blackish. Innerwing coverts mainly brown, with diffuse paler fringes. Underwing generally dark.

TAIL Mainly white, with prominent blackish subterminal band, less broad than on first-years.

BARE PARTS Iris sometimes becoming pale. Bill usually extensively pale with blackish subterminal area, but pattern highly variable. Legs flesh or yellowish-flesh.

Second-summer (Fig. 29D) Acquired by head and body moult, January to April.

As second-winter, except head and underparts whiter or all-white. Mantle and scapulars usually clear dark ash-grey, sometimes with a few brown-barred feathers. Blackish areas on wings and tail faded browner, and brown areas often faded to pale brown. Iris usually obviously pale. Bill and legs often yellowish or bright yellow, bill with subterminal dark area of variable extent.

Third-winter (Fig. 29E) Acquired by complete moult, June to October.

HEAD White, with usually extensive dusky streaking or clouding, concentrated around eye and on crown and lower hindneck.

BODY Underparts mainly white, with variable amount of dark streaking. Rump white. Mantle and scapulars uniform dark ash-grey.

WINGS As adult winter, except black on outer wing less clear-cut and more extensive, white primary tips usually smaller or lacking, and only one mirror, often none;

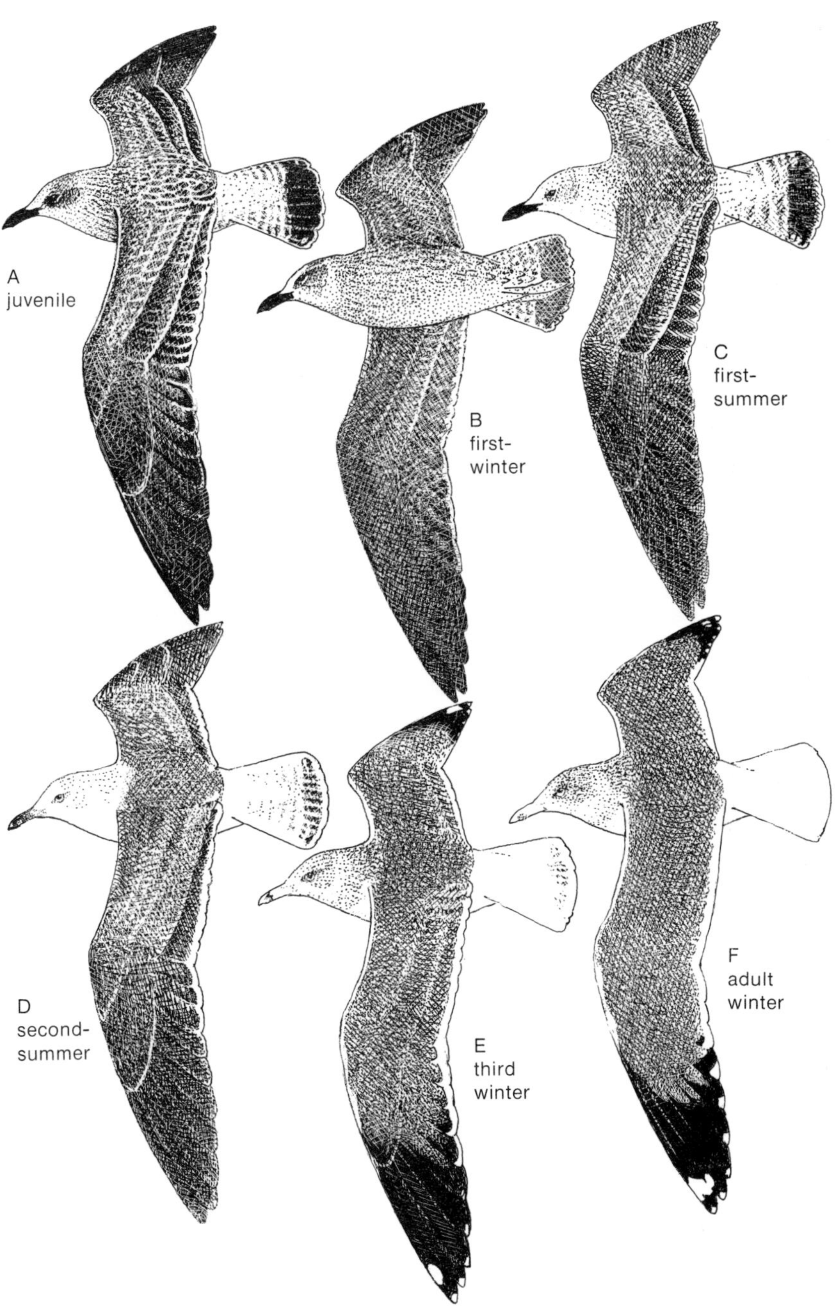

Fig. 29. **Lesser Black-backed Gulls** *Larus fuscus graellsii* in flight.

extensive brown freckling on inner wing, especially on inner greater coverts and tertials, wing thus lacking general smart, uniform appearance of adult.

TAIL White, with usually faint subterminal band of varying extent and pattern.

BARE PARTS As adult, or bill with usually small dark subterminal mark or band, and legs yellowish-flesh, or greyish-flesh.

Third-summer (not illustrated, but wings and tail similar to third-winter, Fig. 29E) Acquired by head and body moult, January to April.

As third-winter, except head and underparts usually white, upperwing faded, patchy brown, especially on median and greater coverts and tertials; white primary tips reduced or lacking through wear.

Adult winter/fourth-winter (Fig. 29F) Acquired by complete moult, June to November.

HEAD AND BODY As third-winter.

WINGS Uniform dark ash-grey; scapular-crescent small, sometimes lacking; tertial-crescent prominent, obvious when perched, but on average less extensive and thinner than on Great Black-backed. Thin white leading edge, white tips to secondaries and inner primaries, forming prominent trailing edge. Black on outer primaries decreasing in extent inwards, usually to small subterminal spot on 7th, forming clear-cut black wing-tip. Outer primaries with neat white tips, smaller than on Great Black-backed, visible only when perched. Small mirror on outer primary (occasionally large and merging with white primary tip) and often another (much smaller) on 2nd. Underwing white, with broad, dark grey subterminal trailing edge, merging with blackish undersides of outer primaries.

TAIL White.

BARE PARTS Iris pale yellow. Orbital ring red. Bill deep yellow, with red or orange-red spot near gonys and whitish tip (colours brighter than on Great Black-backed): some (possibly mainly fourth-winters) have blackish of variable extent on bill. Legs deep- or creamy-yellow: a few (as high as 3% in some large samples) have adult plumage but fleshy or greyish legs. These birds usually also have dark on the bill of variable extent, and are then ageable as probable fourth-winters which have yet to acquire fully adult bare parts coloration.

Adult summer/fourth-summer (not illustrated, but wings and tail similar to adult winter, Fig. 29F) Acquired by head and body moult, January to May.

As adult winter, except head and underparts white, grey of upperparts and wings acquiring brownish tone through fading, white primary tips reduced or lacking through wear, and bill and legs generally bright orange-yellow. As with adult winter/fourth-winter plumage, a few have fleshy or greyish legs: those which also have dark subterminal mark on bill are probably fourth-summers.

GEOGRAPHICAL VARIATION

Barth (1975), in a detailed and convincing review of the taxonomy of Lesser Black-backed Gull, recognised three subspecies, distinguishable in the field mainly by the tone of grey on the upperparts of adults.

L. f. fuscus: Baltic area and northern Norway. Migrates mainly southeastwards, and is apparently the only subspecies wintering in the Middle East and east Africa. Identification and ageing as *graellsii*, except upperparts of adult as black or blacker than Great Black-backed Gull, showing hardly any contrast with black wing-tip, often with brownish cast, probably through fading, and usually only one mirror (on 1st primary) unlike *graellsii*. Photographs and field observations from east Africa indicate that adults of this subspecies have a whiter head in winter than *intermedius* and *graellsii*: some show sparse but prominent spots and streaks, especially on the lower hindneck, but not the extensive dusky streaking or clouding shown by most *intermedius* and *graellsii*. Adults begin the complete autumn moult from August (some two months later than *intermedius* and *graellsii*), sometimes after arrival in the wintering areas.

L. f. intermedius: Southern Norway, west Sweden and Denmark. Migration and winter range as *graellsii*. Identification and ageing as *graellsii*, except upperparts of adult blackish, slightly paler than Great Black-backed Gull, contrasting with black wing-tip. Often shows brownish cast probably through fading. Timing of autumn moults as for *graellsii*.

L. f. graellsii: Iceland, Faeroes, British Isles, Netherlands, Brittany and northwest Spain. Migrates mainly south or southwestwards to wintering areas in western Europe and west Africa. Identification, ageing and timing of moult are covered in the detailed descriptions. Upperparts of adult dull smoky grey or dark ash-grey, obviously much darker than Herring Gull *L. a. argentatus/argenteus* and lacking the blackish tones of both *fuscus* and *intermedius*, and showing obvious contrast with the black wing-tip.

There is a good deal of intergradation in upperparts colour (and occasionally subspecifically mixed pairs) in some breeding colonies in Scandinavia (between *fuscus* and *intermedius*) and western Europe (between *intermedius* and *graellsii*), and in west European and west African migrant and wintering populations, nowhere more obvious than in Britain, where a small proportion of individuals apparently match *fuscus* in their blackness. While typical examples of the three subspecies are readily distinguishable in the field (especially the distinctively pale-backed *graellsii*), fairly close-range observation, with good light (preferably not full sunlight) from behind the observer, is usually necessary for a correct assessment of colour tones. It should be noted that the apparent shade of grey can vary as a bird alters the angle of its body relative to the observer. My own observations of wintering and migrant Lesser Black-backed Gulls in southeast England suggest that the vast majority of blackish-backed Scandinavian birds are within the colour range of *intermedius*: a minority show the blackness of typical *fuscus* as described by Barth (1975) or shown by colour photographs of *fuscus* wintering in east Africa.

On geographical grounds, it seems possible that some *fuscus* from breeding areas in northern Norway or southern Sweden are likely to migrate southwestwards (rather than southeastwards as in the case for the main *fuscus* population) and these may be the areas of origin of the *fuscus*-type Lesser Black-backeds occurring in Britain. An analysis of ringing recoveries would throw light on this possibility.

Great Black-backed Gull

Larus marinus

(Figs 23B and 31, Photographs 294–311)

Adult summer

IDENTIFICATION

Great Black-backed Gull is markedly larger than Herring and Lesser Black-backed Gulls. Compared with the latter, it has a proportionately stouter bill and larger head, and proportionately shorter wings; it is generally much more bulky, and less attenuated at the rear end when perched. The size difference is obvious when the two species are together. In flight, it has broader and proportionately shorter wings, giving a heavier, more lumbering appearance.

The appearance of juveniles, and the differences from the similar juveniles of Herring and Lesser Black-backed Gulls, are described in Table 4 (pp. 90–91), and those of first-winter and first-summer plumages in the detailed descriptions.

The main differences between Great Black-backed and Lesser Black-backed in second-year and subsequent plumages are summarised under Lesser Black-backed on pages 100–101.

AGEING SUMMARY (see general discussion on ageing large gulls on pp. 78–80)

Juvenile: whole plumage fresh and unworn. Underparts uniformly streaked grey-brown, head generally whiter. Neat, contrasting chequered pattern on mantle and scapulars; uniformly barred wing coverts; greater coverts with neat pattern of contrasting barring. Bill mainly black (summer to February).

First-winter: as juvenile, except head and body generally whiter, mantle and scapulars strongly barred in contrasting chequered pattern (August to March).

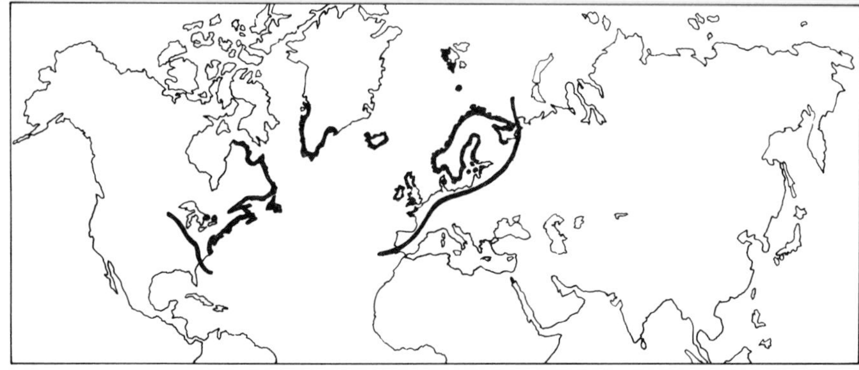

Fig. 30. World distribution of **Great Black-backed Gull** *Larus marinus*, showing approximate breeding range (solid black) and approximate southern limit of winter/non-breeding range (black line).

First-summer: as first-winter, except head and underparts whiter, less contrasting pattern on mantle and scapulars, but no clear blackish as on second-years (March to September).

Second-winter: mantle and scapulars usually with variable amount of clear blackish. Coverts of inner wing, especially greater coverts, generally more uniform grey-brown and less strongly barred than on first-years. No clear-cut black and white on wing-tip. Extensive blackish on tail. Base of bill extensively pale (September to March).

Second-summer: as second-winter, except head and underparts mainly white, mantle and scapulars mainly uniform blackish. Bill often acquires some adult coloration (March to September).

Third-winter: as adult winter, except black on wing-tip less clear-cut and white less extensive; usually much brown freckling on inner wing. Faint tail band. Black subterminal mark or band on bill (September to April).

Third-summer: as third-winter, except wings faded patchy brown and black, and white primary tips reduced or lacking through wear (February to September).

Adult winter/fourth-winter: slight dusky head-streaking, uniform blackish upperparts and wings, extensive white on wing-tip, tail white, no black on bill (September to March).

Adult summer/fourth-summer: as adult winter, except head white, and white primary tips reduced or lacking through wear (February to September).

DETAILED DESCRIPTIONS

Juvenile See Table 4 (pp. 90–91).

First-winter (Figs 23B and 31B, wings and tail similar to juvenile and first-summer, 31A and 31C) Acquired by post-juvenile head and body moult, summer to March.

As juvenile, except white-headed effect often more marked (although some dark streaking visible at close range, especially around eye and on lower hindneck). Mantle and scapulars with more complex barred pattern, but part or all of chequered juvenile scapulars often retained to mid-winter or later. Ground colour on upperparts and wing coverts whiter than on Lesser Black-backed, giving generally paler, less uniformly dark pattern. Bill sometimes paler at base, but not prominently pale-based as on Herring Gull.

First-summer (Fig. 31C, underwing and tail similar to first-winter, 31B) Acquired by head and body moult, January to May.

As juvenile, except head and underparts generally whiter, upperparts sometimes more uniformly dark with less contrasting chequered pattern, and bill often prominently tipped whitish and pale-based. Dark areas on wings and tail often much worn and faded.

Second-winter (not illustrated, but similar to second-summer, Fig. 31D) Acquired by complete moult, May to October.

HEAD White, with faint dark streaking around eye and on lower hindneck.

BODY Underparts with extensive coarse dark streaking especially on breast-sides and flanks. Rump mainly white. Mantle and scapulars usually with much clear dark grey or blackish, feathers otherwise whitish with brown bars; sometimes little different from first-winter (in which case pattern of greater coverts is best age difference).

WINGS Outer wing mainly blackish-brown, inner primaries slightly paler with blackish subterminal marks. Lesser and median coverts barred or with variable amount of rather uniform brownish; greater coverts with very finely barred or vermiculated pattern of dark: inner wing (especially greater coverts) thus lacking strongly barred or chequered pattern of first-years. Secondary bar blackish. Underwing coverts white with dark markings. Outer primary sometimes with trace of mirror.

TAIL Whitish, with extensive blackish subterminal band of highly variable pattern.

BARE PARTS Iris sometimes becoming pale. Bill usually pale at base with extensive dark subterminal areas, but pattern highly variable. Legs as juvenile.

Second-summer (Fig. 31D) Acquired by head and body moult, January to April. As second-winter, except head and underparts sometimes all-white. Mantle and scapulars mainly clear blackish, often with a few brown-barred feathers. Wings and tail worn and faded, coverts of inner wing acquiring general brownish appearance, or even whitish on much-faded individuals. Iris usually pale; orbital ring often red. Bill whitish or fleshy-yellow, with subterminal dark area of variable extent, and often some reddish on gonys.

Third-winter (Fig. 31E) Acquired by complete moult, June to November.

HEAD White, with dark eye-crescent and a few dark streaks mainly around eye and on lower hindneck: looks white-headed at long range.

BODY Underparts and rump white or faintly marked. Mantle and scapulars uniform blackish-grey or with a few brownish fringes.

WINGS As adult winter, except black more extensive and white primary tips and mirror on 2nd smaller; extensive brownish on inner wing, especially on inner greater coverts and tertials, thus wings lacking smart, uniform appearance of adult.

TAIL White, with usually faint subterminal band of variable extent and pattern.

BARE PARTS As second-summer.

Third-summer (not illustrated, but similar to third-winter, Fig. 31E) Acquired by head and body moult, January to April.

As third-winter, except head and underparts white, patchy appearance of upperwing more pronounced, upperparts acquiring brownish tone due to fading, and white primary tips reduced through wear.

Adult winter/fourth-winter (Fig. 31F) Acquired by complete moult, June to January. In view of this species' larger size, it seems likely that a higher proportion do not acquire full adult plumage at this age than is the case with other large gulls, showing signs of immaturity especially on innerwing coverts, tail and bill.

HEAD AND BODY As third-winter.

WINGS Uniform blackish-grey, looking black at long range; scapular-crescent small; tertial-crescent extensive and obvious when perched. Thin white leading edge; white tips to secondaries and inner primaries forming prominent trailing edge. Black on outer primaries decreasing in extent inwards, usually to subterminal mark on 6th,

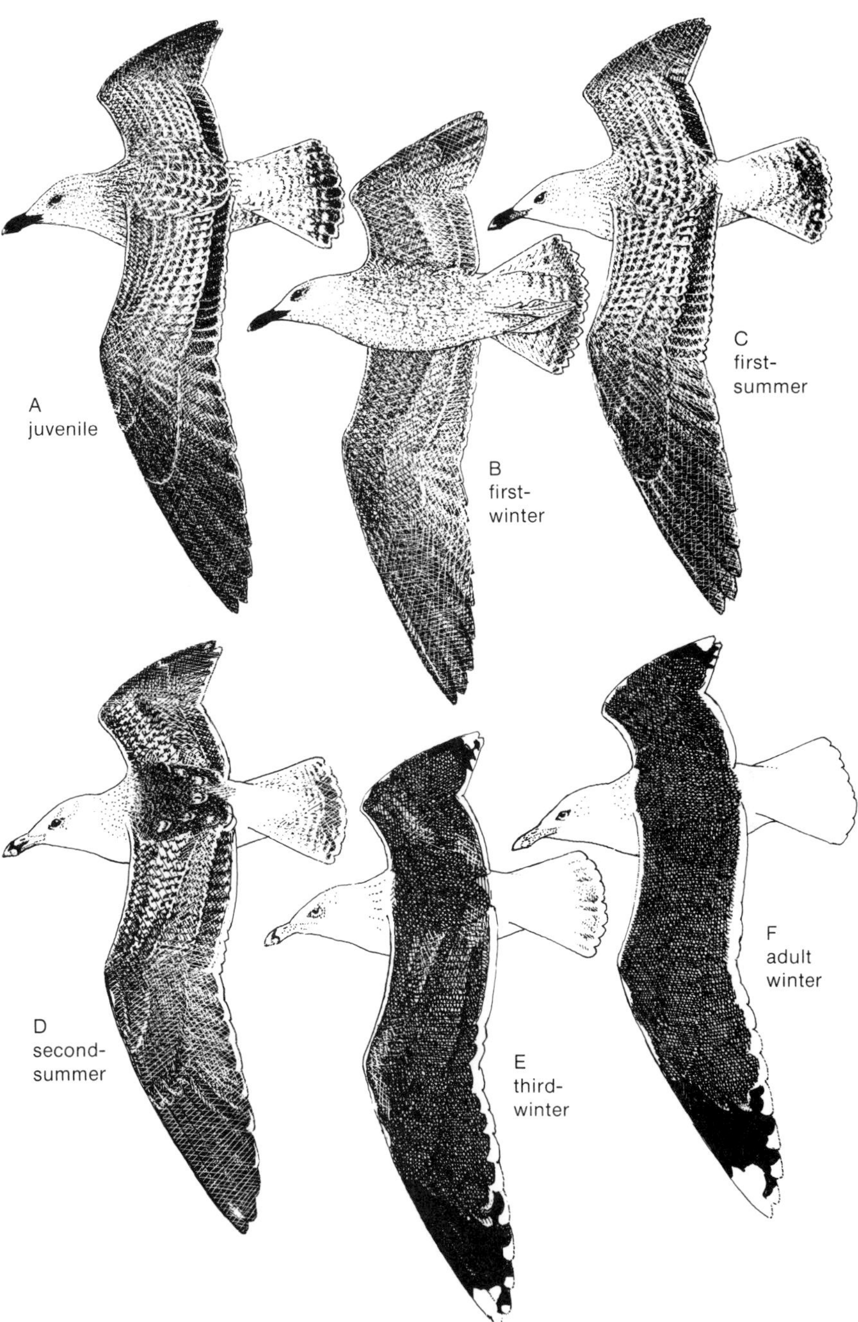

Fig. 31. **Great Black-backed Gulls** *Larus marinus* in flight.

forming black wing-tip which, at close range, contrasts with the blackish-grey remainder. Outer primaries with large white tips, on 1st merging with large mirror to form extensive white end to feather: this, and the large mirror on 2nd form diagnostic wing-tip pattern (rarely, small mirror on 3rd). Underwing white, with broad, dark grey subterminal trailing edge which merges with blackish undersides of outer primaries.

TAIL White.

BARE PARTS Iris pale yellow. Orbital ring red. Bill pale yellow or fleshy-yellow, with orange or red spot on gonys; colours generally paler than Lesser Black-backed. Legs flesh or creamy-flesh.

Adult summer/fourth-summer (not illustrated, but similar to adult winter, Fig. 31F) Acquired by head and body moult, January to May.

As adult winter, except head and body white, blackish-grey of upperparts and wings acquiring brownish tone through fading, white primary tips reduced through wear, and bare parts perhaps generally brighter.

Great Black-headed Gull

Larus ichthyaetus

(Figs 23D and 33, Photographs 312–327)

Adult summer

IDENTIFICATION

Great Black-headed Gull is usually obviously larger than Herring Gull. When perched, it often matches Great Black-backed in length, but its build is not as heavy, the wings are proportionately longer and extend farther beyond the tail (giving a more attentuated rear end), and the legs are proportionately longer; the tertials are sometimes held loosely folded, projecting as a prominent 'hump' from the line of the lower back. The head shape is distinctive; the long, sloping forehead, which peaks well behind the eye, gives a heavy 'snout' effect, which accentuates the length and heaviness of the bill. In flight, the deep chest, long head and heavy bill may give a front-heavy impression; it has proportionately more pointed, slimmer and longer wings than other large gulls. These structural features are important at all ages.

Great Black-headed Gulls, especially immatures, could easily be overlooked when perched among other large gulls, but in flight have a very distinctive appearance at all ages.

The juvenile has a rather pale head and brown mantle and scapulars—the latter with pale fringes giving a prominent scaly pattern—and prominent brownish breast-side patches or complete breast-band (an extension of the dark lower hindneck) which contrast sharply with the clear white remainder of the underparts. Surprisingly in view of its large size, Great Black-headed normally acquires a mainly clear grey mantle and scapulars and white underparts in the first winter, a pattern more like that of some medium-sized gulls of the same age, and unlike the extensively brown mantle, scapu-

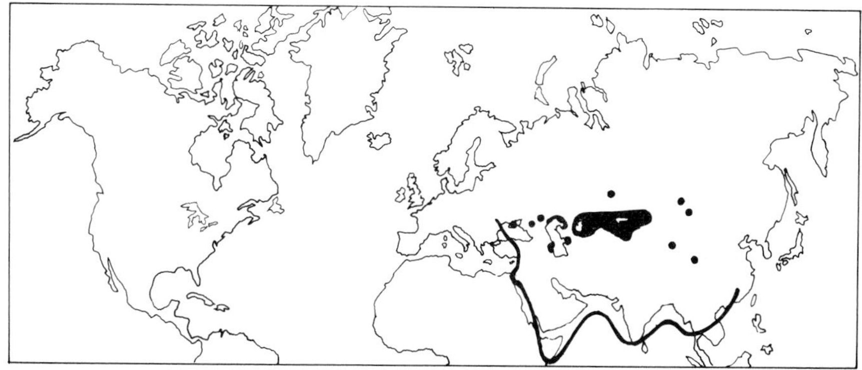

Fig. 32. World distribution of **Great Black-headed Gull** *Larus ichthyaetus*, showing approximate breeding range (solid black) and approximate southern limit of regular winter/non-breeding range (black line). A rare vagrant to western Europe, with five records in Britain prior to 1932 and none since.

lars and underparts of other first-winter large gulls. The head of first-winters is white, with dark markings around eye (which accentuate white crescents above and below the eye); dark markings behind the eye usually forming a prominent dark patch; and dark streaking concentrated on the lower hindneck, often extending to dark breast-side patches. The outer greater coverts are mainly pale grey-brown, forming a uniform and striking pale midwing panel. The underwing is mainly white with an obvious, translucent window, and the tail is white, with a broad, clear-cut black subterminal band: patterns unlike any other first-year large gull. In first-summer plumage, a partial or full hood is sometimes acquired. Throughout the first-year, the bill is pale, with clear-cut black tip or subterminal band.

In second-year plumages, the outer primaries and their coverts are mainly blackish, but the inner primaries and inner wing are mainly clear grey, usually with a few brown coverts and an indistinct secondary bar. The subterminal tail band is thinner than on first-years, and the bare parts usually begin to acquire some adult coloration. A partial or full hood is usually acquired in second-summer plumage.

Third-years closely resemble adults, but have more extensive black on the primaries and less white on the tips, and usually a faint tail band.

Adults are unmistakable: Great Black-headed is the only large gull with a black hood in summer, reduced to a dark mask behind the eye in winter. The wing pattern is diagnostic (the following description based on Harvey, *Brit. Birds* 74: 523–524): the mantle and scapulars are rather dark grey (darker than on Black-headed Gull), shading to pale pearly-grey on the inner wing, with a very broad, rather well-defined white trailing edge, and the outer wing is mainly white, with a neat subterminal crescent of black across the outer primaries. At a distance in flight, the mantle and scapulars may appear rather dark grey, shading paler across the inner wing to mainly white secondaries and primaries: at very long range, the restricted black on the wing-tips of some adults may be difficult to discern. The bill is mainly yellow, with a prominent black subterminal band and reddish tip. The legs are greenish-yellow.

Large gulls with patches of oil on the head, or abnormal concentrations of the usual dark head-streaking in winter, may at times suggest this species, but examination at least of the wing and tail patterns will avoid the slight misidentification risk in such cases.

AGEING SUMMARY

Juvenile: pale head, brownish breast-side patches or broad breast-band, scaly brown mantle and scapulars (summer to October).

First-winter: winter head pattern, white underparts with brownish breast-side patches, mainly uniform pale grey mantle and scapulars. Blackish-brown outer primaries, secondary bar and broad tail band. Brownish wing-coverts, and pale grey-brown midwing panel (August to April).

First-summer: as first-winter, except sometimes hood of variable extent, wings and tail faded, and brownish carpal area reduced (February to September).

Second-winter: winter head pattern; upperparts and wings mainly uniform pale grey; outer primaries and coverts mainly black; clear-cut, thin, black tail band (July to April).

Second-summer: as second-winter, except usually with partial or full hood (February to September).

Third-winter: as adult winter, except outer primaries with more black and less white at tips. Usually a faint tail band (July to April).

Third-summer: as third winter, but hood fully developed (January to September).

Adult winter/fourth-winter: winter head pattern, outer wing mainly white with subterminal crescent of black across outer primaries and extensive white at tips. Tail white (August to February).

Adult summer/fourth-summer: as adult winter, full black hood (January to September).

DETAILED DESCRIPTIONS

Juvenile (Fig. 33A, underwing and tail similar to first-winter, 33B).
HEAD White (sometimes with variable amount of brown streaking behind eye), contrasting with darker hindneck and breast-sides. Thin white crescents above and below eye; eye-crescent dusky.
BODY Underparts white, with brownish mottling on breast-sides, often joining in centre to form fairly clear-cut breast-band, sometimes extending onto flanks. Rump and vent mainly white, usually with a few dark spots on uppertail- and undertail-coverts. Mantle and scapulars rich brown, with pale feather fringes forming strong scaly pattern.
WINGS Carpal-bar brown, with pale feather fringes. Outer greater coverts uniform pale greyish or brownish-grey, with dark centres; inner greater coverts and tertials brown, with clear-cut pale fringes. Secondaries blackish with white fringes, and white on inner webs increasing in extent inwards. Outer wing mainly blackish-brown, inner three or four primaries sometimes with broad, clear-cut pale margins: white on inner webs of primaries increasing in extent inwards from 2nd or 3rd. Underwing coverts and axillaries white with defined dark markings near tips: these markings of variable strength and extent, forming variable pattern of dark lines.
TAIL White, with broad, clear-cut blackish subterminal band, width about one-third of tail length, usually extending to outer web of outer feather, which is, however, often wholly white.
BARE PARTS Iris dark. Orbital ring dark grey. Bill greyish or flesh basally, with extensive diffuse black tip. Legs lead grey, brownish-grey or flesh.

First-winter (Figs 23D and 33B, wing and tail pattern similar to first-summer, 33C) Acquired by post-juvenile head and body moult, summer to September. *As juvenile except:*
HEAD AND BODY White, with dark markings around eye accentuating white crescents above and below eye; and dusky markings forming a usually well-marked dark patch behind eye, extending diffusely over rear crown. Hindneck streaked or neatly spotted with blackish-brown, concentrated in a dense patch on lower hindneck (contrasting sharply with grey mantle), often extending prominently onto breast-sides. Mantle and scapulars clear pale grey, or with a few brown feathers, but sometimes mainly brown.

WINGS Dark areas becoming faded and browner, especially inner primaries which form prominent pale window.

TAIL White tips and fringes often lacking through wear.

BARE PARTS Base of bill paler, sometimes yellowish, with clear-cut black tip or broad subterminal band.

First-summer (Fig. 33C, underwing and tail similar to first-winter, 33B) Acquired by head and body moult, January to April. *As first-winter except:*

HEAD Black usually more extensive; a few may acquire partial or full hood and lose the dark hindneck.

WINGS AND TAIL Becoming much worn and faded, midwing panel often whitish. Some acquire variable number of new, grey tertials, inner lesser coverts, and inner median coverts during moult to first-summer: when perched, these individuals can look plain grey above and be mistaken for second-years or older: dark first-year features, however, visible when wings spread.

BARE PARTS As first-winter, or bill yellowish with clear-cut subterminal band, and legs with greenish tone.

Second-winter (not illustrated, but wing and tail pattern similar to second-summer, Fig. 33D) Acquired by complete moult, April to October.

HEAD White, with dusky markings forming well-defined patch from behind eye, often extending diffusely over crown. Hindneck streaked or spotted blackish, concentrated in patch on lower hindneck.

BODY Underparts and rump white. Upperparts uniform grey, perhaps slightly darker and browner in tone than on adult. Thin white scapular- and prominent tertial-crescent.

WINGS Inner wing grey except for dark-centred outer secondaries and often extensively brown lesser coverts; outer primaries and their coverts with extensive blackish, decreasing in extent inwards to small subterminal marks on 7th to 9th: outer wing thus with much black along leading edge. Underwing white, except for black on outer primaries and a few dusky marks on coverts.

TAIL White with prominent subterminal black band, thinner than on first-year.

BARE PARTS Bill yellowish with clear-cut black subterminal band and pale tip. Legs dusky, greenish or yellowish.

Second-summer (Fig. 33D) Acquired by head and body moult, January to April. As second-winter, except partial or full hood usually acquired, white primary tips and terminal tail fringe reduced or lacking through wear, bill sometimes more orange-yellow, and legs usually yellowish.

Third-winter (Fig. 33E) Acquired by complete moult, May to October. Some probably become indistinguishable from adults at this age. *As adult winter except:*

WINGS Black on outer primaries more extensive and less white at tips; wing-tip looks wholly black at long range.

TAIL Faint or spotted tail band usually present.

Third-summer (not illustrated, but wings and tail as third-winter, Fig. 33E) Acquired by head and body moult, January to April.

As third-winter, except full hood usually acquired, and white primary tips reduced or lacking through wear.

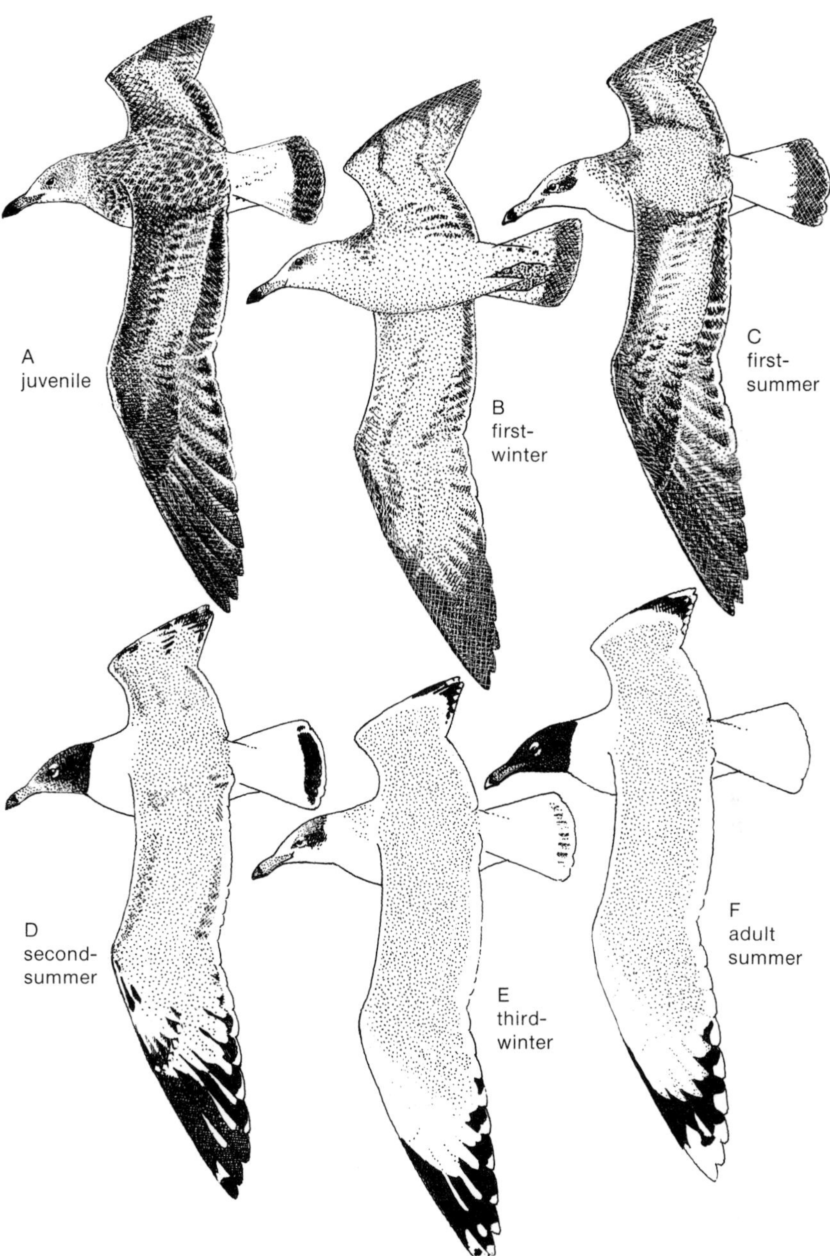

Fig. 33. **Great Black-headed Gulls** *Larus ichthyaetus* in flight.

Adult winter/fourth-winter (not illustrated, but wings and tail similar to adult summer, Fig. 33F) Acquired by complete moult, May to November.

HEAD AND BODY As second-winter, except upperparts grey, with thin whitish fringes to most scapulars, giving delicate scaly pattern.

WINGS Inner wing and inner primaries pale pearly-grey, with thin white leading edge and broad white trailing edge. Outer primary with complete black outer web, extensive subterminal black and large white tip; subterminal black decreasing inwards usually to small spot on 6th, but precise pattern of black and white highly variable. Remainder of outer wing white, forming prominent triangle of white along the leading edge; often whole of outer wing looks white, apart from the subterminal crescent of black across outer primaries. Underwing white, with faint grey bar across greater underwing coverts.

TAIL White.

BARE PARTS As second-winter.

Adult summer/fourth-summer (Fig. 33F) Acquired by head and body moult, January to April. *As adult winter except:*

HEAD White, with extensive black hood. Thick white crescents or oval patches posteriorly above and below eye.

WINGS White primary tips reduced through wear.

BARE PARTS Iris dark brown. Orbital ring red. Bill yellow or orange-yellow, with neat black subterminal band and reddish or orange-red tip. Mouth and gape dull red. Legs yellow or greenish-yellow.

GROUP FOUR

Little, Ross's, Sabine's and Ivory Gulls and Kittiwake

The species in this group (except Ivory Gull *Pagophila eburnea* which is a distinctive odd-one-out and merits a 'group' of its own) are small or medium-sized gulls which share, in their first year, a striking W pattern across the wings in flight (unlike any other western Palearctic gull), causing possible confusion especially at long range. Adults have a more distinctive appearance, making confusion less likely. Ivory Gull is the largest of this group (slightly larger than Common Gull *Larus canus*), and is unmistakable at all ages—white with sparse black spots in its first year, and all-white when adult.

Sabine's Gull *L. sabini* has a complete moult in spring, and a head and body moult in autumn, the reverse of the moult timing of other gulls: a complete early spring moult from first-winter takes place in winter quarters, and in the resultant first-summer plumage most resemble adults except for an incomplete hood. Ross's Gull *Rhodostethia rosea*, Ivory Gull and most Kittiwakes *Rissa tridactyla* acquire adult plumage in their second winter. Little Gull *L. minutus* is exceptional in this group, in that probably the majority are readily ageable in second-year plumages.

Ross's, Sabine's and Ivory Gulls (maps, Figs 37, 39 and 43) are among the most sought-after and beautiful of Arctic rarities; Sabine's is a summer visitor to the northern hemisphere, wintering in the southern oceans. Kittiwake (map Fig. 41) is an almost exclusively marine and coastal gull, familiar in most of the northern hemisphere. Little Gull (map, Fig. 35) typically frequents marshes, inland lakes, and sheltered coasts; on migration and in favoured breeding and wintering areas it may be locally numerous, but in most of its range it is perhaps the least familiar of the commoner gulls. Familiarity with immature Little Gulls and Kittiwakes will greatly aid recognition of Ross's and Sabine's Gulls respectively.

Table 5: Measurements (mm) of five gulls (from Dwight 1925)

	sample	*wing*	*tail*	*bill*	*tarsus*
Little Gull *Larus minutus*	25	210–230	85–97	21–25	25–29
Ross's Gull *Rhodosteithia rosea*	11	248–265	121–138	18–20	30–33
Sabine's Gull *Larus sabini*	25	245–284	108–131	22–28	31–38
Ivory Gull *Pagophila eburnea*	20	320–346	135–160	32–38	35–42
Kittiwake *Rissa tridactyla*	22	285–322	113–140	31–40	31–36

Fig. 34. First-winter **Little** *Larus minutus*, **Ross's** *Rhodostethia rosea* and **Ivory Gulls** *Pagophila eburnea*, and **Kittiwake** *Rissa tridactyla*, and juvenile **Sabine's Gull** *L. sabini*, showing comparative sizes, shapes and stances.

Little Gull
Larus minutus

(Figs 34A and 36, Photographs 328–344)

Second-winter

IDENTIFICATION

Little Gull is the smallest of the world's gulls, with a wing span 20–30% less than that of Black-headed Gull *L. ridibundus* or Kittiwake. On second-years and adults the wing-tip is slightly more rounded than on other similar gulls, and this shape is further accentuated by the even more rounded pattern of the subterminal grey (above) and blackish (below) on the outer primaries. On first-years the wing-tip is not appreciably more rounded than on other gulls. The tail is square-ended or (on some first-years) very slightly forked. It is a dainty, non-scavenging species, which usually feeds by picking from the water surface in flight.

In first-year plumages, the combination of small size and striking W pattern across the wings in flight makes identification straightforward. Of the regular western Palearctic gulls, only first-year Kittiwake (p. 134) has a similar pattern, and in situations where the size difference is not immediately apparent, the best distinctions are juvenile Little Gulls' mainly dark brown mantle, scapulars and back (upperparts grey on juvenile Kittiwake), blackish cap, flesh-coloured or reddish legs (usually dull or blackish on Kittiwake), indistinct, dark secondary bar (Kittiwake has all-white secondaries), and inner greater primary coverts mainly blackish (wholly grey on Kittiwake). Juvenile and some first-winter Kittiwakes have a diagnostic clear-cut, black half-collar on the lower hindneck, but note that a similar mark is shown on the upper mantle by autumn Little Gulls which are in a transitional stage of moult from juvenile to first-winter plumage sometimes as late as November. Little Gulls moulting from first-summer to second-winter often show a strikingly patchy transitional underwing pat-

Fig. 35. World distribution of **Little Gull** *Larus minutus*, showing approximate breeding range (solid black) and approximate southern limit of winter/non-breeding range (black line). Since the first in 1962, there have been several breeding records in the Great Lakes area, together with a general increase in sight records in eastern North America.

tern caused by the contrast of the new, greyish underwing coverts and new inner primaries with the old, white first-year feathers. First-year Bonaparte's *L. philadelphia* (p. 39) and Ross's Gulls (p. 124), both vagrants to Europe, also resemble first-year Little Gull and are only slightly larger: the differences are described in the respective species accounts.

Given good views of the wing pattern, probably the majority of second-year Little Gulls are readily ageable: they resemble adults except for black marks of very variable pattern on the upperside of the wing-tip and the paler, greyish (not uniformly blackish) underwing. Note, however, that a second-year upperwing pattern can be suggested in autumn by adults in a transitional stage of moult from summer to winter plumage, retaining old, worn outer primaries which look darker than the fresh inner ones.

In second-year and adult plumages, Little Gull is unlikely to be confused with any other species; even at long range, the alternation, with each wingbeat, of dark underwing and pale grey upperwing is distinctive. In summer at least, the underparts are usually obviously pink-flushed, unlike other common species.

AGEING SUMMARY

Juvenile: as first-winter, but extensive blackish-brown on mantle and scapulars extending to breast-sides (summer to October).

First-winter: uniform grey mantle and scapulars, bold blackish W pattern across wings in flight, black tail band, winter head pattern (August to April).

First-summer: as first-winter, but W pattern faded, tail band often broken in centre, hood usually developed to variable extent (March to October).

Second-winter: as adult winter, but underwing-coverts paler or whitish, and variable pattern of black marks on wing-tip (August to April).

Second-summer: as second-winter, but hood usually fully developed (March to October).

Adult winter/third-winter: upperwing grey with white border on trailing edge and tip, underwing uniformly blackish, tail white, winter head pattern (August to April).

Adult summer/third-summer: as adult winter, but with full black hood (February to October).

DETAILED DESCRIPTIONS

Juvenile (Fig. 36A. Underwing and tail similar to first-winter, 36C)

HEAD White, with blackish-brown eye-crescent, ear-spot, crown and hindneck.

BODY Mantle, back and scapulars black-brown, with whitish fringes giving scaly pattern most prominent on scapulars. Underparts and rump white, except for blackish-brown patches on breast-sides (extension of mantle colour).

WINGS Coverts of inner wing pale grey, except for clear-cut, broad, blackish-brown carpal-bar: tertials and inner greater and median coverts with neat whitish fringes. Secondaries pale grey, with broad white tips and blackish centres, latter forming broken (sometimes barely visible) dark subterminal bar on trailing edge of

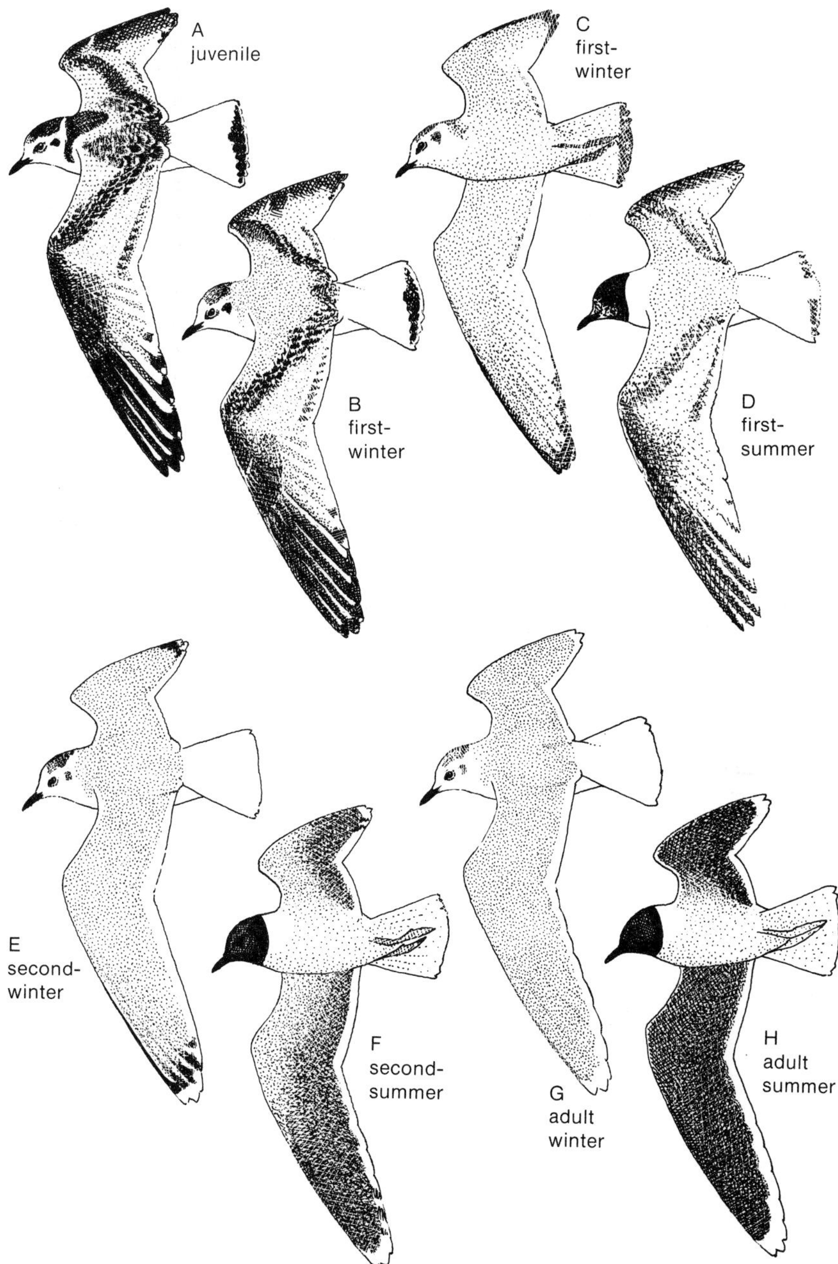

Fig. 36. **Little Gulls** *Larus minutus* in flight.

inner wing. Alula and outer coverts of outer wing mainly blackish, innermost coverts mainly pale grey. Black on outer web and tip of outer primaries decreasing in extent inwards to small subterminal spot on 6th or 7th (rarely 8th); white tips to primaries increasing in size inwards from 2nd or 3rd. Inner primaries grey or outer webs, broadly tipped white. Rare variant has upperwing coverts or whole upperwing almost wholly blackish-brown. Inner webs of all primaries mainly white. Underwing white, except for exposed blackish tips of outer primaries and black leading edge of 1st.

TAIL White, with clear-cut, black band (and narrow, whitish terminal fringe) broadest in centre (accentuating the slightly forked tail-shape of some individuals); sometimes outer pair of feathers, rarely two outer pairs, all-white.

BARE PARTS Iris and orbital ring blackish. Bill blackish; mouth flesh. Legs pale flesh or reddish.

First-winter (Figs 34A, 36B and 36C) Acquired by post-juvenile head and body moult which starts at fledging and is usually complete by November. *As juvenile, except:*

HEAD White, with dark grey or blackish eye-cresent, ear-spot and crown; hindneck grey (extension of mantle colour).

BODY Mantle, back and scapulars pale grey, often with a few retained juvenile feathers on back and scapulars. Breast-sides grey (extension of mantle colour). Individuals in moult from juvenile to first-winter plumage usually go through transitional phase in which there is dark bar across upper mantle (caused by remaining juvenile mantle feathers) resembling dark bar on lower hindneck of juvenile and some first-winter Kittiwakes: this bar may be shown as late as November.

WINGS AND TAIL White terminal spots on primaries, and terminal fringe on tail, reduced or lacking through wear.

First-summer (Figs 36D depicts typical worn and faded individual in late summer. Underwing and tail similar to first-winter, 36C) Acquired by moult of head, body, and usually one or more pairs of central tail feathers and some innerwing coverts, February to May. *As first-winter except:*

HEAD Partial or full hood of grey, brown or black usually acquired, and grey on hindneck lost.

BODY Some acquire pink flush on underparts and lose grey breast-sides.

WINGS Becoming much worn and faded by late summer, and dark areas, especially carpal-bar (which is often less extensive), often fade to pale brown.

TAIL Band often faded to pale brown and white terminal fringe lacking through wear; tail band often broken in centre by one or more pairs of newly-grown, all-white feathers. Tail rarely wholly white.

BARE PARTS Legs and mouth dull red.

Individuals in transition from first-summer to second-winter plumage in autumn have strikingly patchy greyish and white underwing patterns.

Second-winter (Fig. 36E. Underwing and tail similar to second-summer, 36F) Acquired by complete moult, June to October. *As adult winter except:*

WINGS Outer webs of two to six outer primaries with subterminal or terminal blackish marks of variable extent and pattern. Sometimes, outer greater primary coverts, alula, inner secondaries and tertials have small blackish-brown marks which are occasionally extensive. Axillaries white; median and lesser underwing coverts whitish or grey, contrasting with grey or blackish remainder of underwing (underwing thus never uniformly blackish as on adult).

An unknown proportion probably become indistinguishable from adults at this age. Blackish subterminal marks on outer primaries are certain indication of second-year, and individuals with these marks invariably also have obviously pale underwing coverts. Individuals with adult-type upperwing pattern and obviously pale underwing-coverts are probably second-years. Black marks on wing-tip are most easily visible on closed wing when perched, but should not be confused with black underside of the outer primaries shown by perched adults, or (on adults moulting from summer to winter plumage) with old (worn and dark) outer primaries which contrast with new, pale grey inner ones.

Second-summer (Fig. 36F. Upperwing and tail similar to second-winter, 36E) Acquired by head and body moult, February to May.

As adult summer, except upper- and underwing as second-winter, although white border and dark marks on wing-tip reduced through wear. Hood usually fully developed or white-flecked, but a few have winter head pattern. Legs dull red.

Adult winter/third-winter (Fig. 36G. Underwing and tail as adult summer, 36H) Acquired by complete moult, June to November.

HEAD White, with blackish eye-crescent and ear-spot, and grey crown and hindneck.

BODY Mantle, back and scapulars uniform pale grey with white scapular-crescent faint or lacking. Breast-sides grey (extension of mantle colour), rump and remainder of underparts white; underparts sometimes flushed pink.

WINGS Upperwing uniformly pale grey, all primaries and secondaries broadly tipped white, forming prominent white border on trailing edge and tip of wing. Axillaries pale grey, median and lesser underwing coverts dark grey, remainder of underwing blackish with white border on trailing edge and tip.

TAIL White, square-ended.

BARE PARTS Iris and orbital ring blackish brown. Bill blackish; mouth red or orange-red. Legs dull red.

Adult summer/third-summer (Fig. 36H. Upperwing and tail as adult winter, 36G) Acquired by head and body moult, January to May.

As adult winter, except black hood extending over whole head and upper neck. Whole underparts and hindneck often flushed with pink, usually obvious on breast. Bill dark reddish-brown. Legs scarlet.

Ross's Gull

Rhodostethia rosea

(Figs 34B and 38, Photographs 345–355)

Adult summer

IDENTIFICATION

This beautiful small gull of the high Arctic resembles Little Gull in some plumages, and could be overlooked as such as long range. In body size, it is only slightly—if at all—larger than Little Gull, but the wings and tail are proportionately much longer, giving a strikingly attenuated rear end when swimming or on the ground. In flight, the wing-tips are pointed (not slightly rounded as on Little Gull), and the end of the tail is diagnostically wedge-shaped (although this may be difficult to discern at long range), with the central pair of feathers more elongated and projecting farther than the rest. When feeding it has a leisurely, buoyant flight, with noticeably long wings, hovering to take food from the surface or dropping momentarily onto the water, or sometimes plunge-diving like a Kittiwake. It also feeds when swimming, picking at the surface in the manner of a phalarope *Phalaropus*. In direct flight, it has rather pigeon-like, fast, deep wing-beats. On the ground, it is strikingly reminiscent of a dove *Streptopelia*, a compound effect of its small bill, rather small, domed head, full chest, short legs, feathered thighs and, especially, its short-stepping, head-nodding gait.

In first-year plumages, it has a striking W pattern across the wings in flight, but the black on the outer primaries is less extensive than on Little Gull, and the secondaries are clear white without a dark bar, forming a broad white trailing edge to the inner wing which extends across the outer wing almost to the leading edge near the wing-tip. The black on the tail is more confined to the centre, not forming an almost complete band as

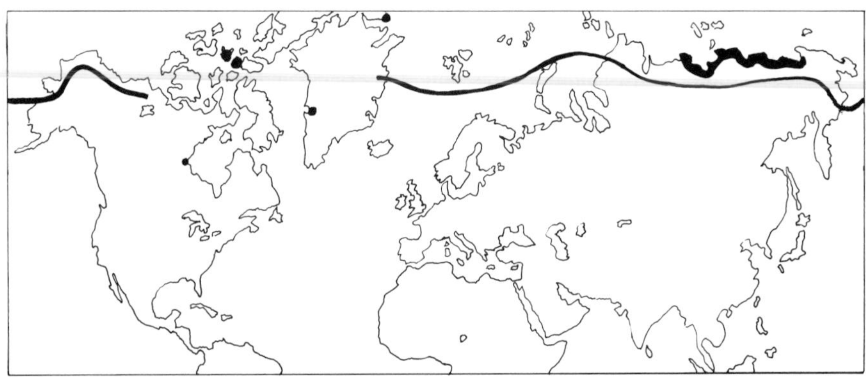

Fig. 37. World distribution of **Ross's Gull** *Rhodostethia rosea*, showing approximate regular breeding range (solid black), and approximate sites of recent proved breeding in Greenland, Canadian Arctic and Manitoba. Approximate southern limit of winter/non-breeding range of Siberian population is shown by black line. Rare south of Arctic seas, in Britain and Ireland averaging one or two annually.

on Little Gull. In first-summer plumage, the wing-pattern may become much faded, and some acquire an adult-type neck-ring.

Probably the majority acquire adult plumage in their second winter. Occasionally, however, individuals in otherwise adult plumage show such immature characters as traces of a carpal-bar, dark marks near the tips of the outer two or more primaries, or dusky marks on the innermost secondaries, and such birds can be safely aged as second-years; individuals which retain winter-type head and body plumage in summer may be in second-summer plumage.

In addition to the structural features, adults in winter differ from adult Little Gull in lacking a prominent dark cap, the underwing is grey (but shadow often makes it appear blackish like Little Gull's), the upperwing has a broad, white trailing edge confined to the secondaries and inner primaries (not a complete, comparatively thin border as on Little Gull), the hindneck is usually obviously grey (often extending to the breast-sides or as a complete breastband), and there is a thin black leading edge to the outer primary (lacking on Little Gull). The underparts are often obviously pink-flushed in winter. Summer adults are unmistakable, with diagnostic black neck-ring and, usually, intensely pink underparts, this colour being most obvious in overcast condition.

An identification pitfall is provided by immature and adult Little Gulls in autumn, which, at a transitional stage of moult, may have a wedge-shaped tail (caused by outer tail feathers which are not fully grown) and unfamiliar plumage patterns. At long range, the black of the centrally-broken tail band on some first-summer Little Gulls may not be discernible, so that the tail appears to be all-white and wedge-shaped.

AGEING SUMMARY

Juvenile: as first-winter, but extensive blackish-brown on mantle and scapulars, extending to breast-sides (summer to October).

First-winter: uniform grey mantle and scapulars, bold blackish W pattern across wings in flight, black bar on tail, winter head pattern (August to April).

First-summer: as first-winter, but W pattern faded; some acquire partial or complete neck-ring and/or pink flush on underparts (March to September).

Adult winter/second-winter: upperwing grey with broad white trailing edge to inner wing, tail white, winter head pattern, underparts often pink (August to April).

Adult summer/second-summer: as adult winter, but with full neck-ring and usually intensely pink underparts (February to October).

DETAILED DESCRIPTIONS

Juvenile (Fig. 38A)

HEAD White, with blackish-brown eye-crescent, ear-spot, crown and hindneck.

BODY Mantle, back, upper rump and scapulars blackish-brown, with buff or golden fringes, giving scaly effect most prominent on scapulars. Underparts and lower rump white, except for blackish-brown patches on breast-sides (extension of mantle colour).

WINGS Coverts of inner wing pale grey, except for clear-cut, blackish-brown carpal-bar (individual feathers fringed whitish) and mainly very pale grey or whitish greater coverts. Innermost secondaries with small black marks, remainder white. Alula and outer coverts of outer wing mainly blackish, innermost coverts grey. Outer web and half of inner web of outer three primaries black, except sometimes for small white area on outer web near tip of 3rd and occasionally also 2nd. Blackish on base of outer web of 4th decreasing in extent inwards to 6th or 7th; black on tips decreasing in extent inwards from 4th to small black subterminal marks on 7th or 8th; remainder of 4th to 10th whitish. Marginal coverts of inner and outer wing white. Underwing coverts washed grey, with broad translucent trailing edge to underwing on secondaries and inner primaries; outer web of 1st and exposed tips of outer primaries black.

TAIL Long uppertail-coverts finely tipped black. Tail markedly wedge-shaped, white with broad black subterminal area on elongated central pair (terminal fringe buff), black decreasing in extent outwards, usually to small terminal mark on 3rd outermost (two outer pairs usually all-white). Black on tail sometimes confined to only two central pairs of feathers. From below, black on tail often obscured by long, white undertail-coverts.

BARE PARTS Iris and orbital ring blackish, sometimes with reddish-brown at base; mouth flesh. Legs brown, dull flesh or dull red.

First-winter (Figs 34B and 38B) Acquired by head and body moult, summer to September. *As juvenile except:*

HEAD White, with grey-washed crown and hindneck (extension of mantle colour) often extending to sides of breast or as complete broad breast-band below line of adult's neck-ring; blackish ear-spot (often appearing as dark crescent along line of adult's neck-ring); and blackish eye-crescent, latter usually extensive in front of and below eye, often appearing as dark mask. Thin white crescents above and below eye.

BODY Mantle and scapulars uniform pale grey, often with retained blackish juvenile back feathers and sometimes also a few among mantle feathers and scapulars; thin white scapular- and tertial-crescents. Breast-sides or whole upper breast and upper flanks washed grey (extension of mantle colour). Remainder of underparts sometimes faintly pink-washed.

First-summer (Fig. 38C depicts a particularly faded individual in late summer) Acquired by head and body moult, February to May. *As first-winter, except:*

HEAD Partial or full neck-ring often acquired.

BODY Many acquire pink flush on underparts and/or lose grey on breast and flanks.

WINGS Becoming much worn by late summer, and dark areas, especially the carpal-bar, often fade to brownish.

TAIL Black faded and reduced through wear.

BARE PARTS Orbital ring sometimes reddish.

Second-winter and **second-summer**

Some second-year individuals may be aged, as described in identification section, page 125.

Adult winter/second-winter (Fig. 38D) Acquired by complete moult, June to September.

HEAD As first-winter, but eye-crescent and ear-spot sometimes very faint or lacking. Partial or full neck-ring.

BODY As first-winter, but without retained juvenile feathers. Underparts often

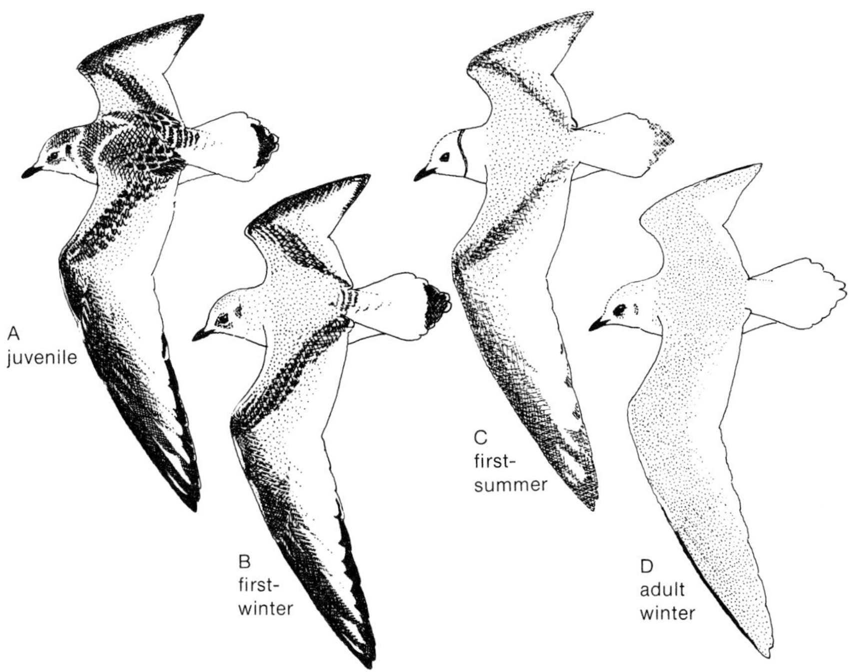

Fig. 38. **Ross's Gulls** *Rhodostethia rosea* in flight.

obviously pink-flushed.

WINGS Upperwing uniform pale grey except for black outer web almost to tip of 1st primary, white or pinkish-white shaft of 1st primary, white or pinkish-white tips to inner primaries increasing in extent inwards from 6th to almost all-white or pinkish-white 10th, and all-white or pinkish-white secondaries: thus broad white or pinkish-white triangular area on trailing edge of wing. Underwing coverts and undersides of outer primaries pale grey of same tone or perhaps sometimes slightly darker than upperwing, but often appearing blackish through effect of shadow. Axillaries and innermost coverts of underwing white, pinkish-white or washed grey. White secondaries and tips of inner primaries form broad translucent trailing edge to underwing. Marginal coverts of inner and outer wing white or pinkish-white.

TAIL White or pinkish-white. Central feathers sometimes worn to a point or broken short.

BARE PARTS Much as juvenile, but legs sometimes red.

Adult summer/second-summer (not illustrated, but head as first-summer, Fig. 38C, and wing and tail pattern as adult winter, 38D) Acquired by head and body moult, February to May. *As adult winter except:*

HEAD White or pinkish-white, with thin black neck-ring around nape and lower throat, thickest on nape (especially when neck erect, often appearing as broad band on nape), and thinnest on throat, sometimes incomplete or lower portion concealed by feather overlap. Crown sometimes washed grey.

BODY Usually, whole underparts and neck pink of apparently varying strength, usually intense: this variation may be largely illusory, the pink being most obvious in overcast conditions. Rump white, sometimes washed pink.

BARE PARTS Iris blackish-brown, orbital ring red. Bill blackish, mouth red. Legs orange-red or red.

Sabine's Gull

Larus sabini

(Figs 34c and 40, Photographs 356–371)

Juvenile

IDENTIFICATION

Away from the breeding grounds, Sabine's Gull is almost wholly pelagic. The breeding population of Canada and Greenland migrates on a diagonal route across the north Atlantic to wintering areas off southwest Africa; sightings from west European coasts are usually the result of westerly gales, the majority during September and October. The breeding population of Siberia and Alaska migrates down the Pacific to winter off South America.

Sabine's Gull is exceptional in having a complete moult in early spring (prior to the northwards migration), and a partial one in autumn (after arrival in winter quarters); this is the reverse of the moult seasons of other gulls, which have a complete moult in autumn and a partial one in spring. Also unlike most other gulls, which start the post-juvenile moult at or shortly after fledging, Sabine's Gull retains full juvenile plumage throughout the first autumn until arrival in the southern wintering areas,

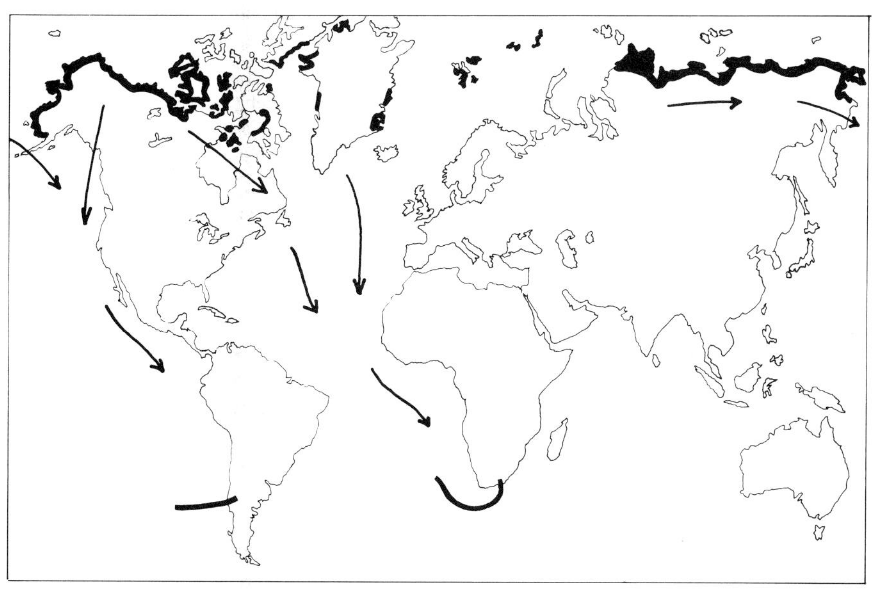

Fig. 39. World distribution of **Sabine's Gull** *Larus sabini*, showing breeding range (solid black), approximate migration routes (arrows), and southern limit of winter/non-breeding range (black lines) of Canadian and Greenland population off southwest Africa, and of Siberian and Alaskan population off west coast of South America. Scarce in coastal Europe; in Britain and Ireland an average of about 20–30 records annually, mainly in southwest in autumn.

where the post-juvenile head and body moult to first-winter plumage takes place during November and December. This is followed by a complete moult during the following February to April, from first-winter to a very adult-like first-summer plumage but lacking a full hood. I am indebted to Piet Meeth for providing an invaluable series of photographs which complemented museum and other photographic evidence, and which was the first material located by the author to indicate the appearance of first-winter plumage and to confirm the extent and timing of the complete moult to first-summer plumage (Photo 360).

Sabine's Gull is between Little Gull and Kittiwake in size, with a forked tail-shape which is difficult to discern except at close range. Its shape in flight resembles a scaled-down Kittiwake, although (largely a function of its smaller size) it has a more bouyant, tern-like flight, making less confident or powerful progress. In flight at all ages, it has a sharply-contrasting, tri-coloured wing pattern, at close range rendering confusion impossible. At long range, however, in the illusory conditions of sea-watches, a major pitfall is provided by first-year Kittiwakes (or possibly even first-year Little Gulls), on which the blackish carpal bar is sometimes impossible to discern, giving a wing pattern which can appear very similar to that of Sabine's, although never matching its actually very striking and clear-cut contrasts of black, grey (greyish-brown on juveniles), and white, the latter almost separating the black and grey near the carpal joint. Caution over this potential identification trap is always advisable, never more than in northern seas in winter when, apart from the occasional straggler (very rarely as late as mid-December in Europe), all Sabine's Gulls should be in equatorial and southern oceans (see map, Fig. 39).

Juveniles (which usually make up the majority of autumn records in Europe) have extensive greyish-brown on the head and breast-sides, giving an almost wholly dark appearance to the bird's front end: at long range, this combined with firm and precise observation of the diagnostic wing pattern, is perhaps the best means of distinguishing juvenile Sabine's Gull from juvenile and first-winter Kittiwake, which usually appear mainly white-headed. At close range, the scaly, greyish-brown mantle, scapulars and coverts of the inner wing; the dusky bar on the inner underwing; and pale legs (usually dull coloured or blackish on Kittiwake) are further differences.

Individuals in first-winter plumage (which presumably do not occur in northern seas) retain the juvenile wing pattern, black-banded tail, a presumably variable amount of juvenile wing-coverts, and all-black bill, but otherwise have uniform grey upperparts and winter adult-like head pattern.

After the complete moult in spring, the first-summer plumage resembles summer adult, except that a full hood is apparently never acquired (the actual extent of the black on the head is highly variable, often with a partial hood or blackish half-collar on the nape, and smudges below this onto the sides of neck). Other, less obvious distinctions of first-summer plumage are in the detailed description. The small number of records of first-summer plumage in Europe suggests that the majority of birds of this age remain in or near the southern wintering areas, and do not return north with the adults in spring.

Adults have uniform grey upperparts and coverts of inner wing, a prominent, clear-cut yellow bill-tip, all-white tail, and (in summer) a full black hood or (in winter) black head markings typically confined to a patch or half-collar on the nape.

AGEING SUMMARY

Juvenile: extensive grey-brown on head and breast-sides; scaly, grey-brown upperparts and coverts of inner wing, black tail-band (summer to December).

First-winter: as adult winter, except for variable amount of retained juvenile inner wing-coverts, black tail band, and all-black bill (November to April).

First-summer: as adult summer, but hood incomplete and usually some other signs of immaturity such as smaller white tips on primaries and/or small, subterminal dark marks on tertials and tail. Yellow bill-tip usually smaller (March to September).

Second-winter: as adult winter, except sometimes traces of immaturity on wings and tail as on first-summer: most are probably indistinguishable from adults in the field (August to April).

Adult summer/second-summer: full hood, uniform grey upperparts and innerwing coverts, white tail, black bill with clear-cut yellow tip (March to October).

Adult winter/third-winter: as adult summer, but black on head confined to patch or half-collar on nape (September to March).

DETAILED DESCRIPTIONS

Juvenile (Figs 34C, 40A and 40B)

HEAD Forehead, narrow eye-ring, lores, chin and throat white. Eye-crescent blackish, remainder of head grey-brown with thin whitish feather fringes.

BODY Mantle, back and scapulars brown to brown-grey, larger feathers with blackish subterminal crescents and neat, whitish or gingery fringes giving scaly effect most prominent on scapulars. Underparts and rump white, except for extensive grey-brown on breast-sides (extension of mantle colour).

WINGS Coverts of inner wings mainly brown to brown-grey, lesser, median and inner greater coverts with blackish subterminal crescents and whitish or gingery fringes giving scaly patterns as on scapulars. Tertials and innermost secondaries grey-brown with clear-cut white fringes, remainder of secondaries and outermost greater coverts white. Alula and most of coverts of outer wing black, inner coverts of outer wing white. Six outer primaries black on outer web with small white tips from 3rd, 4th or 5th inwards; remainder of primaries white, except for blackish of variable extent on outer web of 6th and sometimes also at base of 7th. Inner webs of all primaries mainly white, increasing in extent inwards to wholly white on 6th or 7th, visible as white lines on outer upperwing when wing is fully spread. Underwing white except for exposed black tips of outer primaries (which form a thin dark trailing edge to outer wing), and mainly grey greater underwing coverts which form a dusky bar on the inner under-wing; white secondaries and inner primaries form a broad, translucent white triangle on the trailing edge of the inner wing, reflecting the upperwing pattern.

TAIL Obviously forked (but appearing square-cut when fully spread), white, with complete, clear-cut black band (and narrow pale terminal fringe) broadest in centre (accentuating the forked tail-shape) and narrowing outwards to terminal spot on inner web (and sometimes outer web) of outer tail feather.

BARE PARTS Iris brown, orbital ring blackish. Bill black, mouth flesh. Legs pinkish- or greyish-flesh.

First-winter (wing, tail and bill much as juvenile, Figs 34C, 40A and 40B; head and body much as adult winter, Fig. 40E) Acquired by moult (on or near wintering areas) of head and body feathers and variable amount of innerwing coverts, November and December.

As juvenile, except head pattern, upper body and variable amount of coverts of inner wing as adult winter, and black on wings and tail becoming much worn and faded. Legs presumably become dark at this age on some individuals.

First-summer (Fig. 40C) Acquired by complete moult, February to April. *As adult summer except:*

HEAD White with always incomplete grey or blackish hood of variable pattern, usually mainly confined to ear-coverts and nape, often with blackish rear border, and blackish smudges or grey wash extending below this onto sides of neck and sometimes also breast-sides.

WINGS White primary tips smaller, sometimes reduced by late summer through wear; blackish on 6th sometimes more extensive; tertials sometimes with dusky subterminal marks.

TAIL Sometimes a few feathers have subterminal dark marks.

BARE PARTS Yellowish bill tip lacking or smaller and less well-defined. Legs dull flesh or blackish.

Second-winter (upperwing and tail similar to first-summer, Fig. 40C; head as adult winter, 40E) Acquired by head and body moult in autumn, probably August to October.

As first-summer, except head pattern as adult winter, and white on primary tips often lacking through wear. Only those which show signs of immaturity on wings and tail are separable from adults.

Adult summer/second-summer (Fig. 40D) Acquired by complete moult, December to April.

HEAD Uniform grey hood (appearing dark or rather pale grey, much depending on light) to nape, bordered along lower edge by complete black collar, broadest on nape. Clear white division between hood and mantle.

BODY Mantle, scapulars and back uniform grey, with thin white scapular- and tertial-crescents. Underparts and rump white.

WINGS Striking, clear-cut, tri-coloured pattern: inner wing-coverts and innermost two or three secondaries mainly uniform grey; remainder of secondaries, most of outer greater coverts, outermost median and lesser coverts, and inner primaries and their coverts white; alula and outer coverts of outer wing black (greater primary coverts often with small white tips), and outer five primaries black with large, clear-cut white tips and white tongues on inner webs (the latter visible as white lines on the outer upperwing when wing fully spread). Pattern of black on 6th primary variable, but usually confined to half of outer web and base of inner web. White coverts of inner wing often visible when perched, appearing as white division between grey upperparts and black primaries, merging with white terial crescents. Underwing white, except for exposed black at tips of outer primaries and faint grey bar on greater underwing coverts; white secondaries and inner primaries form broad, translucent white triangle on trailing edge of inner wing, reflecting upperwing pattern.

TAIL Forked, perhaps more prominently than on juvenile, white.

BARE PARTS Iris blackish-brown, orbital ring red. Bill black with clear-cut, bright yellow tip; mouth and gape reddish. Legs blackish or dark grey.

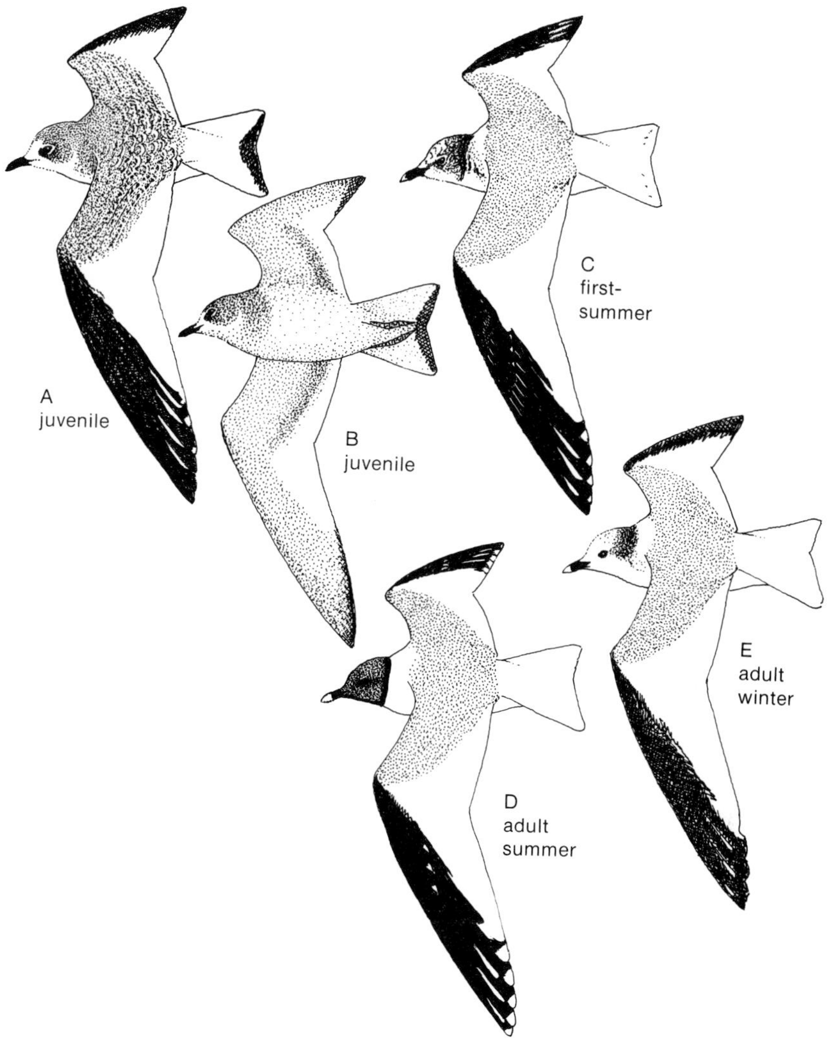

Fig. 40. **Sabine's Gulls** *Larus sabini* in flight.

Adult winter/third-winter (Fig. 40E) Acquired by head and body moult in autumn, probably August to October.

As adult summer, except head white with blackish eye-crescent and variable pattern of blackish-grey, usually confined to fairly defined patch on nape and upper hindneck, but sometimes extending to rear ear-coverts, rear crown, lower hindneck and sides of neck. Outer primaries often brownish and lacking white tips through fading and wear. Bare parts as adult summer, except legs in some colour slides appear to be flesh-coloured or even reddish.

Kittiwake

Rissa tridactyla

(Figs 34D and 42, Photographs 372–391)

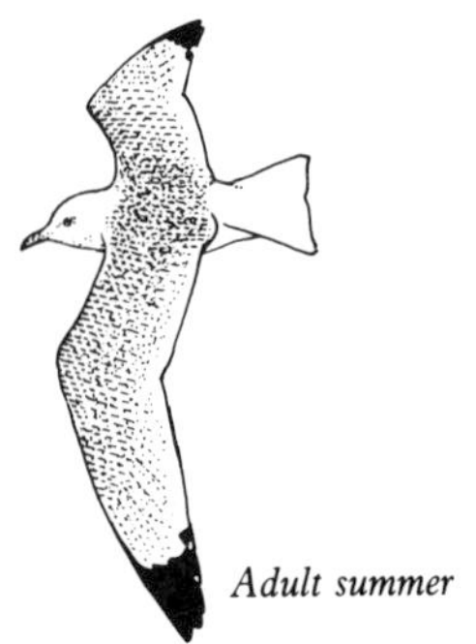

Adult summer

IDENTIFICATION

Kittiwake is between Black-headed and Common Gull *L. canus* in size, with a slightly forked tail-shape (which is usually impossible to detect in the field), very short legs, and rather more upright posture than other gulls when perched. It is an adept marine scavenger, especially around fishing ports and boats at sea, feeding mainly by picking from the surface in flight. In calm conditions, it has a leisurely flight much like other gulls, but in strong winds it adopts a distinctive, powerful flight action which combines deep, stiff wingbeats (with wings sharply angled at the carpal joint) and accomplished shearing (Photo 388). The outer wing is narrower and appears more curved-back than on other gulls, giving a distinctive shape and action in flight.

The differences of first-year Kittiwakes from Sabine's (p. 129) and first-year Little Gulls (p. 119) are described in the respective species accounts.

Juvenile Kittiwake has black bill and legs, black ear-spot and half-collar on the lower hindneck, striking W pattern across the wings in flight, and black tail band. The upperparts are uniform grey like the adult, lacking the brown coloration of other juvenile gulls. First-winter plumage resembles that of the juvenile, except that the black half-collar is usually reduced or lacking, the bill often begins to acquire some greenish-yellow coloration, and the legs are sometimes dull flesh, occasionally orange-flesh; in first-summer plumage, the wing pattern usually becomes extremely worn and faded, and in July and August the moult to second-winter plumage produces a great variation in appearance which may be confusing.

It is probable that some second-years are indistinguishable from adults, but at close range many can be aged by one or more immature characters such as a partially black bill, more extensive black on the outer wing (extending up outer webs of outermost primaries sometimes onto primary coverts), black marks on the tertials, and partial or

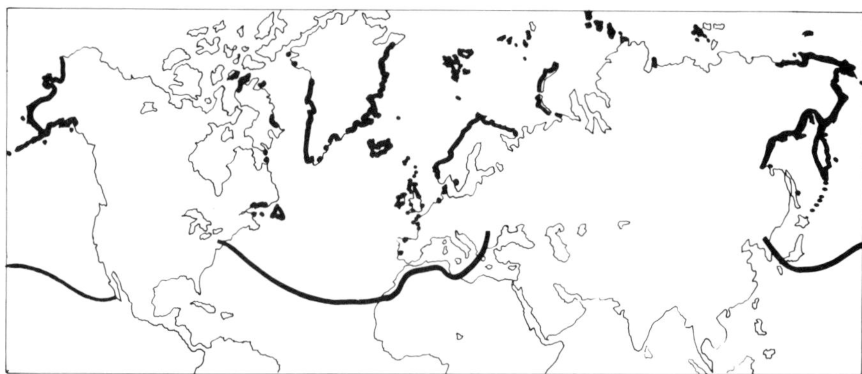

Fig. 41. World distribution of **Kittiwake** *Rissa tridactyla*, showing breeding range (solid black) and approximate southern limit of winter/non-breeding range (black line).

full winter head pattern in summer (not pure white as on adults) indicating second-summer plumage (see summary at end of adult winter/second-winter description). Identifiable second-years apparently lacking in populations of west coast North America.

Adults have a white head in summer (dusky markings in winter), white tail, a distinctive flight pattern (dark grey upperparts, mantle and wing-coverts, shading to whitish on the trailing edge and primaries before the clear-cut triangle of black on the wing-tip), greenish-yellow or yellow bill, and black legs.

AGEING SUMMARY

Juvenile: as first-winter, except black half-collar on lower hindneck always present, and bill always wholly black (summer to September).

First-winter: uniform grey mantle and scapulars, bold blackish W pattern across wings in flight, black tail band, winter head pattern with or without black half-collar, bill sometimes becoming pale at base (August to April).

First-summer: as first-winter, but W pattern faded and much less striking, carpal-bar often reduced, bill usually mainly pale (March to September).

Second-winter and *second-summer:* see detailed descriptions.

Adult winter/second-winter: as adult summer, but head with dusky markings (August to April).

Adult summer/second-summer: white head, underparts and tail, wholly yellowish bill, grey mantle, scapulars and upperwing with clear-cut triangle of black on wing-tip (February to October).

DETAILED DESCRIPTIONS

Juvenile (Fig. 42A. Underwing and tail as first-winter, 42B).

HEAD White, with dusky eye-crescent, blackish ear-spot and broad black half-collar on lower hindneck, remainder of hindneck faintly washed grey.

BODY Mantle, back and scapulars uniform dark grey, latter finely fringed paler. Underparts and rump white.

WINGS Coverts of inner wing dark grey becoming paler outwards, except for clear-cut, broad, blackish carpal-bar (which rarely extends to all lesser coverts, giving solid blackish triangle on leading edge of inner wing: K. M. Olsen *in litt.*); inner greater coverts and tertials broadly edged dark grey. Secondaries white. Alula and outer coverts of outer wing mainly blackish, remainder mainly pale grey. Black on outer web and tip of outer primaries decreasing in extent inwards to subterminal spot on 6th or 7th; small white tips to primaries increasing in size inwards from 5th or 6th. Primaries otherwise pale grey or whitish, with white tongue covering most of inner web from 1st or 2nd inwards. Underwing white, except for exposed black tips of outer primaries (forming a neat, dark trailing edge to outer wing), leading edge of 1st, and speckles on marginal coverts of outer wing.

TAIL White, with clear-cut, black terminal band, broadest in centre (accentuating the slightly forked tail-shape) usually extending to small spot on inner web of outer pair.

BARE PARTS Iris, orbital ring, bill, mouth and legs blackish.

First-winter (Figs 34D and 42B, from above resembles juvenile, 42A) Acquired by head and body moult, summer to October.

As juvenile, except rear crown and hindneck pale grey (rarely dark grey like mantle and extending to whole crown and ear-coverts giving half-hooded effect: K. M. Olsen *in litt.*), and black half-collar usually reduced or replaced by dark grey (but retained on about 20%: K. M. Olsen *in litt.*). Carpal-bar averages less extensive, and K. M. Olsen (*in litt.*) reports two (from 15,000 to 20,000 migrants in Denmark in October 1983) at close range which lacked the carpal-bar, giving an effect very similar to Sabine's Gull. Bill often acquiring variable pattern of greenish-yellow. Legs usually blackish, but sometimes partially or wholly dull-flesh to orange-flesh, rarely bright pink or orange-red.

First-summer (Fig. 42C depicts a particularly worn and faded individual in late summer. Underwing and tail similar to first-winter, 42B) Acquired by moult of head and body feathers and usually some coverts on inner wing, February to May. *As first-winter except:*

HEAD Usually whiter with less dark or extensive markings.

WINGS Becoming much worn and faded, especially by late summer: carpal-bar reduced in extent and faded to pale brown, and black on outer wing much faded and pattern less defined.

TAIL Black band faded and often reduced by wear.

BARE PARTS Bill often extensively pale yellowish or greenish-yellow.

Adult winter/second-winter (resembles adult summer, Fig. 42E, but with dusky head markings much as second-winter, 42D) Acquired by complete moult, June to October.

As adult summer, except rear crown and hindneck pale grey (extension of mantle colour), merging with ill-defined, often crescentic, dark grey or blackish ear-spot which often extends upwards over rear of crown; ill-defined, small dusky eye-crescent.

At least some second-winters are probably indistinguishable from adults, but at close range many are ageable by one or more immature characters such as more black on wing-tip (extending to subterminal marks on 6th, rarely also 7th or even 8th primaries, and up outer web of 2nd and sometimes also 3rd); small dark marks on outer median and greater primary coverts, alula, lesser coverts and tertials; very rarely, tail has a few dark subterminal marks; grey on upperwing subtly less 'clean' and uniform, appearing marginally paler and rather patchy; bill often has yet to acquire full adult coloration, retaining some black; and legs retaining some patchy pale coloration. Typical second-year wing and bill pattern illustrated in Fig. 42D.

Adult summer/second-summer (Fig. 42E) Acquired by head and body moult, February to May.

HEAD White.

BODY Mantle, scapulars and back dark grey, obviously darker than Common Gull *L. c. canus*, with thin white scapular- and tertial-crescents. Underparts and rump white.

WINGS Coverts of inner wing dark grey as mantle, shading to white on trailing edge and to whitish immediately before black of wing-tip. Black on wing-tip confined to outer web of 1st primary, and to clear-cut triangle on inner and outer webs of outer four primaries; subterminal black area on 5th and sometimes also 6th; tiny white tip on 4th increasing in extent inwards. Underwing white, except for black on wing-tip as on upperwing, and pale grey marginal coverts of outer wing.

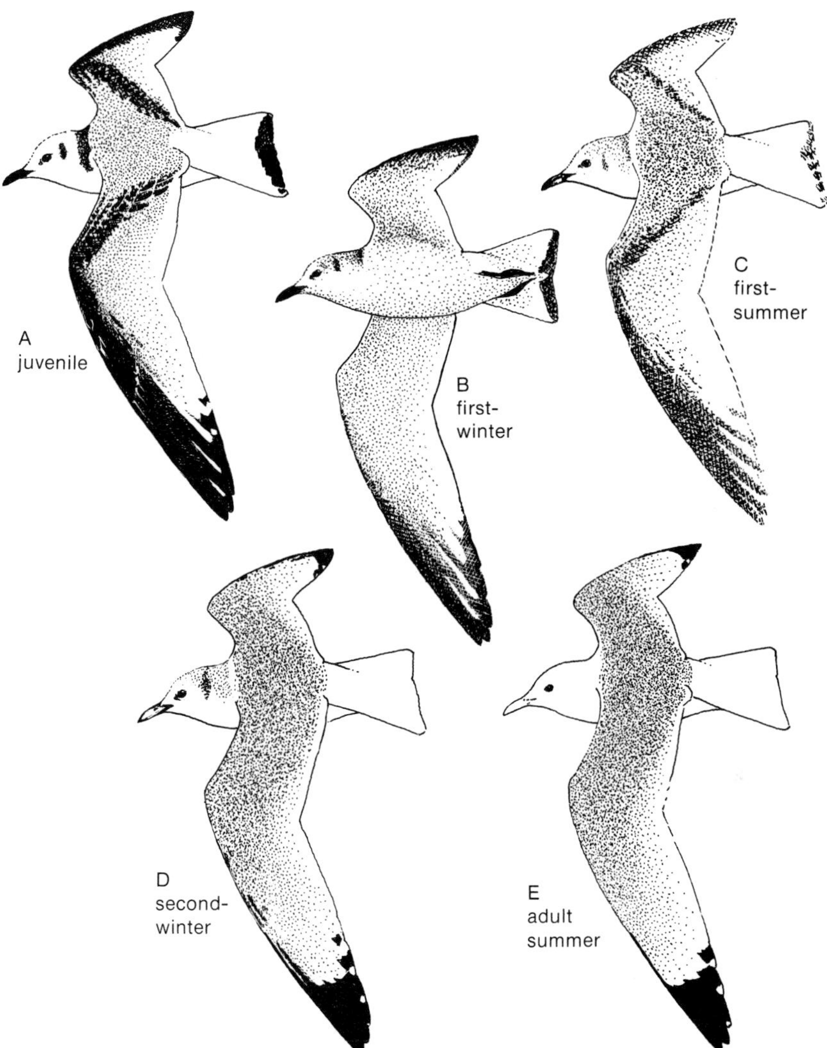

Fig. 42. **Kittiwakes** *Rissa tridactyla* in flight.

TAIL White.

BARE PARTS Iris blackish-brown, orbital ring orange-red or red. Bill greenish-yellow or yellow, sometimes whitish at tip; mouth and gape orange. Legs blackish or dark grey. Variants, apparently very rare, have legs partially or wholly yellow, orange, pink or red.

Some second-summers show one or more of the immature characters described for second-winter, and retain partial or full winter head pattern throughout summer.

Ivory Gull
Pagophila eburnea

(Figs 34E and 44, Photographs 392–398)

Adult summer

IDENTIFICATION

Ivory Gull is slightly larger than Common Gull *L. c. canus*, but more stockily built, with shorter neck, plumper body, and short, strongly-built legs and feet which frequently hang down in flight. On the ground, its full chest, short legs and rolling gait give it an appearance recalling a pigeon *Columba*. The white plumage accentuates its graceful, long-winged flight-jizz. Most commonly it is a scavenger on carrion, but it may also pick food from the surface in flight, often pattering its feet on the surface. It is strong and aggressive, and often more than a match for larger gulls. Contrary to the impression given by most literature, it swims readily.

At all ages, Ivory Gull has a totally distinctive appearance. The first-year's 'ermine' pattern of white with black spots is subject to a great deal of individual variation in the size and distribution of the spots: those on the primary tips, tail and coverts of outer wing are always present and invariably the most easily visible at a distance, as is the dusky 'face' of juvenile and first-winter birds. The base of the pale-tipped bill is blackish on juveniles, paling to greyish by the first winter. The legs and feet are blackish at all ages.

Adult plumage is acquired in the second winter, a surprisingly short period of immaturity for a gull of this size. Adults in summer and winter have all-white plumage (actually very faintly ivory-toned when viewed against snow); sight of the greyish bill with yellow and orange tip, and the black legs is essential to rule out the risk of confusion with all-white albinistic gulls.

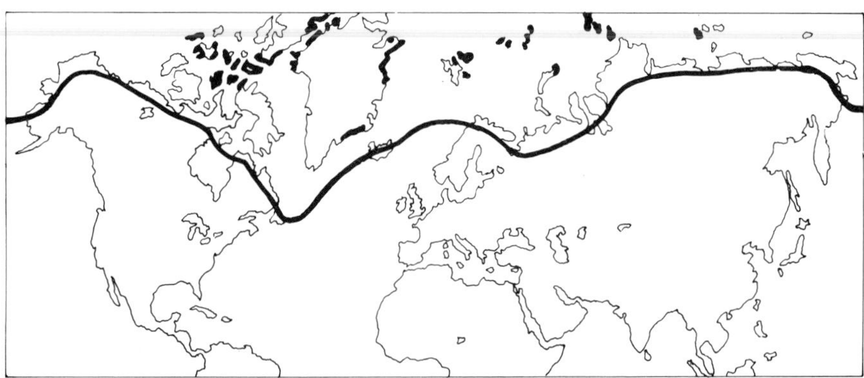

Fig. 43. World distribution of **Ivory Gull** *Pagophila eburnea*, showing approximate breeding range (solid black) and approximate southern limit of winter/non-breeding range (black line). Rare south of Arctic seas, with one or two records annually in Britain and Ireland.

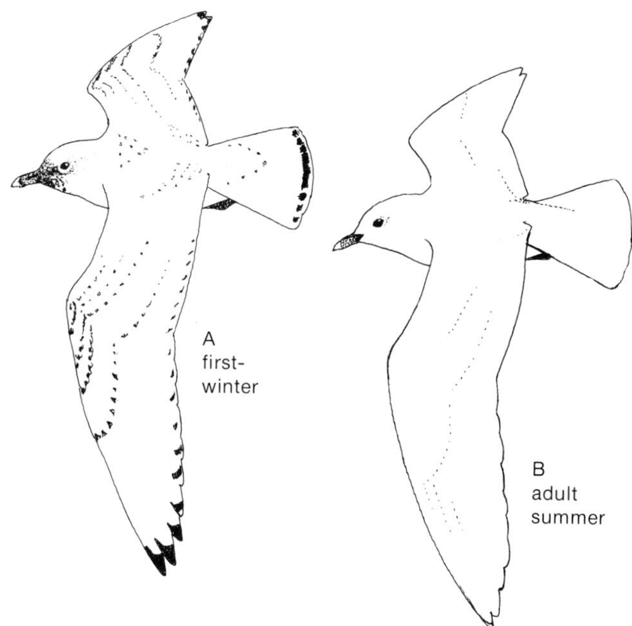

Fig. 44. **Ivory Gull** *Pagophila eburnea* in flight.

AGEING SUMMARY

Juvenile: as first-winter, but more black spots on head, mantle, scapulars and breast; base of bill blackish (summer to September).

First-winter: white with dusky 'face' and variable amount of black spotting on wings, upperparts and tail band. Bill greyish with yellowish tip (August to April).

First-summer: as first-winter, but dusky 'face' reduced or lacking, and black spotting on upperparts and coverts of inner wing reduced or lacking (March to September).

Adult winter/second-winter: plumage wholly white. Bill greyish with yellow and orange tip (August to April).

Adult summer/second-summer: as adult winter (March to September).

DETAILED DESCRIPTIONS

Juvenile (wings and tail as first-winter, Figs 34E and 44A).
As first-winter, except crown, nape, hindneck, ear-coverts, mantle, scapulars, and occasionally breast sparsely spotted with black. Base of bill blackish, tip yellowish.

First-winter (Figs 34E and 44A) Acquired by head and body moult, summer to September.
HEAD White, with grey or blackish 'face' of variable extent on forehead, lores and

chin, often extending behind eye. White eye-ring usually prominent in front of eye. Occasionally, a very few spots on crown and nape.

BODY White, with variable amount of black spotting on mantle, scapulars and (rarely) breast.

WINGS White: inner wing with small black subterminal spots on greater, median and lesser coverts (number of spotted feathers varies individually); secondaries white, with or without small black subterminal spots (majority have spots on at least outer secondaries); tertials with usually prominent subterminal black crescents. On outer wing, alula and lesser, median and greater primary coverts have small subterminal black spots. Primaries tipped with black crescentic marks of variable size, decreasing in size inwards to small subterminal marks on 5th to 10th. Underwing white, except for exposed black tips of primaries and secondaries, and dusky marks on marginal coverts of outer underwing.

TAIL White, with black subterminal bars or crescents on all feathers of variable thickness, forming thin, often broken tail band. Uppertail-coverts with or without small, black subterminal spots.

BARE PARTS Iris brown, orbital ring black. Bill grey or grey-green with yellowish or fleshy-yellow tip, sometimes suggestion of orange at tip of lower mandible. Legs blackish or grey.

First-summer (wings and tail much as first-winter, Figs 34E and 44A) Acquired by head and body moult, January to May.

As first-winter, except dusky 'face' reduced or lacking, and black spotting on head, mantle, scapulars, and coverts of inner wing reduced or lacking. Bill coloration often as adult.

Adult winter/second-winter (as adult summer, Fig. 44B) Acquired by complete moult, May to August.

Whole plumage uniformly white with very faint ivory tone. Shafts of primaries and tail feathers straw-yellow. Iris brown, orbital ring red. Basal two-thirds of bill blue-grey or grey-green, remainder yellowish with orange at tip of lower mandible of variable strength and extent, occasionally lacking. Bill rarely all-yellow. Mouth and gape flesh or orange-flesh. Legs blackish.

Adult summer/second-summer (Fig. 44B) Acquired by head and body moult, January to April.

Much as adult winter, but bill coloration brighter.

GROUP FIVE

Glaucous and Iceland Gulls

Glaucous *Larus hyperboreus* and Iceland Gulls *L. glaucoides* are large gulls which lack any black or blackish on the wings and tail in immature plumages and have all-white wing-tips when adult. These two white-winged gulls are therefore distinctive amongst other large west Palearctic species.

Glaucous Gull (map, Fig. 46) is rare in most of Europe, but is of sufficiently regular occurrence in mainly coastal northern Europe (especially during November to March) to make worthwhile a check for its presence in gatherings of large gulls. Identification is usually straightforward, but small or small-looking individuals may be confused with Iceland Gull, and all-white albinistic or (apparently rare) leucistic other gulls (especially Great Black-backed Gull *L. marinus*), and especially the rather frequent examples of hybrid Glaucous X Herring Gull *L. argentatus* may cause problems.

Iceland Gull (map, Fig. 48) of the white-winged nominate race *L. g. glaucoides* breeds in Greenland and is usually rarer than Glaucous Gull in Europe, but has arrived in larger-than-usual numbers in some recent winters. Identification is usually straightforward, but large or large-looking individuals may be confused with Glaucous Gull, and all-white albinistic or (apparently rare) leucistic other large gulls (especially Herring Gull), and hybrid Glaucous X Herring Gulls may cause problems.

The northeast Canadian subspecies of Iceland Gull *L. g. kumlieni*, known as Kumlien's Iceland Gull, is a vagrant to Europe, and is described separately under 'Geographical variation' on p. 152. Adults have a distinctive pattern of grey on the wing-tips.

IDENTIFICATION

Because the two species are similar at all ages, and because there is no consistent difference in the progression of immature plumages, it is convenient to discuss their identification together, under appropriate headings.

Plumage: First- and second-years in fresh plumage look rather uniformly coffee-coloured or pale grey-brown at a distance: the complex pattern of barring on the

Table 6: Measurements (mm) of **Glaucous** Larus hyperboreus *and* **Iceland Gulls** L. glaucoides *(from Dwight 1925)*

	sample	*wing*	*tail*	*bill*	*tarsus*
Glaucous Gull *L. hyperboreus*	21	430–477	180–210	56–67	64–77
Iceland Gull *L. glaucoides*	13	378–433	156–178	39–45	52–63

upperparts, wings and tail are usually visible only at close range. First-years are more uniformly coloured on the head and underparts than first-years of other large gulls. At all ages, the whitish primaries and secondaries are a prominent feature in flight, especially when viewed from below, when they appear wholly translucent. There is apparently no consistent plumage difference between the two species at any age, but, on average, first-year Icelands have a neater pattern of barring on the wings and uppertail- and undertail-coverts; and a generally greyer-brown, less coffee-coloured appearance. The first-year plumages of both species show a good deal of individual variation in the darkness and pattern of plumage.

Size: The size of most Glaucous Gulls is from that of a large Herring Gull to that of an average Great Black-backed Gull. There is very little size overlap with Iceland Gull, which is typically slightly smaller than an average Herring Gull. Thus, for practical field purposes, size alone is a valid distinction for individuals which are obviously at least as large as the largest Herring Gull (thus Glaucous), or obviously smaller than an average Herring Gull (thus Iceland). For birds which are not side-by-side with other relevant species (and thus do not allow an accurate size assessment), or those which are about the size of an average Herring Gull, structure and (on first-years) bill pattern should be checked.

Structure: A typical Glaucous Gull has a long, heavy, often massive bill, and a long, rather flat-profiled contour to the forehead and crown (but note that it can raise its crown feathers, giving a more rounded look at times); bill and head shape combine to give a strong, aggressive look. Iceland Gull has a comparatively short bill (but still occasionally as large as that of a small Herring Gull), more rounded profile to the forehead and crown, and a proportionately slightly larger eye: these features combine to give a more gentle expression, even recalling that of a Common Gull *L. canus* at times. A useful general rule is that Iceland Gull's bill is less than half its head length, whereas that of Glaucous is greater, but this may be complicated by the effect on apparent head length which different postures may produce. Perhaps the best impression of the bill size/head shape differences can be obtained by studying the series of photographs of the two species included here.

The small-eyed/large-billed appearance of Glaucous compared with the large-eyed/small-billed impression given by Iceland can be measured in full-profile photographs (or assessed in the field) by comparing the width of the eye (the diameter from front to back of the eye) with the bill length (from the feathering on the culmen to the tip). On 22 photographs of Glaucous, the bill was 4.2 to 7.5 times the eye diameter; on 20 photographs of Iceland the bill was 2.2 to 4.5 times the eye diameter: a safe rule would seem to be that a bill:eye ratio of 5 or more indicates Glaucous, and 4 or less indicates Iceland.

When perched, the projection of the primaries beyond the tail is a good distinction: on Glaucous the projection is comparatively short, always the same or less than the bill length (from the forwardmost extension of feathering on the upper mandible to the tip), whereas on Iceland the projection is obviously much longer than its bill length. This distinction applies throughout the first year and on older individuals which have not dropped or partially regrown the outermost primaries during the complete autumn moult.

The whole build of Glaucous is typically more massive than Iceland, with large, full-chested body; bunched tertials and secondaries 'fuller' and bulkier; and proportionately slightly longer legs. Iceland Gull resembles a long-winged small or average

Fig. 45. First-winter **Glaucous** *Larus hyperboreus* and nominate **Iceland Gulls** *L. g. glaucoides*, showing comparative sizes and structure.

Herring Gull in general build, and never gives the very large, bulky impression of a typical Glaucous.

On typical Glaucous, the larger size and bulkier structure is obvious in flight, when it looks broad-winged, full-chested and lumbering, with heavy head and bill prominent. Iceland Gull is more elegantly proportioned, with longer, slimmer wings and relatively small head and bill. Even so, these structural differences are often very difficult to assess, especially on lone birds.

The structural differences are obvious on typical birds, but on individuals which are indeterminate on size alone, the structural differences too, may be contentious: bill size and shape, bill: eye ratio, and primary projection are then usually the most reliable structural characters.

Glaucous Gulls breeding in northwest Alaska and wintering on the west coast of North America south to California are slightly smaller on average than other populations, with adult upperparts slightly darker grey on average: they have been given the subspecific name '*barrovianus*' by some authors. Some individuals are also significantly smaller-billed and longer-winged than typical Glaucous Gulls, and extreme examples might be confusible with Iceland Gull. Special care is therefore needed over claims of Iceland Gull in this region, where it is extremely rare. My own field experience of '*barrovianus*' confirms their smaller-billed, longer-winged look on average compared with typical Glaucous Gulls, and some showed a primary projection slightly longer than the bill. They were all, however, obvious Glaucous Gulls in their general structure, bulk, bill: eye ratio, and bill colour of first-years.

Bill pattern and colour: On first-years there is a diagnostic difference in bill pattern. Glaucous Gull always has the basal two-thirds bright flesh-pink to yellowish-cream and a sharply contrasting, square-cut black tip extending very slightly, if at all, back along the cutting edges; this bill pattern is not shared by any other first-year large gull, and it is often the first feature by which Glaucous can be located among perched flocks. Iceland Gull has a slightly variable bill pattern, typically with at most the basal half of the bill dull flesh or greyish and an extensive black tip which usually shades into the pale base and extends back in a wedge along the cutting edges. At long range (especially on juveniles and first-winters), the bill may look wholly dark, which is never the case on Glaucous. The bill pattern difference holds good throughout the first year at least (after which the black area usually begins to diminish and the distinctions become lost), but may be evident on some individuals well into the second year. On third-winter and older, the yellow on the bill of Iceland Gull often shows an obvious greenish tone which is never present on Glaucous Gull (on which the bill is fleshy, yellowish or bright yellow).

Identification pitfalls: The possibility of all-white albinistic or (apparently rare) leucistic examples of other large gulls, or hybrid Glaucous X Herring Gulls (there is apparently no proven case of hybridisation between Iceland and Herring Gull) needs to be eliminated when identifying Glaucous and Iceland Gulls. The simple rule is that true or pure Glaucous or Iceland Gulls will never show any characters such as a contrasting darker tail band or secondary bar (but note that immatures of both species often show a tail band or secondary bar of uniform coloration of similar tone to the rest of the upperparts); a prominent blackish area around the eye or on the ear-coverts; or outer primaries (on immatures) darker than the inner ones or (on adults) with dark markings, however small, near the wing-tip. Typically, the primaries on Glaucous and Iceland are the palest part of the wing, but on some dark first-years they are as dark as the remainder. The presence of one or any combination of these characters is a certain indication of hybridity or leucism. See also discussion of hybrids of Glaucous-winged Gull on west coast of North America (p. 184).

Reference in some literature to an all-white second-year plumage for Glaucous and Iceland Gulls is misleading. Some faded second-years or even first-years, especially in spring and summer, may appear white at a distance, but they are actually pale buff-toned and close examination will reveal at least a trace of the normal barring of these ages (especially on areas which are less susceptible to fading such as the undertail-coverts, lower scapulars, or underwing), and normal bill coloration. Any large gull which is genuinely all-white is certainly albinistic and then the only clues to identity are usually the bill pattern (on immatures), bare parts colours (on adults), or general size and structure. The difficulty of judging size on any lone bird, and the illusory effects of all-white plumage on apparent size, wing shape and jizz, render even an all-white albinistic (or leucistic) medium-sized species (such as Common Gull) subject to misidentification as Iceland Gull in brief fly-by views.

Another pitfall is provided by adult Herring Gulls which have moulted or only partially regrown the outer two or three primaries during September to November, towards the end of the complete autumn moult. On such birds, the only black visible on the upperside of the wing-tip in flight is the usually small amount on the 4th and 5th primaries, which is difficult to discern at long range. The extensive black on the partially grown 1st to 3rd primaries is however, always evident along the leading edge of the outer wing when viewed from below.

AGEING SUMMARY

The difficulties of accurately ageing a proportion of immature large gulls after their first year (see pages 78–80) apply equally to Glaucous and Iceland Gulls. There is a further complication in that there is more individual variation in the strength of the dark patterning of juveniles than in the cases of other large gulls. This, combined with the fact that their paler plumage is more prone to fading, means that what started out as 'pale-morph' juveniles can appear very whitish in first-winter (from as early as January) and first-summer plumages, and at long range they may be difficult to separate from the normal, pale, less barred and often whitish plumage of second-years. Thus, during January to April (after which second-summers are usually obvious as such by at least some clear grey on the upperparts), it is safest to leave the age of pale buff or whitish individuals as indeterminate (i.e. 'first- or second-winter', or 'first- or second-summer'), unless views are close enough to determine the age-diagnostic characters of most second-years, such as a pale iris, smaller extent of black on the bill-tip (with prominent pale area at extreme tip), less prominently barred wings (especially the greater coverts and tertials), presence of any clear grey on the mantle and/or scapulars, or the slightly rounded outer primary tips and square-tipped tail feathers (pointed and rounded respectively on first-years). Extremely worn primaries, on which the tips are sharply pointed or on which only the shafts remain at the tips are typical of some late first-winters and most first-summers; such extreme wear is never evident on second-years.

Juvenile: whole plumage fresh and unworn. Head and underparts rather uniform brown. Mantle and scapulars neatly patterned. Wing-coverts neatly barred. First-year bill pattern (summer to October).

First-winter: as juvenile, except head and underparts averaging paler, and mantle and scapulars more coarsely patterned (September to March).

First-summer: as first-winter, except head and underparts usually very pale or whitish, mantle and scapulars often whitish with coarse dark barring, and wing-coverts very pale or whitish through wear. Wings and tail very worn (March to September).

Second-winter: whole plumage generally whitish or generally paler and more uniform, less barred, than juvenile/first-winter. Head and underparts sometimes rather coarsely streaked. Bill much as first-year, but usually with obvious pale area at extreme tip. Iceland Gull may acquire an age-diagnostic black-tipped bill during the second-year with pattern like that of first-year Glaucous. Iris usually becoming pale (August to March).

Second-summer: as second-winter, but whole plumage generally faded paler or whitish. Mantle and scapulars with variable amount of clear grey. Iris pale (March to September).

Third-winter: as adult, except obvious brownish areas on upperwing, underwing and tail (looking uniform at distance), usually obvious sparse barring on wing coverts and uppertail- and undertail-coverts, and usually obvious dark subterminal area on bill (October to April).

Third-summer: as third-winter, except head and underparts white and brownish areas on wings and tail faded (February to September).

Fourth-winter/fourth-summer: as adult, except for pale brown-washed areas on wings, occasionally also tail, and small, if any, dark subterminal mark on bill.

Adult winter: head heavily streaked; upperparts and wings uniform grey; tail all-white; adult bill pattern (November to March).

Adult summer: as adult winter, except head white (February to September).

DETAILED DESCRIPTIONS

For Glaucous Gull see facing page: for Iceland Gull see page 151.

Glaucous Gull

Larus hyperboreus

(Figs 45A and 47, Photographs 399–422)

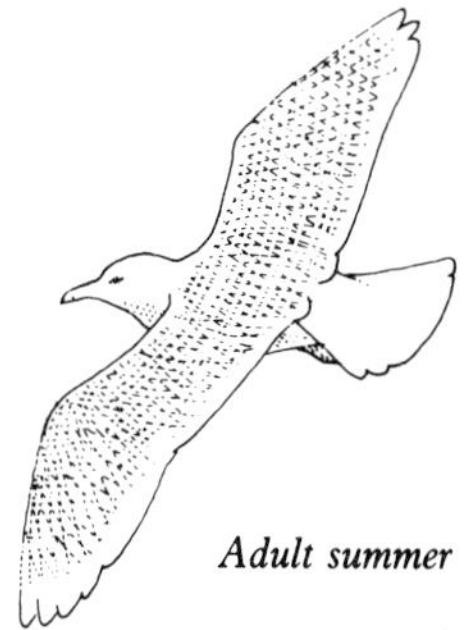

General factors relating to identification and ageing, especially distinctions from Iceland Gull, are discussed on pp. 141–146.

DETAILED DESCRIPTIONS

Juvenile (similar to first-winter, Figs 45A and 47A)

HEAD Rather uniform light brownish-grey or buff, shading to whitish on chin and around base of bill. Streaking fine and inconspicuous. Eye-crescent dusky; whitish crescents above and below eye.

BODY Underparts uniform brownish-grey or buff, usually darkest on belly, with mottles or faint bars especially on breast-sides and flanks; underparts often generally darker than upperparts. Mantle and scapulars pale buff with intricate, neat pattern of brownish bars or chevrons of various strength, with barring strongest on lower scapulars. Rump strongly barred.

WINGS Coverts of inner wing pale buff with neat pattern of dark bars, but greater coverts more strongly and coarsely marked (pattern highly variable), but becoming progressively more uniform grey-brown outwards. Tertials coarsely patterned as inner greater coverts. Primaries and secondaries mainly uniform grey-brown or buff (as dark or paler than general colour of rest of wing) with broad whitish tips and fringes which combine to form strikingly whitish wing point when perched, dusky subterminal mottling or chevrons of variable pattern and strength, and whitish or straw-coloured shafts. Underwing coverts and axillaries mottled with dark, of similar general coloration to underparts.

TAIL Typically rather plain pale grey or buff, with highly variable marbled or

Fig. 46. World distribution of **Glaucous Gull** *Larus hyperboreus*, showing approximate breeding range (solid black) and approximate southern limits of winter/non-breeding range (black line).

'watered' pattern of whitish and dark mottles and bars, or broad subterminal band of uniform grey or buff. Uppertail- and undertail-coverts strongly barred.

BARE PARTS Iris dark brown. Basal two-thirds of bill bright flesh-pink to pale flesh, with sharply-demarcated black tip; mouth flesh. Legs pale flesh.

First-winter (Figs. 45A and 47A) Acquired by post-juvenile head and body moult, summer to October.

As juvenile, except head and underparts averaging slightly paler, and mantle and scapulars basically whiter, usually with coarser, more irregular pattern of bars; sometimes indistinguishable from juvenile plumage. From January onwards, some become worn and faded, acquiring generally whitish appearance as moult to first-summer progresses.

First-summer (Fig. 47B) Acquired by head and body moult, January to May.

As first-winter, except head and body very pale buff or whitish, with faint mottling or streaking, and mantle and scapulars whitish, with irregular, often sparse brown barring which may become inconspicuous through fading. Wings and tail becoming much worn and faded, in extreme cases acquiring very whitish appearance as base colour fades and dark juvenile markings become faint or disappear. Bill sometimes acquires small pale area at extreme tip, and yellowish-flesh at base.

Second-winter (Fig. 47C) Acquired by complete moult, April to September. *As first-winter, except:*

HEAD AND BODY Head and underparts basically pale buff or whitish, sometimes rather coarsely streaked or mottled, less uniform. Mantle and scapulars patchy buff and whitish, or with sparse pattern of barring less intricate than first-winter. Some acquire a few clear grey feathers among mantle feathers and scapulars.

WINGS Generally pale buff and plainer, without neat, defined barring on coverts and terials; greater coverts mainly plain pale buff or whitish, with any patterning much finer and paler, usually confined to innermost. Tertials as inner greater coverts. Underwing mainly dusky, similar to underparts. Primaries and secondaries plainer; pale buff or whitish.

TAIL Typically more uniform and paler, with fainter markings. Uppertail- and undertail-coverts less strongly barred.

BARE PARTS Iris often pale at this age. Black on bill usually less extensive, extreme tip usually obviously pale, and base pink, yellowish or yellowish-flesh.

Second-summer (not illustrated, but plumage similar to second-summer Iceland Gull, Fig. 49C) Acquired by head and body moult, January to May.

As second-winter, except head and underparts pale buff or whitish. Mantle and scapulars invariably with some clear grey or whitish grey, usually extensive. Wings and tail acquiring uniform whitish or very pale buff appearance through wear and fading. Iris pale, sometimes obvious only at close range; orbital ring sometimes yellowish. Bill pattern as second-winter or with thick, subterminal dark band.

Third-winter (not illustrated, but plumage similar to third-winter Iceland Gull, Fig. 49D) Acquired by complete moult, April to January.

HEAD As adult winter.

BODY Underparts white or with some brownish mottling. Mantle and scapulars clear pale grey or with some patchy whitish on scapulars. Rump white or faintly mottled.

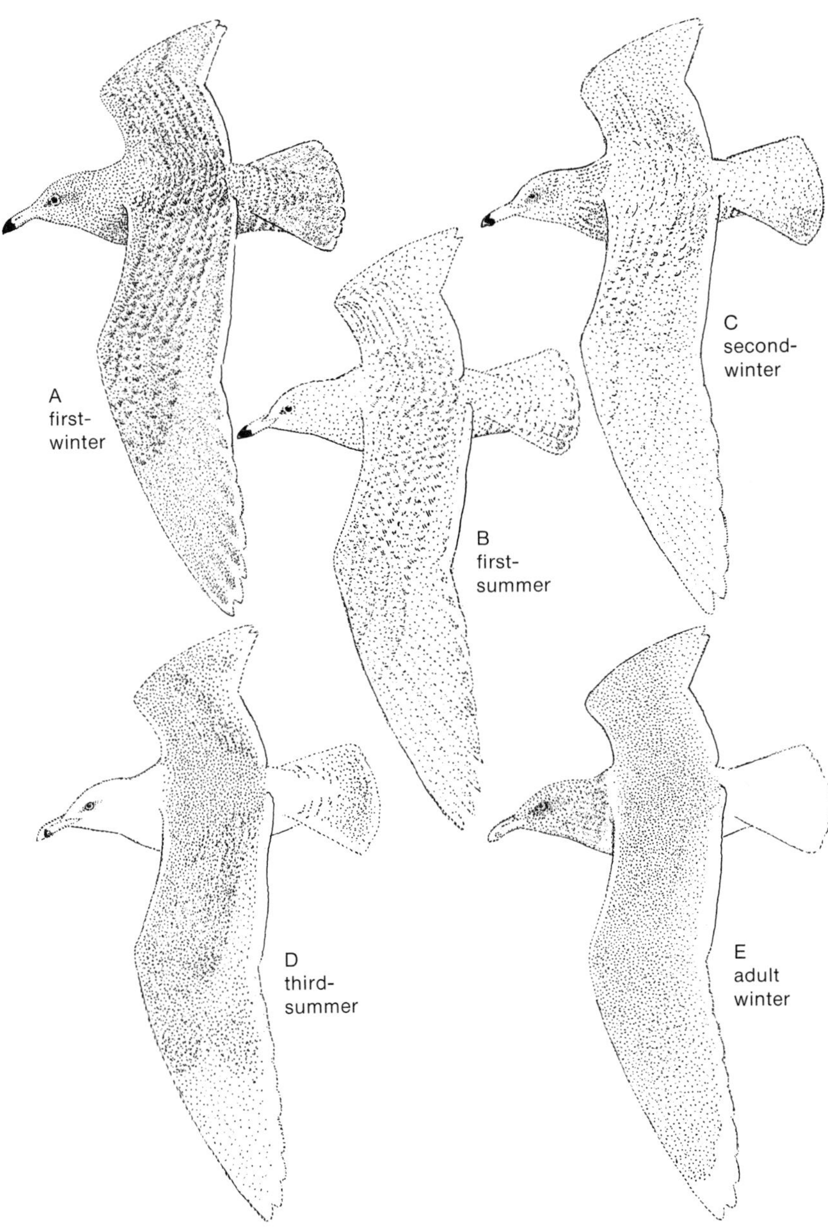

Fig. 47. **Glaucous Gulls** *Larus hyperboreus* in flight.

WINGS As adult, but grey areas patchy or whitish, with age-diagnostic areas of obvious uniform pale brown especially on greater coverts (sometimes faintly freckled with brown), primaries and secondaries, and often sparse barring on median and lesser coverts. Primaries sometimes whitish without clear grey or brown. From distance in flight, wings and tail have uniform pale brown areas, giving patchy, faded look. Underwing mainly white, faintly marked with pale brownish.

TAIL White, typically with often extensive areas of uniform pale brown or faint brownish freckling; uppertail- and undertail-coverts usually sparsely barred or washed with brown.

BARE PARTS As adult except bill with usually obvious blackish subterminal marks, and sometimes lacking red on gonys.

Third-summer (Fig. 47D) Acquired by head and body moult, January to April.

As third-winter, except head and underparts white or faintly streaked, and brown areas on wings and tail faded.

Adult winter/fourth-winter (Fig. 47E) Acquired by complete moult, June to February.

HEAD White, with often dense brownish or orange-brown streaking confined to head and upper breast. Eye-crescent dusky; whitish crescent above and below eye.

BODY Underparts and rump white. Upperparts uniform pale grey, slightly paler than those of Herring Gull *L. a. argenteus*, with prominent white scapular- and tertial-crescents when perched.

WINGS Upperwing pale grey with thin white leading edge and broad white trailing edge. Primaries and secondaries broadly tipped white; shafts straw-coloured. Underwing white.

TAIL White.

BARE PARTS Iris pale yellow; orbital ring yellowish, yellowish-pink, or yellowish-orange. Bill yellowish or bright yellow, with pale orange or orange-red spot near gonys and whitish at extreme tip. Legs pale or bright pink.

Individuals as adult except for pale brown-washed areas on wings (occasionally also tail), and sometimes also small, dark subterminal mark on bill are typical fourth-years.

Adult summer/fourth-summer (not illustrated, but plumage similar to adult summer Iceland Gull, Fig. 49E) Acquired by head and body moult, January to March.

As adult winter, except head and underparts white, and yellow and red on bill brighter.

Iceland Gull

Larus glaucoides

(Figs 45B, 49 and 49(a), Photographs 423–439)

Adult summer

General factors relating to identification and ageing, especially distinctions from Glaucous Gull, are discussed on pp. 141–146.

DETAILED DESCRIPTIONS

Juvenile (similar to first-winter, Figs 45B and 49A)
Description as for juvenile Glaucous Gull, except: general coloration greyer-brown, less buff or coffee-coloured on average; pattern of dark barring on mantle, scapulars and wings neater, denser and less coarse on average; barring on uppertail- and undertail-coverts finer on average; and dark crescentic mark near tip of each primary more prominent on average. Exceptionally, however, barring on wings and tail much stronger and more contrasting than usual (see Photo 425). Bill pattern slightly variable, typically with at most basal half dull flesh or greyish, and black tip more extensive, usually shading into pale base and extending back in wedge along cutting edges; bill usually appears all dark at long range.

First-winter (Figs 45B and 49A) Acquired by post-juvenile head and body moult, summer to September.
Text as for first-winter Glaucous Gull.

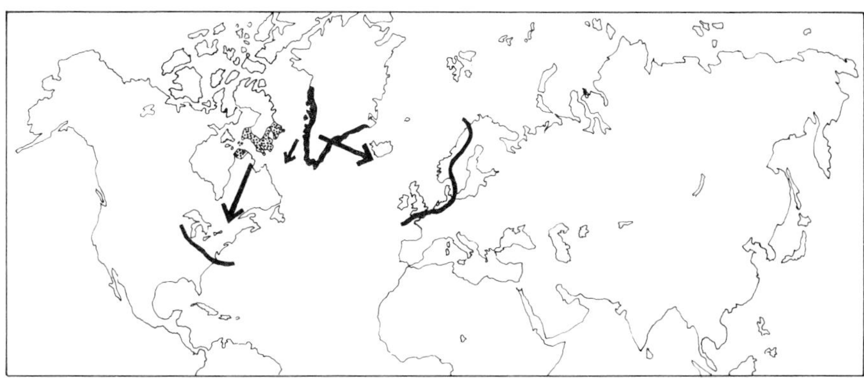

Fig. 48. Approximate breeding ranges of **Iceland Gull** *Larus glaucoides glaucoides* (solid black), and **Kumlien's Iceland Gull** *L. g. kumlieni* (spotted). Nominate *glaucoides* largely sedentary or wintering Iceland or (in smaller numbers) mainly coastal northwest Europe (these probably mainly from east Greenland), or wintering sparingly in northeast North America (these probably from west Greenland); *kumlieni* winters in northeast North America, vagrant to Europe. Black lines indicate approximate limits of winter/non-breeding range.

First-summer (Fig. 49B) Acquired by head and body moult, January to April. Text as for first-winter Glaucous Gull.

Second-winter (not illustrated, but plumage similar to second-winter Glaucous Gull, Fig. 47C) Acquired by complete moult, April to September.
Test as for second-winter Glaucous Gull. Distinctive first-year bill pattern often retained, but with obvious pale area at extreme tip, or black area reduced so that pattern resembles that of first-year Glaucous.

Second-summer (Fig. 49C) Acquired by head and body moult, January to April. Text as for second-winter Glaucous Gull. Distinctions from Glaucous Gull of first-year bill pattern usually lost by this age.

Third-winter (Fig. 49D); **third-summer** (plumage similar to Glaucous Gull, Fig. 47D); **adult winter/fourth-winter** (plumage similar to adult winter Glaucous Gull, Fig. 47E); and **adult summer/fourth-summer** (Fig. 49E): descriptions and moult timing much as for Glaucous Gull, except orbital ring of adult summer usually red, not yellowish; bill of third-winter and older often obviously greenish-yellow (Glaucous always lacks obvious greenish tone).

GEOGRAPHICAL VARIATION

*L. g. **kumlieni**:* (Kumlien's Iceland Gull) Fig. 49(a), Photo 439. Subspecies of Iceland Gull, breeding in northeast Canada and wintering there or in mainly coastal eastern North America (map, Fig. 48). It has only recently been added to the British list (a few earlier claims have not yet been officially accepted) and there are now about six accepted records in Britain and a few others in Europe. Most have occurred in winters when exceptional numbers of nominate *glaucoides* have also been recorded.

Identical to *glaucoides* in size, structure, progression of immature plumages and moult timings: differences from *glaucoides* are summarised below. Firm notation of *glaucoides*-like structure is the essential starting point for identification of ***kumlieni***, as this will eliminate possible confusion such as with leucistic Herring Gull or hybrid Glaucous × Herring Gull. There appears to be no proved case of hybridisation between Iceland Gull and Herring Gull, but if such ever occurred it would complicate matters.

Unlike adult *glaucoides* (which has all-white wing-tips), adult *kumlieni* has pattern of obvious frosted grey markings on outer primaries when fresh, which initially wear darker, then fade to pale grey-brown when feathers old. Judging from personal study of photographs and museum specimens, and comments from E. Mills (*in litt.*), pattern of wing-tip markings and their colour seems very consistent, contradicting some previous literature which speaks of highly variable pattern and colour. All photographs and specimens examined showed dark markings on outer five primaries as follows: line on basal two-thirds of outer web of 1st; similar mark on 2nd not reaching greater primary coverts and separate from or joining subterminal mark which extends across both webs; line on terminal half or third of outer web of 3rd joining subterminal mark which extends across both webs; small subterminal mark across both webs of 4th; small or tiny subterminal mark on outer web (or separate spot on both webs) of 5th, this marking on 5th so small that probably sometimes absent on some individuals. From below, outer primaries appear all-white, except for the dark leading edge on 1st and dark marks near tips of 2nd to 4th or 5th. On closed wing, wing-tip markings combine to form dark

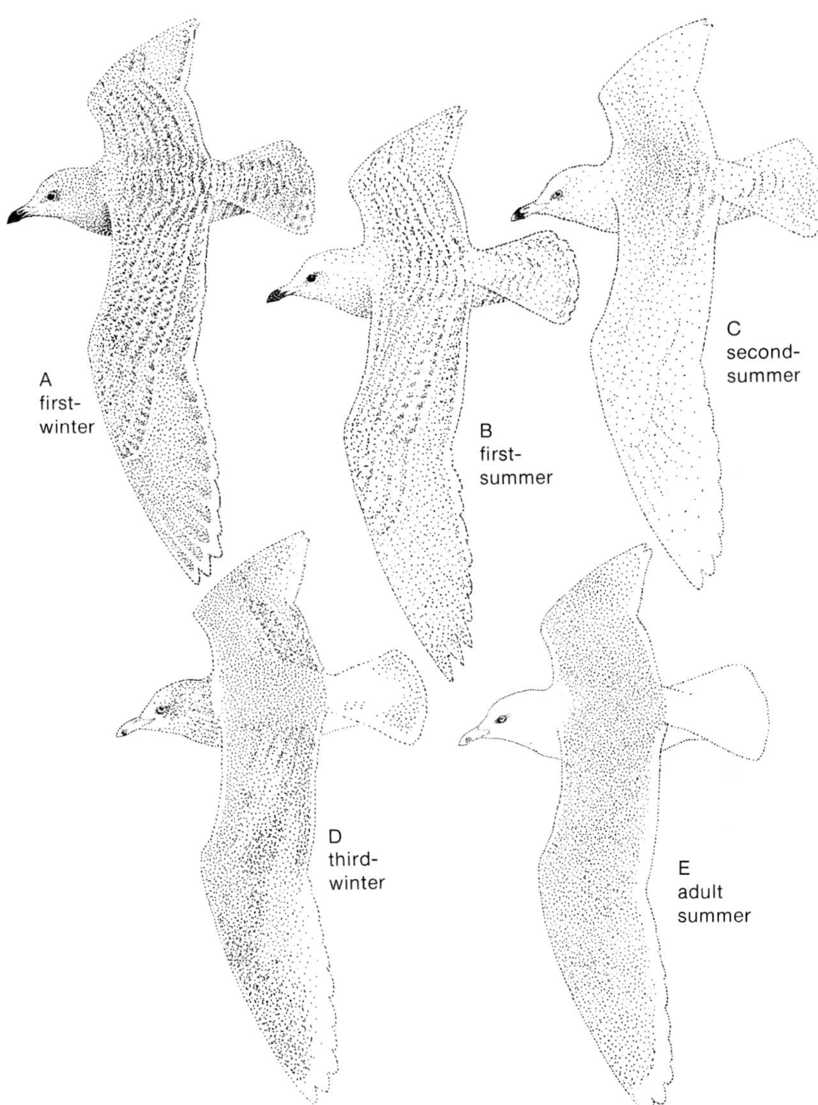

Fig. 49. **Iceland Gulls** *Larus g. glaucoides* in flight. The first-winter is towards the darkest extreme of variation.

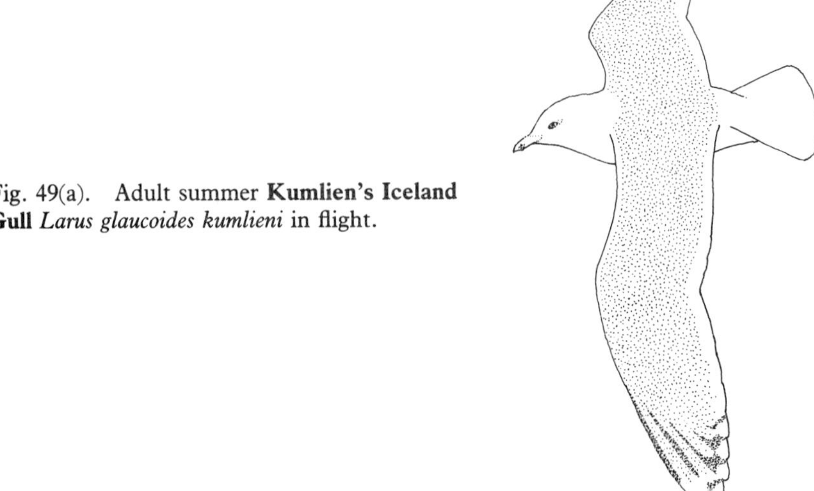

Fig. 49(a). Adult summer **Kumlien's Iceland Gull** *Larus glaucoides kumlieni* in flight.

subterminal area and white tip (latter formed by white tips of 1st to 3rd) and prominent separate white tips to 4th and usually 5th. In field, determination of precise pattern difficult in flight, and at long range markings sometimes totally invisible, especially small ones on 4th and 5th: this, and effect of wear, fading and different light conditions on strength of dark markings, may have falsely prompted reference to 'highly variable' pattern and colour of *kumlieni* wing-tips. Future study is needed to ascertain whether the wing-tip pattern of *kumlieni* is as consistent as proposed here, and whether Greenland-breeding *glaucoides* always have all-white wing-tips. Some have dark iris when adult, unlike *glaucoides*.

At present there is no evidence that Greenland-breeding *glaucoides* ever has other than all-white wing-tips, so any adult Iceland Gull (which is certainly such on size and structure) which also shows *any* pattern of distinct dark markings on the tips of the outer primaries, even if the precise pattern cannot be discerned, is arguably **kumlieni**.

Second- and third-years as *glaucoides*, except outer webs of outer three or four primaries extensively uniform brownish (fading to pale brown when old) contrasting with always pale secondaries and inner primaries. From below, primaries whitish, except for dark tips to outermost. Third-years may also show clear-cut white tips to outer primaries. Secondaries and tail as *glaucoides*, never showing a secondary bar or tail band which is obviously darker than general tone of rest of plumage.

First-years probably not certainly distinguishable from *glaucoides*. It is possible that *kumlieni* averages darker than *glaucoides* on outer web of outer three or four primaries, with more prominent subterminal dark arrowheads, and tail probably averages more solidly dark, less barred, but these features probably matched by variation within *glaucoides*. Bill usually all-black (not pale-based as on typical *glaucoides*), but this also probably within variation of first-year *glaucoides*, many of which in any case look dark-billed at distance.

GROUP SIX

Sooty and White-eyed Gulls

These two Middle East specialities (maps, Figs 51 & 53) are of medium size, and share rather similar plumage patterns and structural features. At all ages, they have a generally dark coloration, blackish underwings, and long-winged silhouette, which at long range in flight may recall a skua *Stercorarius* or first-year Lesser Black-backed Gull *Larus fuscus*. Both have exceptionally long bills and, when perched, long wings which form an elongated rear end; unlike any other western Palearctic gull, the hoods of adults extend as a bib onto the upper breast. These features combine to give the two species a general appearance which is strikingly different from all other western Palearctic gulls.

The following summaries and descriptions are almost entirely based on photographs and museum specimens, and the value of many of the identification and ageing characters requires testing or confirmation in the field.

First- and most second-years are readily ageable. The timing of the breeding season varies greatly for different populations of both species; the timing of the post-juvenile and subsequent moults is fixed by the fledging date, so temporal limits cannot be set for the incidence of the various plumages.

IDENTIFICATION

Sooty Gull *L. hemprichii* is the same size or slightly smaller than Common Gull *L. c. canus*; White-eyed Gull *L. leucophthalmus* is slightly smaller, between Black-headed Gull *L. ridibundus* and Common Gull, closest to the latter; the dark coloration and rather languid flight of both species, however, recall immatures of some larger western Palearctic gulls, and on lone birds may give a misleading impression of much larger size.

Sooty Gull has an exceptionally long and thick bill, proportionately much larger and heavier than that of any other western Palearctic gull; the bill of White-eyed is just as long, but slimmer, exaggerating its length. Sooty Gull is generally more heavily built than White-eyed, with broader, less pointed wings in flight. Structure, especially bill shape, is among the best specific differences at all ages.

The plumage of Sooty Gull is generally pale brown on first-years to grey-brown on adults, and the hood of adults is dark brown marked by a prominent white crescent above the eye, and sometimes also a faint white crescent below the eye. The general

Table 7: Measurements in (mm) of **Sooty** Larus hemprichii *and* **White-eyed Gulls** L. leucophthalmus (from Dwight 1925)

	sample	*wing*	*tail*	*bill*	*tarsus*
Sooty Gull *L. hemprichii*	24	318–352	114–132	44–52	48–59
White-eyed Gull *L. leucophthalmus*	11	305–332	107–125	43–52	44–50

coloration of White-eyed Gull is greyer, less brown, at all ages, and the hood of adults is jet black with very prominent, thick white crescents above and below the eye. Contrary to descriptions in most literature, the iris of White-eyed Gull is dark at all ages, never white. In winter, the head markings of both species are apparently duller or less well-defined, and, according to the literature, the white half-collar on the lower hindneck is sometimes obscured or lacking.

In first-year plumages, both species have clear pale fringes on the wing coverts and tertials, forming an obvious scaly pattern. In first-winter and first-summer plumages, the head pattern of Sooty Gull is rather plain, pale brown, whereas White-eyed has a rather well-defined blackish mask and nape, whitish throat, and ill-defined, fine blackish streaks on the head and breast. Sooty Gull has a greyish bill with sharply contrasting black tip, whereas White-eyed has a wholly black bill. The legs of Sooty Gull are greyish, whereas those of White-eyed Gull are greenish.

Second-years of both species resemble adults, but typically show immature characters such as black or black-and-grey on the tail of highly variable pattern, more extensive blackish bar on the secondaries, paler and less well-defined head pattern, and bare parts lacking full adult colour.

DETAILED DESCRIPTIONS

For Sooty Gull see facing page; for White-eyed Gull see page 160.

Fig. 50. First-winter **Sooty** *Larus hemprichii* and **White-eyed Gulls** *L. leucophthalmus*, showing comparative sizes and structure.

Sooty Gull

Larus hemprichii

(Figs 50A and 52, Photographs 440–453)

Adult summer

General distinctions from White-eyed Gull are discussed on pp. 155 to 156.

DETAILED DESCRIPTIONS

Juvenile (not illustrated, but wings and tail similar to first-winter, Figs 50A and 52A)
HEAD Pale brown, paler than mantle, shading to brown on nape and whitish on chin and face. Whitish crescent above eye. Dark eye-crescent.

BODY Broad breast-band and flanks pale brown with some mottling; belly and undertail-coverts whitish. Mantle and scapulars brown, with pale fringes forming scaly pattern; rump and uppertail-coverts pale grey-brown or whitish.

WINGS Secondaries and outer primaries blackish, inner primaries paler; inner three or four primaries and secondaries fringed and tipped whitish, forming thin white trailing edge to inner wing; tertials pale brown, clearly fringed whitish. Coverts of inner wing pale brown, fringed whitish, forming scaly pattern, and thin whitish lines across tips of greater and median coverts in flight. Underwing wholly grey-brown.

TAIL Mainly black, with thin white terminal fringe and white basally on inner webs of outer feathers; tail thus often appearing wholly black from above, but with very broad subterminal band when fully spread or from below.

BARE PARTS Iris dark brown. Base of bill greyish or blue-grey, tip black. Legs greyish or blue-grey, a shade darker than bill-base.

First-winter (Figs 50A and 52A) Acquired by post-juvenile head and body moult, probably August to March, depending on fledging-date.

As juvenile, except breast-band and flanks grey-brown, mantle and scapulars grey-brown, rump and uppertail-coverts whitish, and wings and tail becoming worn and faded.

First-summer (similar to first-winter, Figs 50A and 52A) Acquired by head and body moult, probably March to October.

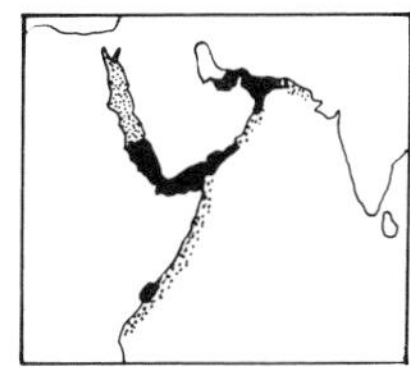

Fig. 51. World distribution of **Sooty Gull** *Larus hemprichii*, showing approximate breeding range (solid black) and approximate non-breeding range (spotted). Apparently rare in southeastern Mediterranean.

As first-winter, except wings and tail becoming much worn and faded, wing coverts and tertials usually losing pale fringes.

Second-winter (Fig. 52B) Acquired by complete moult, probably August to May. *As adult winter except:*

HEAD Usually little different from first-winter.

BODY Mantle, scapulars, breast-band and flanks usually patchy and browner, less uniform grey-brown.

WINGS Blackish bar on secondaries broader and more extensive, white trailing edge on inner wing thinner, and white tips and fringes on inner primaries less prominent and often confined to innermost.

TAIL White, with highly variable pattern of black subterminal marks or black and grey, varying from little different from first-year pattern to subterminal black spots on only one or two pairs of feathers.

BARE PARTS Bill pattern and colour usually little different from that of first-year.

Second-summer (not illustrated, but wings and tail similar to second-winter, Fig. 52B) Acquired by head and body moult, probably March to October.

As second-winter, except hood and bare parts varying from like adult to little different from second-winter.

Adult winter/third-winter (not illustrated, but wings and tail similar to adult summer, Fig. 52C) Acquired by complete moult, probably August to May. *As adult summer except:*

HEAD Brown of hood paler, and white half-collar less well-defined or occasionally lacking.

WINGS Primaries, primary coverts and alula black, shading to blackish-brown inwards; white tips to primaries from 3rd or 4th, increasing in size inwards to large white tips on innermost. Secondaries and tertials blackish-brown, with white tips forming broad trailing edge to inner wing. Coverts of inner wing uniform dark grey-brown. Underwing dull brown, coverts and axillaries blackish-brown.

BARE PARTS Somewhat duller.

Adult summer/third-summer (Fig. 52C) Acquired by head and body moult, probably March to October.

HEAD Shape of hood unlike any other western Palearctic gull except White-eyed, covering whole head and extended to narrow rounded bib on upper breast; hood very dark brown (looking black at distance), shading to blackish on lower nape and bib. White crescent above eye invariably prominent, and sometimes also inconspicuous thin white crescent or mark below eye. Hood bordered by white half-collar on lower hindneck and sides of heck.

BODY Broad grey-brown breast-band bordering bib, extending onto flanks; belly and undertail-coverts white. Mantle and scapulars uniform brown-washed dark grey; rump and uppertail-coverts white.

WINGS As adult winter, except faded browner, and white primary tips often lacking through wear except on innermost.

TAIL White.

BARE PARTS Iris dark brown; orbital ring red. Bill yellow or greenish-yellow with blackish area or band of variable extent before bright red tip: extreme tip often yellowish. Gape red, mouth flesh. Legs dull yellow or greenish-yellow.

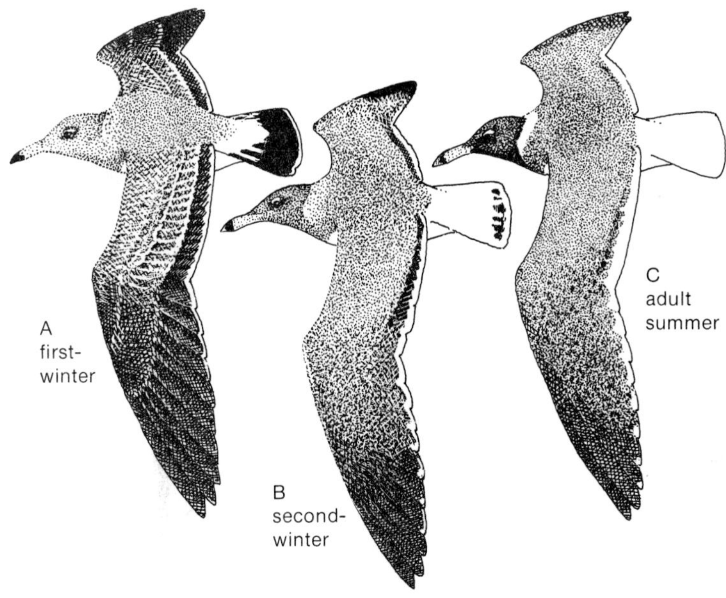

Fig. 52. **Sooty Gulls** *Larus hemprichii* in flight.

White-eyed Gull

Larus leucophthalmus

(Figs 50B and 54, Photographs 454–465)

Adult summer

General distinctions from Sooty Gull are described on pp. 155–156.

DETAILED DESCRIPTIONS

Juvenile (not illustrated, but wings and tail similar to first-winter, Figs 50B and 54A)
HEAD Brown, shading to whitish on face and throat; eye-crescent and ear-coverts dusky; whitish crescents above and below eye.

BODY Breast brownish, extending to flanks; belly and undertail-coverts whitish. Mantle and scapulars grey-brown, slightly darker and greyer, less brown, than on Sooty Gull, with pale feather-fringes; back and upper rump greyish, lower rump and uppertail-coverts white, latter with dark subterminal marks.

WINGS Primaries and secondaries blackish, with narrow white trailing edge on secondaries and innermost primaries; tertials grey-brown with pale fringes. Coverts of upperwing mainly grey-brown, with pale fringes. Underwing wholly grey-brown.

TAIL Black, with white terminal fringe and small white area basally on inner web of outer feathers; when tail fully spread, or from below, black terminal band broader than on Sooty Gull, but tail usually appearing wholly black.

BARE PARTS Iris dark brown. Bill glossy black with brownish area at base of lower mandible. Legs greenish-grey.

First-winter (Figs 50B and 54A) Acquired by post-juvenile head and body moult, probably June to December, depending on fledging date.

As juvenile, except head with more defined blackish mask through eye to nape, with fine dark streaking on crown; breast-band, flanks, mantle and scapulars uniform grey-brown, a shade darker and greyer, less brown, than on Sooty Gull.

First-summer (similar to first-winter, Figs 50B and 54A) Acquired by head and body moult, probably December to July.

As first-winter, except wings and tail becoming much worn and faded.

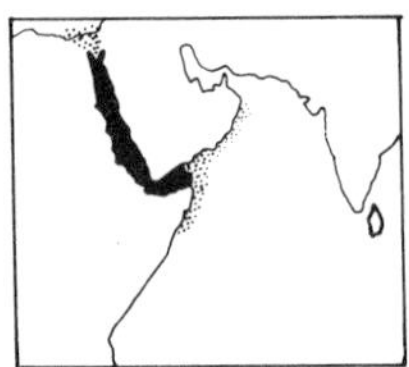

Fig. 53. World distribution of **White-eyed Gull** *Larus leucophthalmus*, showing approximate breeding range (solid black) and approximate non-breeding range (spotted).

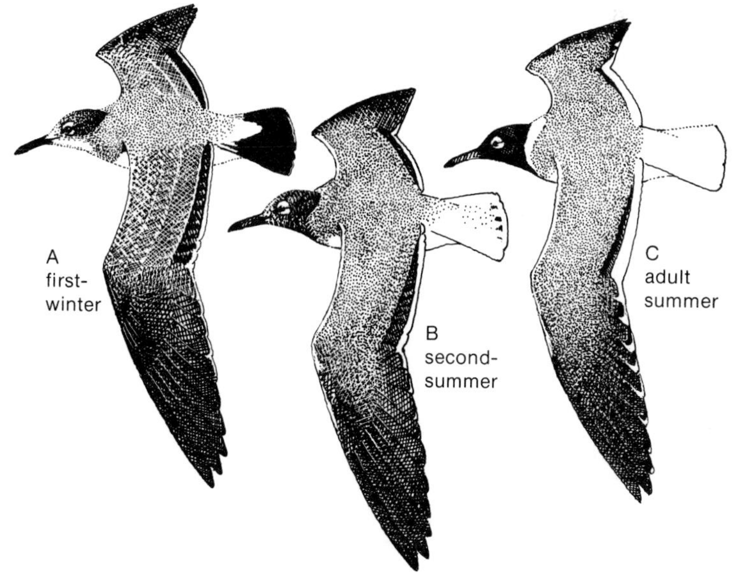

Fig. 54. **White-eyed Gulls** *Larus leucophthalmus* in flight.

Second-winter (not illustrated, but wings and tail similar to second-summer, Fig. 54B) Acquired by complete moult, probably June to December. *As adult winter except:*

HEAD Hood and bib basically browner, perhaps often little different from first-winter.

BODY Mantle, scapulars, breast-band and flanks less immaculate grey. Rump usually clouded with grey.

WINGS Outer primaries, their coverts and alula blackish, shading to greyer inwards; white fringes at tips of primaries from 7th inwards, less prominent than on Sooty Gull. Secondaries blackish with less broad white trailing edge. Coverts of inner wing a shade browner, less immaculate grey.

TAIL White, or with highly variable pattern of black and grey, usually forming broken subterminal tail band. Uppertail-coverts white, grey-brown, or with dark tips.

BARE PARTS Bill and legs duller than adult summer; bill-base often brownish.

Second-summer (Fig. 54B) Acquired by head and body moult, probably December to July.

As second-winter, except hood and bare parts varying from like adult to little different from second-winter.

Adult winter/third-winter (not illustrated, but wings and tail similar to adult summer, Fig. 54C) Acquired by complete moult, probably July to January. *As adult summer except:*

HEAD Hood and bib peppered with white flecking; white half-collar less well-defined.

WINGS Primaries and outer primary coverts black, shading to dark grey inwards;

white tips to primaries smaller than on Sooty Gull, from 3rd, 4th or 5th increasing in size inwards. Secondaries and tertials blackish with white tips forming broad trailing edge to inner wing. Wing-coverts uniform dark grey. Thin white leading edge to inner wing, usually lacking on Sooty Gull (S. C. Madge *in litt.*). Underwing dull grey-brown, coverts and axillaries blackish-brown.

BARE PARTS Somewhat duller.

Adult summer/third-summer (Fig. 54C) Acquired by head and body moult, probably January to August.

HEAD Shape of hood and bib much as adult summer Sooty Gull, but uniform glossy black, not dark brown, and with prominent, thick white crescents above and below eye. White half-collar as on adult Sooty Gull.

BODY Breast-band and flanks pale grey, less extensive than on Sooty Gull; belly and undertail-coverts white. Mantle, scapulars and back dark grey without obvious brownish tone as on Sooty Gull; rump and uppertail-coverts white.

WINGS As adult winter, except white primary tips usually lacking through wear except on innermost.

TAIL White.

BARE PARTS Iris dark brown; orbital ring black or red. Bill bright red with black tip (extreme tip sometimes pale). Legs bright yellowish.

GROUP SEVEN

West coast North American gulls: Heermann's, California, Thayer's, Slaty-backed, Yellow-footed, Western and Glaucous-winged Gulls and Red-legged Kittiwake

Seventeen species of gulls are common or of regular occurrence on the west coast of North America. Nine have already been fully described, namely: Bonaparte's, Common (of North American subspecies *L. c. brachyrhynchus*, called Mew Gull in North America and subsequently in this section), Ring-billed, Laughing, Franklin's, Herring (of North American subspecies *L. a. smithsonianus*), Sabine's and Glaucous Gulls and Kittiwake (called Black-legged Kittiwake in North America and subsequently in this section). The other eight are dealt with here as a separate group. The main identification features and age characters are described and illustrated for each species, together with distribution notes or maps and a selection of photographs. This treatment is intended as a detailed review of west coast gull identification.

First-time visitors will find gull identification in the region most challenging. Three particular aspects of gull identification on the west coast may be especially difficult for newcomers. They are the confusingly 'intermediate' characters of California Gull (p. 166); the problems of Glaucous-winged × Western Gull hybrids (p. 184); and (for Europeans) the surprisingly different appearance of immature Mew Gull from that of the European subspecies of Common Gull. In addition, for observers new to North America as a whole, the different appearance of the North American subspecies of Herring Gull *L. a. smithsonianus* from other subspecies in first- and second-year plumages may also be confusing. Awareness and mastery of these areas will help greatly.

Heermann's Gull

Larus heermanni

(Fig. 56, Photographs 466–475)

Adult summer

Similar to Ring-billed Gull in size, but slimmer and more elegant in build with proportionately longer legs, attenuated rear end when perched, and appearing longer-winged in flight. The timing and sequence of moults and the progression of immature plumages are like those of other medium-sized gulls (eg Ring-billed), with identifiable first-year, second-year and adult plumages.

At all ages, uniform 'all-dark' coloration (with white head and grey underparts in adult summer plumage) renders Heermann's Gull unmistakeable among other west coast gulls, even at long range. It is an almost exclusively coastal or offshore species at all seasons.

MEASUREMENTS (Sample 24) Wing 329–368 mm; tail 132–154 mm; bill 37–48 mm; tarsus 49–58 mm (from Dwight 1925).

First-year Juvenile all dark brown with pale fringes to mantle, scapulars and wing coverts giving scaly pattern; primaries, secondaries, underwing and tail plain blackish-brown. First-winter and first-summer uniform brown on head and body; retained pale-fringed juvenile wing coverts contrast with uniform brown body and upperparts, especially in first-summer when much paler and faded. Bill pale flesh or yellowish-flesh at base, with usually clear-cut blackish tip of variable extent; legs blackish.

Second-year As first-year, except: upperparts brown-washed grey, with neat white scapular- and tertial-crescents when perched; underwing and underparts uniform grey-brown (thus body greyer, less brown than first-year); wing coverts

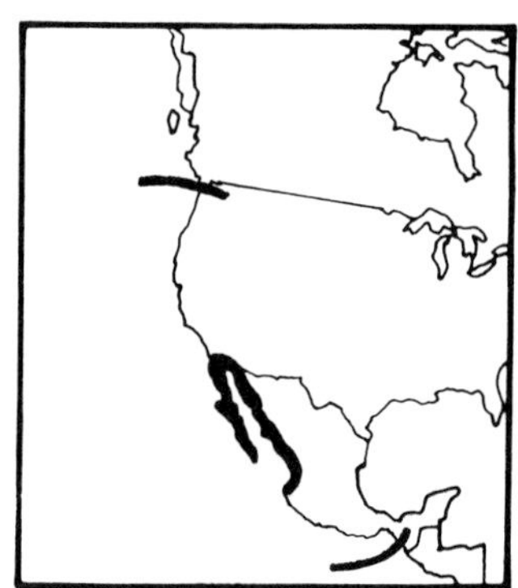

Fig. 55. World distribution of **Heermann's Gull** *Larus heermanni*, showing approximate breeding range (solid black) and northern and southern limits of winter/non-breeding range (black lines).

Fig. 56. **Heermann's Gulls** *Larus heermanni* in flight.

uniform brown, not contrastingly paler or scaly as on first-year; usually obvious thin pale crescent above and below eye; bill orange or reddish at base, with black tip; narrow whitish terminal fringe to tail; narrow white trailing edge to wing in flight.

Adult Uniform dark grey upperparts and underwing; grey underparts; pale grey rump and vent; thin white fringes at tips of outer primaries; white tips to inner primaries and all secondaries form prominent white trailing edge to wing in flight, primaries and secondaries otherwise blackish contrasting with grey upperwing coverts; tail blackish with prominent white border at end. In summer, head and neck white, shading into grey body; in winter, head and neck white densely flecked with grey. Bill bright red or duller in winter, with clear-cut black tip or subterminal band; iris dark; orbital ring red; legs blackish.

California Gull
Larus californicus
(Fig. 58, Photographs 476–487)

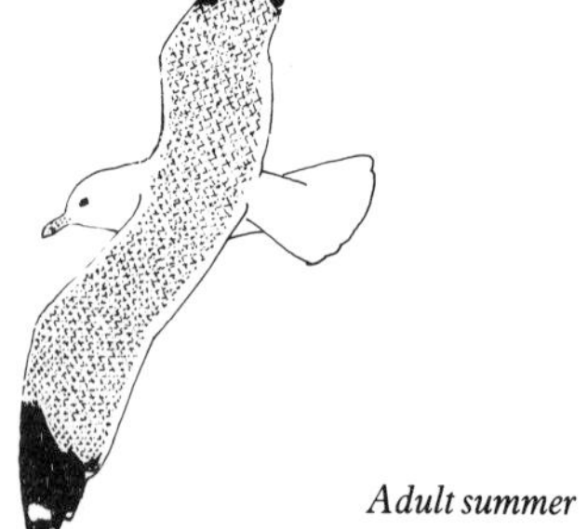
Adult summer

California Gull is intermediate in size, structure and many plumage features between the medium-sized species (eg Ring-billed and Mew Gulls) and the large species (eg Herring and Western Gulls) of western North America. The timing and sequence of moults and the progression of immature plumages are like those of a large gull (eg Herring Gull), with identifiable first-year, second-year, third-year and adult plumages.

Compared with Ring-billed Gull it is longer-bodied and slimmer when perched, with proportionately shorter legs, and the bill is slightly longer. In flight it is long-winged and distinctively skinny-bodied (with a flat or often slightly concave profile to the underparts behind the bulge of the breast). The iris is dark at all ages.

MEASUREMENTS (Sample 23) Wing 368–415 mm; tail 150–162 mm; bill 42–56 mm; tarsus 53–63 mm (from Dwight 1925).

First-year Head and underparts uniform rather dark brownish, slightly paler around base of bill and on belly (head often whitish in first-summer plumage); upperparts and wing coverts barred and patterned with dark to variable extent (some rather uniform in general appearance, others neatly barred). In flight, primaries and secondaries uniformly blackish (latter with narrow whitish trailing edge), without obvious pale window on inner primaries; greater coverts and tertials mainly uniform grey-brown, paler than secondaries, with pale fringes and variable amount of barring on inner greater coverts; underwing rather uniform brownish; rump whitish, boldly barred with dark; tail mainly uniform blackish-brown, appearing all dark. Juvenile may have extensively dark bill, but at least from first-winter always has pale flesh base

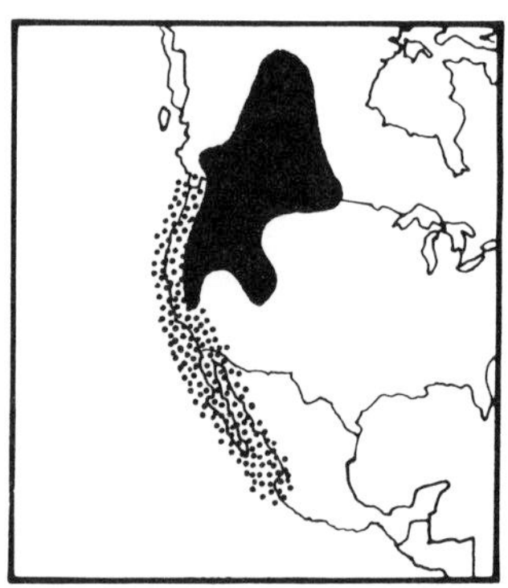

Fig. 57. World distribution of **California Gull** *Larus californicus*, showing approximate breeding range (solid black) and approximate winter/non-breeding range (spotted). Rare in winter on coasts of Gulf of Mexico.

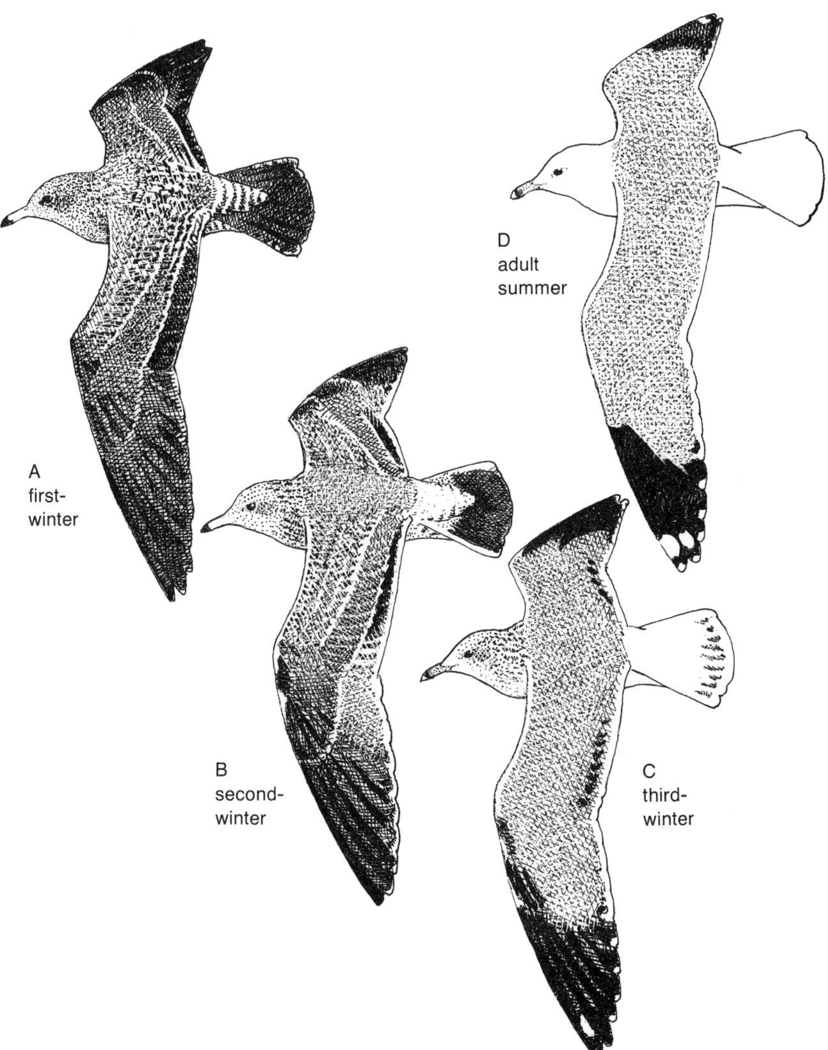

Fig. 58. **California Gulls** *Larus californicus* in flight.

and clear-cut black tip (black extending back farther on lower than upper mandible), recalling pattern of first-year Glaucous Gull: this, in combination with rather uniformly dark head and body, pale legs, and barred upperparts provides best distinction from all other first-winter west coast gulls. Legs pale flesh or pinkish, often with bluish or greenish tones especially by first summer.

Second-year Mantle and scapulars uniform rather dark grey like adult. Otherwise like first-year, except: greater coverts uniform brownish-grey; median and lesser coverts more uniform (less barred); usually prominent pale window on inner primaries; rump mainly white (not strongly barred); head and underparts less uniformly dark; underwing whiter with spots and bars forming pattern of dark lines; and dark tail with prominent white terminal fringe and sides. Variable amount of head streaking in second-winter, usually extensive. Bill distinctively dull blue-grey or grey-green, with dark tip like first-year or black subterminal band. Leg colour as bill-base.

Third-year Like adult, except: variable amount of black markings on primary coverts and tail (latter forming narrow or broken tail band); black on wing-tip less well-defined, with smaller white primary tips (or none) and smaller mirror on first primary; wing coverts and tertials often brown-washed; bill-base and legs often bluish-grey like second-year.

Adult Upperparts and wings rather dark blue-grey, slightly darker than Mew Gull and obviously darker than Ring-billed Gull or Herring Gull *L. a. smithsonianus*, with prominent white scapular- and tertial-crescents. In flight, wing-tip pattern similar to Ring-billed, but black slightly more extensive (adjoining grey primary coverts bluntly rather than as point and with less of 'hook-back' on trailing edge) and white trailing edge of wing more prominent through greater contrast; from below, grey bases of secondaries show through to form faint grey subterminal bar along trailing edge of inner wing, lacking on Ring-billed. In winter, nape and hindneck (and often also rest of head and breast-sides) obviously streaked and spotted with dark. Bill yellow with red spot near gonys to rear of, and merging with, black subterminal mark of variable extent: tip yellowish or whitish. In winter, black subterminal mark is usually thin bar across both mandibles, but frequently in summer is only small, difficult-to-see area of black confined to lower mandible, or (rarely) completely lacking. This black-and-red bill marking diagnostic among fully adult west coast species, but similar colour and pattern is often shown by immatures of other species which have red bill-spot when adult, as they approach adult plumage, or occasionally, too, by individuals which otherwise appear to be fully adult. In winter, bill-base often greenish-yellow and subterminal black more extensive. Gape and orbital ring red. Iris dark brown. Legs yellow or greenish-yellow, often greenish or grey-green in winter.

Thayer's Gull

Larus thayeri

(Fig. 60, Photographs 488–494)

Adult summer

Thayer's Gull is intermediate in appearance between Iceland Gull *L. g. kumlieni* and Herring Gull. In the past it has been regarded as a subspecies of either, or (erroneously) as a hybrid between the two. Recent identification literature (eg Gosselin & David 1975, Lehman 1980) have shown adults and immatures to be consistently distinctive in appearance, and at least on these grounds specific status seems reasonable; it is treated here as a full species, in accordance with the current opinion of the American Ornithologists' Union.

Identification of Thayer's ideally requires close-range viewing and firm notation of the full range of its distinctive features, as well as familiarity with the variations of similar species and the possible problems of some hybrids.

Thayer's Gull has not been recorded in Europe, but this is a possibility bearing in mind its northeast Canadian breeding range and its (infrequent) occurrence on the east coast of North America.

The timing and sequence of moults and the progression of immature plumages are like those of other large gulls (eg Herring Gull), with identifiable first-year, second-year, third-year and adult plumages. Thayer's Gull averages between Herring and Iceland Gulls in size. Structure is similar to Iceland Gull, but with slightly longer or larger bill on average, and a slightly more sloping forehead giving a slightly less rounded profile to the head. Its general appearance is usually closer to Iceland Gull than to Herring Gull, often still recalling Iceland's 'gentle' appearance.

At all ages, the dark on the outer primaries is on the outer web of each feather, except at the tip where it extends onto the inner web. This means that the full extent of the dark is visible only when the wing is viewed from above. From below, only the pale

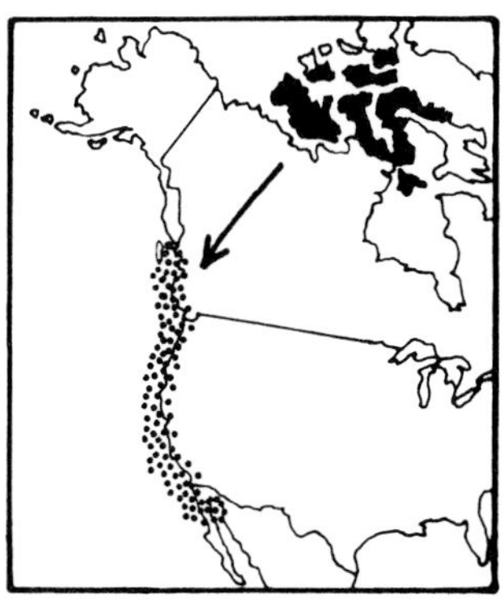

Fig. 59. World distribution of **Thayer's Gull** *Larus thayeri*, showing approximate breeding range (solid black) and approximate winter/non-breeding range (spotted). Rare in winter in eastern North America.

inner webs of the primaries are visible, so that the underwing appears silvery or whitish except at the extreme tips where the small area of dark on both webs is visible, forming a thin, dark trailing edge to the outer primaries. Especially at a distance, the impression is often of a wholly translucent, pale underwing-tip like that on true white-winged gulls (eg Glaucous Gull and nominate Iceland Gull *L. g. glaucoides*).

The following descriptions cover the features which distinguish Thayer's from Herring Gull *L. a. smithsonianus* and Iceland Gull *L. g. kumlieni*, which are perhaps the main confusion species. Note that Iceland Gull is accidental in western North America, so it should not normally present confusion with Thayer's in that region: the comparison is covered mainly to assist observers in eastern North America. In its wintering range on the west coast of North America, Thayer's has also to be distinguished from the usually coastal Glaucous-winged Gull, which differs at least in its larger size, much heavier bill, and – in first-year plumage – in its colder grey-brown and plainer (less patterned) upperparts, wing coverts and wing-tip, the latter the same colour or slightly paler than the rest of the upperparts (not obviously darker as on Thayer's), and also especially from Glaucous-winged × Western Gull and Glaucous-winged × Herring Gull hybrids, which differ at least in their larger size and much heavier bill (see discussion of hybrids under Glaucous-winged Gull on p. 184). An important step in the identification of Thayer's at all ages is the firm notation of its intermediate size and structure between Herring and Iceland Gulls.

First-year Pattern of dark barring on upperparts and wing coverts like Iceland Gull, thus more intricate and giving paler general impression than on *smithsonianus*. The darkness of the grey-brown barring is variable, usually much as on average Iceland Gull (and similarly often much faded by first summer), but apparently sometimes as dark as on Herring Gull. Head and underparts rather uniform pale grey-brown like Iceland (paler than on *smithsonianus*), shading paler around bill-base. Often shows diffuse darker area around eye, like some *smithsonianus* but unlike Iceland Gull. Head not contrastingly whitish as on some first-winter *smithsonianus*. When perched, wing-tip brown or dark brown, not blackish as on Herring Gull. Wing-tip obviously darker than general coloration of tertials and upperparts, always with neat, complete pale fringe around tip of each primary: pale fringes give distinctive pattern of obvious pale Vs along closed wing-tip, which on 'dark' Thayer's provides one of best distinction from perched first-year *smithsonianus* (on which wing-tip solidly blackish or occasionally with *faint* pale Vs). Tertials pale brown, matching rest of upperparts (not blackish, matching wing-tip as on Herring). Darker wing-tip is important distinction from Iceland Gull, both subspecies of which have wing-tip paler than, or matching, rest of upperparts, and which often also shows subterminal dark arrowhead marks on each outer primary which Thayer's always lacks. Dark on outer five or six primaries restricted to outer webs except at tips: in flight, dark thus appears much less extensive than equivalent blackish on Herring Gull which is extensive on both webs. When wing fully spread, Thayer's shows dark outer webs and pale inner webs, giving distinctive pattern of dark lines on outer primaries. From below, wing-tip appears silvery-white and translucent (like that of true white-winged gulls), except for thin, dark trailing edge to outer primaries, visible only at close range. Secondaries also dark only on outer webs, thus secondary bar appears as broken bar of dark spots, not solidly blackish as on Herring Gull. Iceland Gull of both subspecies completely lacks any darker secondary bar, providing important difference from Thayer's. Broad band on tail solidly brownish (matching colour on outer primaries), obviously darker than general coloration of rest of upperparts (first-year *smithsonianus* has thinly pale-edged, wholly

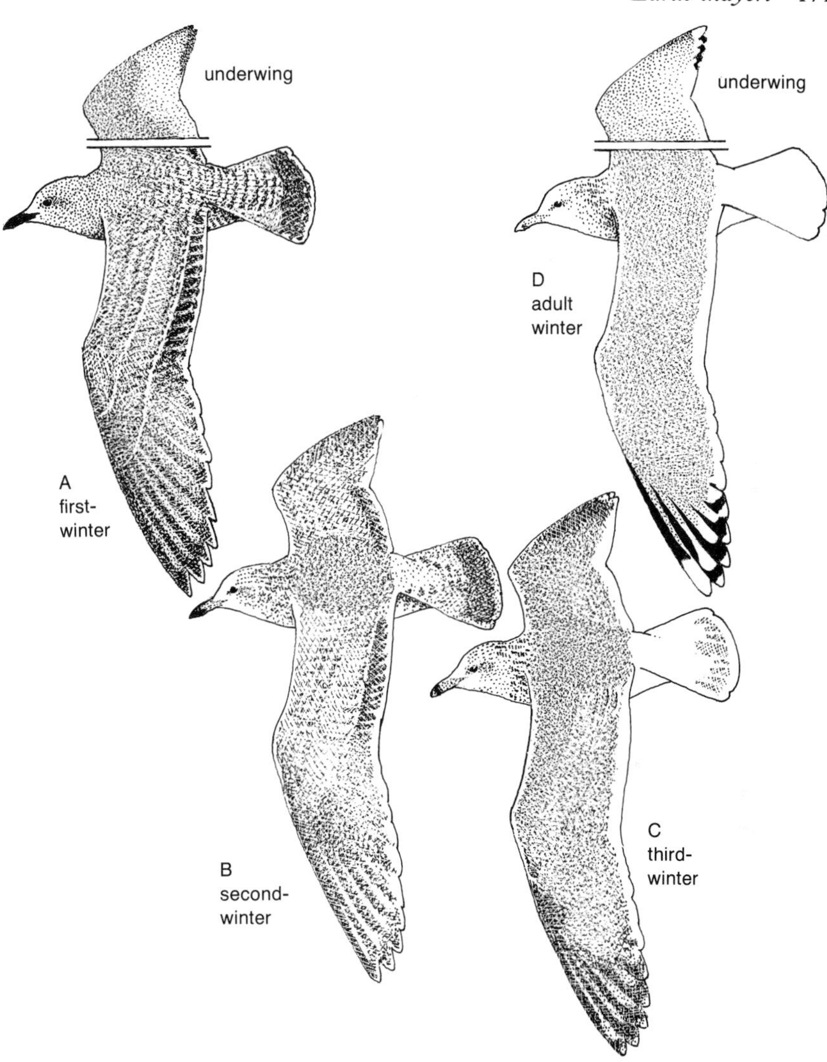

Fig. 60. **Thayer's Gulls** *Larus thayeri* in flight.

blackish tail); tail has pale fringe at sides and tip and faint barring on outermost feathers; tail band contrasts with paler tail-base and with barred uppertail-coverts and rump. Tail pattern thus unlike Iceland Gull of both subspecies, on which general coloration much paler and matching general colour of upperparts, usually with intricate pattern of barring. Bill all-black, usually at least to end of first calendar-year (bill-base of Herring usually obviously pale from early in first winter). Iris dark. Legs typically deep rose-pink (usually pale pink on Herring and Iceland Gulls).

Second-year Clear adult grey acquired on mantle and scapulars; lower scapulars, wing coverts and tertials plain pale creamy-brown, all with broad white fringes, latter giving upperparts patchy and 'washed-out' look; rump whiter. Bill pink-based with dark tip of variable extent. Iris dark, like adult (most *smithsonianus* and *kumlieni* begin to show pale iris during second year). Otherwise, identification and pattern of wings and tail much as for first-year, but dark areas on outer primaries and tail band average paler brown (but still darker than general coloration of rest of upperparts), often much faded by second-summer.

Third-year As adult, but grey on wings sometimes faintly brown-washed, and tail usually marked with greyish in variable pattern typical of third-year large gull. Pattern of black on wing-tip often less sharply defined than on adult (sometimes brownish, fading to pale brown by third-summer), sometimes extending onto greater primary coverts. Bill with dark tip or subterminal dark mark or band, often with some reddish near gonys; base flesh, yellowish or greenish-yellow; sometimes as adult.

Adult Grey of upperparts and wings a shade darker than on *smithsonianus*, thus obviously darker than on Iceland Gull. Pattern of dark on outer primaries very similar to that described for adult *kumlieni* (p. 152), but typically more extensive with small subterminal mark also on 6th, and definitely black when fresh, not frosted grey as on fresh *kumlieni*. Very variable amount of dark head markings in winter, often extending over whole head and neck, averaging more extensive than on Herring Gull; often appears uniform pale brown rather than grey or grey-streaked as on Herring. Bill pale yellow or greenish-yellow, with red or orange-red spot near gonys and often whitish tip. Iris usually dark, but some have brown flecking in pale iris (none has entirely clear yellow iris), eye often appearing large and prominent, adding to gentle appearance. Orbital ring dark red or purple (coloration less obvious in winter). Legs usually distinctively deep rose-pink or purple-tinged pink, unlike typically pale pink of Herring and Iceland Gulls. Closed wing-tip appears black with white primary tips like Herring, so best told from that species when perched by structure; less black on wing-tip with larger white primary tips on average; slightly darker grey upperparts; greenish tone to bill, if present (adult Herring's bill yellow, never greenish-toned); deep pink legs; dark iris (pale yellow on Herring); and dark orbital ring (yellow or orange on Herring). In flight, compared with Herring Gull, black on wing-tip much less extensive on upperwing (when wing fully spread, white inner webs and black outer webs often give black-and-white lined effect), and underwing-tip white with small dark spots at tips of outer primaries (these often visible only at close range). Beware adult Herring Gulls in October to December with still-growing outer three primaries: such birds show much less black on upperwing-tip, suggesting Thayer's-like pattern. On these problematic moulting Herring Gulls, however, the more extensive black on the still-growing outer primaries can be seen from below on leading edge of outer wing, giving underwing-tip pattern quite unlike that of Thayer's Gull. Told from *kumlieni* by darker grey upperparts, black pattern on wing-tip (not grey), more extensive black on wing-tip, dark iris (most *kumlieni* have pale iris), and deep pink legs. In Europe, some individuals of Scandinavian subspecies of Herring Gull *L. a. argentatus* apparently can show Thayer's-like wing-tip pattern (see p. 94 for discussion of differences), and hybrids in Europe and elsewhere (especially Glaucous × Herring Gull) need to be excluded when identifying Thayer's, which should be possible on consideration of full range of distinguishing features described here, especially structure and bill size.

Slaty-backed Gull

Larus schistisagus

(Fig. 61, Photographs 495–510)

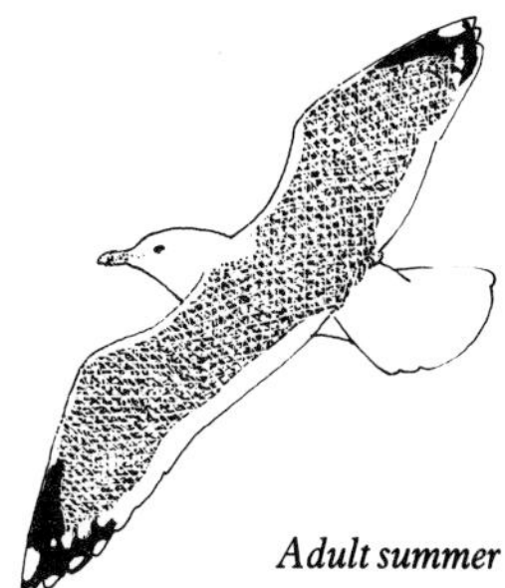

Adult summer

An exclusively coastal gull of northeastern Asia, breeding around the Kamtchatka Peninsula and the Sea of Okhotsk south to northern Japan. In summer, wanders north to coasts of Bering Sea, occurring annually in usually small numbers in the Aleutian Islands and on mainly western and northern coasts of Alaska: accidental farther south on west coast of North America and in USA. In winter reaches southern Japan: rare farther south on coast of China at least to Hong Kong.

A large gull, similar in size and structure to the North American subspecies of Herring Gull *L. a. smithsonianus*: it is typically slightly smaller than Glaucous Gull, with neat, straight bill, more rounded head profile, and longer neck when alert; these features combine to give more elegant, less massive general appearance, but some, perhaps males, may be more heavily structured. The timing and sequence of moults and the progression of immature plumages are like those of other large gulls (eg Herring Gull), with identifiable first-year, second-year, third-year and adult plumages.

Slaty-backed is the only blackish-backed gull likely to be found in Alaska (only one record of any other: a Western Gull on the Alaskan Peninsula), making identification there straightforward from at least second-summer plumage onwards when the adult upperparts coloration is evident. The upperparts coloration is a shade or two darker than that of the southern, darker-backed subspecies of Western Gull *L. o. wymani*, matching that of the southern Scandinavian subspecies of Lesser Black-backed Gull *L. f. intermedius*, thus obviously blackish-backed and much darker than any subspecies of Herring Gull in this region: the grey on the upperparts of the east Siberian subspecies of Herring Gull *L. a. vegae* (which is darker than *smithsonianus*, and is regular in small numbers in northwestern Alaska) is the same as that of California Gull or Black-legged Kittiwake, thus clearly grey not blackish.

Notes by P. Alström (*in litt.*) and photographs by Urban Olsson, from Japan in November, have been extremely useful in compiling the following descriptions, as have comments on a first draft of this section by Ronald E. Goetz and Phoebe Snetsinger.

MEASUREMENTS (Sample 19) Wing 405–447 mm; tail 165–197 mm; bill 49–60 mm; tarsus 60–72 mm (from Dwight 1925).

First-year Juvenile differs from Herring Gull *L. a. vegae* in rather plain, dark upperwing, lacking obvious pale window on inner primaries or strongly patterned coverts; also, has neat, isolated dark subterminal marks on 7th to 10th primaries (these marks less sharply-defined and more extensive on *vegae*); outer primaries dark brown on outer webs and fringed pale at tips, giving first-year Thayer's-like pattern when perched and in flight (blackish with faint pale fringes on *vegae*); greater coverts mainly plain, any barring confined to tips or innermost feathers (greater coverts fully barred on *vegae*); greater coverts dark, contrasting little with blackish-brown secondary bar (sharp contrast on *vegae*); tertials brown with pale fringe (darker, with pale-notched sides on *vegae*); tail almost wholly blackish (contrasting little with rather dark rump) with narrow pale fringe at tip and sides, and vermiculated slightly paler base (*vegae* has broad blackish tail band contrasting with mainly white base and dark-barred, whitish rump); and mantle and scapulars rather plain with pale fringes (barred and notched with pale on *vegae*). Plumage of first-year Slaty-backed seems exceptionally prone to fading, especially on retained juvenile wing and tail feathers. Some differences from *vegae* described for juvenile plumage may be lost by first-winter and especially first-summer plumages: rump becomes whitish and contrasts with all-dark tail (*vegae*, however, still shows broad tail band, not all-dark tail); inner primaries fade to whitish (thus window now prominent, like *vegae*); dark subterminal marks on 7th to 10th increase in contrast and become more obvious (these marks ill-defined on *vegae*); greater coverts fade to uniform whitish; dark brown areas on wings and tail fade to pale brown (paler than on *vegae* of same age); and head and body rather uniformly dark in first-winter (when *vegae* whitish-headed), but whitish in first-summer. Bill all-black, becoming pale at base and tip by first-summer plumage. Legs pink.

Second-year In second-winter plumage, outer primaries and tail much as first-winter, but inner primaries and whole inner wing uniformly rather pale with only slightly darker secondary bar; mantle and scapulars mainly dingy grey; rump mainly white, contrasting with dark tail. Blackish mantle and scapulars, like adult, acquired at least during spring moult to second-summer plumage, producing blackish saddle contrasting sharply with now much faded and whitish inner wing and with usually pure white head, underparts and rump; tertials, outer primaries and tail much faded and brownish. Bill pale with subterminal dark band of variable pattern: by second summer, bill-base yellowish and sometimes also some red near gonys. Iris becoming pale. Legs pink.

Third-year As adult, except: upperwing patchy, not uniform blackish; black on wing-tip more extensive and less well-defined; white spots across 3rd–6th primaries often less prominent; small white mirror on 1st, sometimes lacking; sometimes mirror also on 2nd; smaller white tips on outer primaries; white trailing edge to wing often less broad; tail with variable amount of black, usually forming prominent, broken tail band; bill often with subterminal black markings.

Adult Mantle, scapulars, back and upperwing uniform blackish grey, with thin white leading edge to upperwing. Exposed part of all but outermost secondaries all-white, forming extremely broad white trailing edge to inner wing (which can be matched by some Western Gulls) continued outwards by broad white tips to inner primaries. Pattern of white, black and grey on wing-tip diagnostic: from above, black on outer primaries mainly on outer webs except near tips, decreasing in extent inwards to small subterminal bar on 5th or 6th; subterminal black on 3rd to 5th or 6th primaries divided from blackish-grey remainder of each feather by broad white band mainly on inner web, forming distinctive line of white spots (or white 'divide') across wing-tip; large white mirror (or long, all-white tip like Great Black-backed Gull) on 1st primary and usually also smaller mirror on 2nd; prominent white tips to outer primaries, obvious on closed wing. From below, primaries grey with broad white spots across 3rd to 5th or 6th primaries before subterminal black; primaries and secondaries otherwise grey below, contrasting with white underwing coverts and broad white trailing edge. When perched, prominent white scapular-crescent and very broad, white tertial-crescent. All similar species have a narrower white trailing edge to inner wing (averaging only slightly narrower on Western Gull, however), lack prominent white

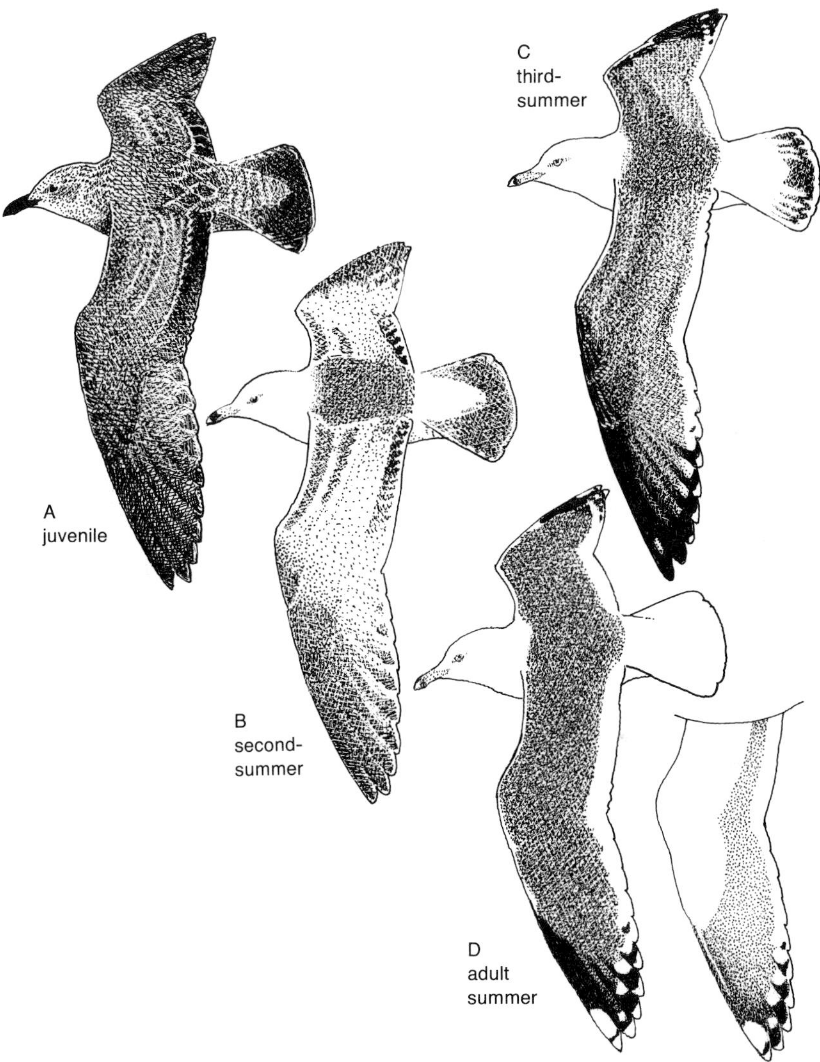

Fig. 61. **Slaty-backed Gulls** *Larus schistisagus* in flight.

dividing spots on 3rd to 6th primaries, and have more extensive black on wing-tip from above and especially from below. Whole head white in summer, usually heavily mottled and streaked with grey-brown or brown in winter, often with concentration forming distinctive dark patch around eye which sometimes extends back in upward curve towards hind crown. Underparts, rump and tail white. Bill yellow with red spot near gonys. Iris clear yellow or cream. Orbital ring reddish or pink. Legs bright deep pink or reddish-pink.

Yellow-footed Gull

Larus livens

(Fig. 62, Photographs 511–520)

Formerly regarded as a third subspecies of Western Gull *L. occidentalis livens*, Yellow-footed Gull was given full specific status by the American Ornithologists' Union in 1982. Its distribution and identification were described in detail by McCaskie (1983), on which this account is largely based.

Apart from very rare occurences of Western Gull, Yellow-footed is the only blackish-backed large gull likely to be found in the Gulf of California and at the Salton Sea in southeastern California (see map, Fig. 63, p. 178). The pale grey-backed and much commoner Herring Gull is the only other large gull regularly to be found in the same region: it is similar to Yellow-footed Gull only in juvenile and first-winter plumages, and then only superficially. Identification of Yellow-footed Gull in its usual areas is therefore straightforward on range alone. It closely resembles the southern, darker-backed subspecies of Western Gull *L. o. wymani* in adult upperparts colour and structure, but is perhaps on average slightly larger, slightly larger-billed, and with a slightly more elongated slope to the forehead. The diagnostic yellow coloration of the adults legs and feet can be evident as a faint yellowish tinge as early as in first-winter plumage: Western Gull is always pink-legged.

The other major difference is that, unusually for such a large gull, Yellow-footed normally acquires full adult plumage in its third winter, not the fourth winter as is the case for other large gulls, including Western Gull. It therefore has identifiable first-year, second-year and adult plumages. This rapid progress to maturity is perhaps connected in some way with its earlier breeding season than for the more northerly-breeding species of large gulls: eggs are laid by early April, and juveniles are fledged by late June. Also, the moults are completed 3 to 4 months earlier than for typical northern large gulls, for example the adult's partial moult to summer plumage is from December to February, and the complete moult to winter plumage is from May to August.

First-year Differs from juvenile and first-winter *smithsonianus* especially in extensive white underparts (*smithsonianus* rather dark below); whiter rump; lack of obvious pale window on inner primaries; and heavier, 'blob-ended' bill (like Western Gull's): in first-summer plumage also by usually extensive blackish on mantle and scapulars. Differs from juvenile Western Gull especially in extensive clear white on belly, vent and undertail-coverts, which contrasts rather sharply with dark head, breast and flanks (Western Gull has uniformly rather dark head and underparts); conspicuously whiter rump; more contrastingly-patterned scapulars and wing coverts (pattern more like Herring Gull than Western); and more streaked, less plain, neck- and breast-sides. First-winter usually shows mixture of faded brownish and new blackish-grey feathers on mantle and scapulars; whitish scapular-crescent; faded plain grey-brown wing coverts (thus contrasting juvenile pattern lost); mainly white breast and head, latter often with heavy dark streaks on hindneck (thus whole head and underparts mainly white, whereas Western Gull still has mainly dark head and underparts); pale flesh base to bill often obvious (Western Gull still has mainly black bill); and some show hint of diagnostic adult leg colour, thus yellowish-flesh, not pink. First-summer plumage has

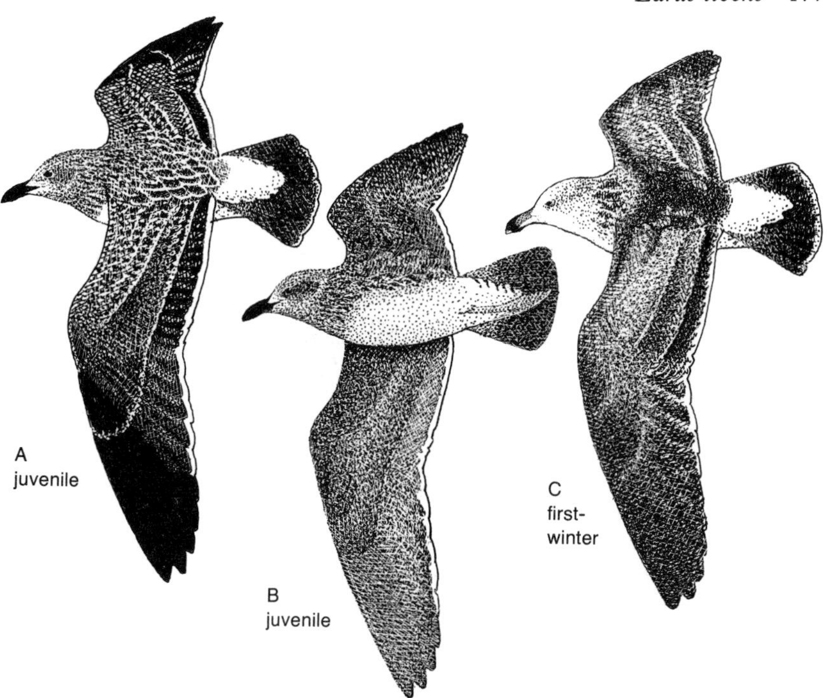

Fig. 62. **Yellow-footed Gulls** *Larus livens* in flight. First-summer resembles second-summer Western Gull *L. occidentalis* (Fig. 64D) except rump white, legs yellowish (not pink), and wing coverts more faded, often whitish; second-year resembles third-winter Western Gull (Fig. 64E) except more black on tail, and legs yellow (not pink); adult resembles Western Gull (Fig. 64F) except legs yellow (not pink).

usually extensive blackish on mantle and scapulars, often forming solid blackish saddle which contrasts with now often very faded and whitish wing coverts; legs yellowish. Plumage pattern of first-summer thus closely resembles that of second-summer Western Gull, so notation of yellowish legs and firm age-diagnosis important to identification. Iris usually starts to pale during first-winter.

Second-year General appearance like that which would be expected for a third-year large gull, thus adult-like except for brownish tones on upperwing coverts; wing-tip pattern less well-defined, with smaller white tips to primaries and lacking obvious mirror on first primary; and tail mainly black. Resembles third-year Western Gull, but averages more black on bill and tail, and has yellowish or bright yellow legs. Bill colour varies from yellowish with solid dark tip (especially on some second-winters) to like adult (especially on some second-summers); leg colour varies similarly, from yellowish to bright yellow like adult.

Adult Plumage and bare parts like adult Western Gull *L. o. wymani*, except legs bright yellow. Some third-years may show few dark marks on tail, but are otherwise like adult.

Western Gull

Larus occidentalis

(Fig. 64, Photographs 521–533)

Adult summer

Western Gull is a mainly resident, coastal species which very rarely wanders far inland. It is the only large blackish-backed gull in much of western North America, so it can be easily identified from second-year plumages onwards, when it begins to show the adult upperparts colour. Outside the usual range of Western Gull there are two other confusible, blackish-backed species in western North America: they are Slaty-backed Gull (Alaska) and Yellow-footed Gull (Gulf of California and Salton Sea), but Western Gull is very rare in both these areas. First-years resemble Herring Gulls of the North American race *L. a. smithsonianus*, and a major further complication in the otherwise fairly straightforward identification of Western Gull is the fact that they commonly hybridise with Glaucous-winged Gull, as discussed under that species on pp. 184–185.

Western Gull is about the size of *smithsonianus* or slightly smaller, but it is very stockily built, with heavily domed forehead, very stout and 'blob-ended' bill (depth of bill obviously greater near the tip than at the base), and proportionately shorter- and broader-winged. The compound effect of these structural differences is to give a generally much larger impression, and – especially in the white-headed, blackish-backed adult or near-adult plumages – recalls Great Black-backed Gull when an observer sees

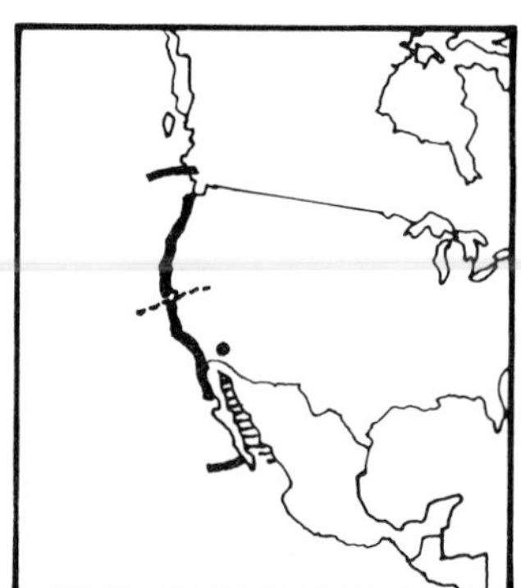

Fig. 63. World distribution of **Western Gull** *Larus occidentalis* and **Yellow-footed Gull** *L. livens*. Shows approximate breeding range of Western Gull (solid black), and approximate northern and southern limits of winter/non-breeding range (black lines): rare farther south to coastal central Mexico, and north to Alaskan Peninsula (where one record). Dotted line marks division near San Francisco between northern, paler-backed nominate subspecies *L. o. occidentalis*, and the southern, darker-backed subspecies *L. o. wymani*. Cross-hatching marks range of mainly resident Yellow-footed Gull in Gulf of California, and black spot marks Salton Sea in southeastern California where sometimes large numbers regular from late summer to early winter: very rare on Pacific coast north to southern California.

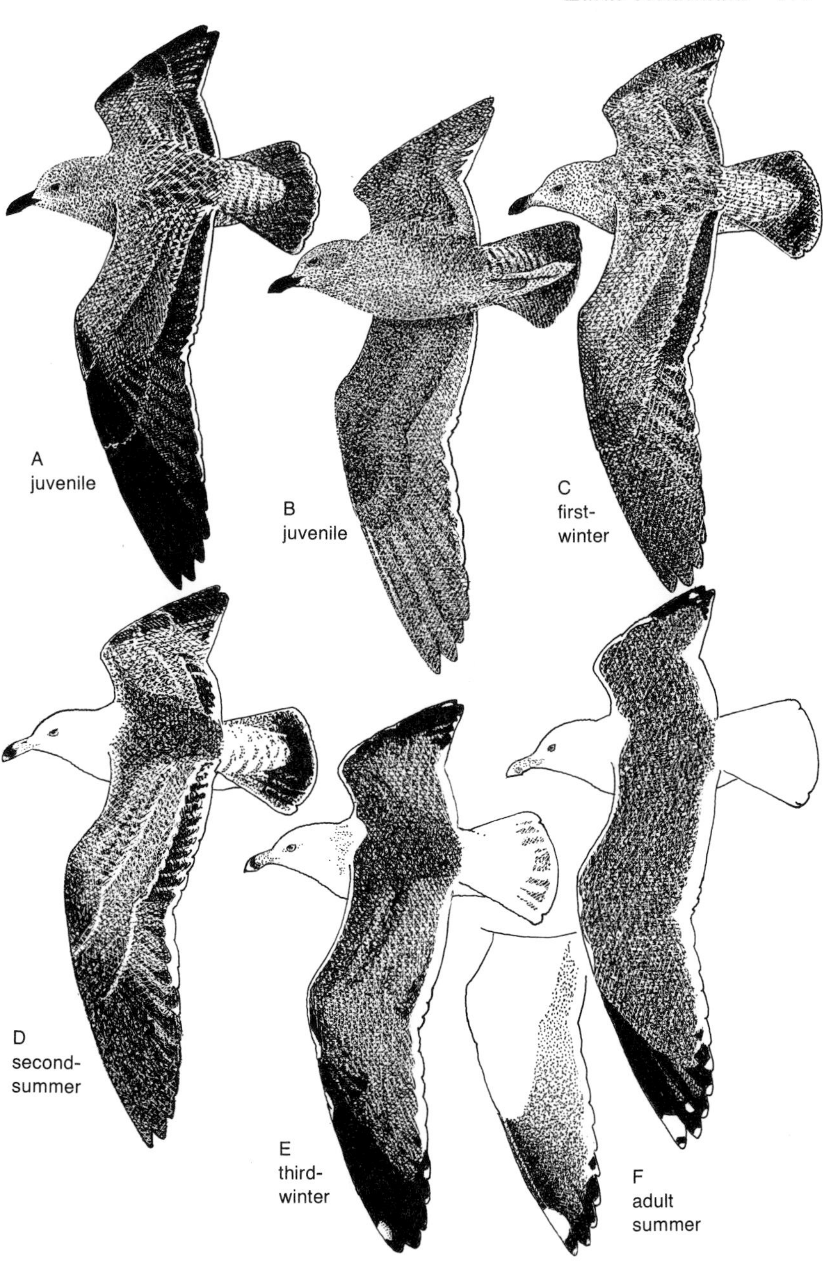

Fig. 64. **Western Gulls** *Larus occidentalis* in flight.

Western Gull for the first time: Great Black-backed Gull is actually much larger, however, and is unrecorded on the west coast of North America. It is about the same size and structure as Glaucous-winged Gull. The timing and sequence of the moults and the progression of immature plumages are like those of other large gulls (eg Herring Gull), with identifiable first-year, second-year, third-year and adult plumages. The large size and heavy, all-black bill alone distinguish first-year Western Gull from other, smaller west coast species such as California Gull, and the blackish or black wing-tips from first-winter pale-winged large gulls such as Glaucous-winged.

There are two subspecies of Western Gull. The northern, nominate subspecies *L. o. occidentalis* is slightly larger on average, and adults more often have faint grey markings on the head in winter, tend to be darker-eyed, and have paler blackish-grey upperparts (typically slightly paler than the west European subspecies of Lesser Black-backed Gull *L. f. graellsii*); the southern subspecies *L. o. wymani* is slightly smaller on average, adults are usually white-headed in winter, tend to be paler-eyed, and have darker upperparts (typically matching the west European subspecies of Lesser Black-backed Gull *L. f. graellsii*, or Yellow-footed Gull). The difference in adult upperparts colour is clinal, with darkest in the south and palest in the north of the species' range. Hybrid Glaucous-winged × Western Gulls, which show every shade of grey intermediate between the two parents, need to be borne in mind.

MEASUREMENTS (Sample 45) Wing 380–420 mm; tail 147–177 mm; bill 46–65 mm; tarsus 61–74 mm (from Dwight 1925).

First-year Juveniles similar to *smithsonianus*, and best distinguished by combination of following average differences: heavier structure (especially heavily domed forehead and heavy, blob-ended bill); all-black bill (*smithsonianus* sometimes has pale-based bill); darker general coloration with darker, more uniform sooty grey on head and underparts, and less intricate and rather narrower pattern of pale markings on mantle, scapulars and wing coverts; solidly dark outer greater coverts (forming stronger dark bar in flight); lack of obvious pale window on inner primaries in flight; and whitish, dark-barred rump and uppertail-coverts (rather uniform brownish on *smithsonianus*) which contrasts more with (*smithsonianus*-like) all-dark, pale-fringed tail. Much same applies for differences in first-winter plumage and, in addition, Western's new mantle and scapular feathers rather dingy, uniform grey-brown with washed-out buff fringes (*smithsonianus* more patterned, paler); head and underparts remain uniform, sooty grey-brown whereas *smithsonianus* usually whiter headed; and bill remains all-black or slightly paler at base, whereas bill more often obviously pale-based on *smithsonianus*: first-winter Westerns thus have rather distinctive dingy or sooty general coloration, whereas *smithsonianus* generally 'cleaner-looking'. By first-summer plumage, head and body sometimes generally whiter, wing coverts often much faded to whitish, and primaries, secondary bar and tail often much faded, making some individuals difficult to separate from Glaucous-winged × Western hybrids.

Second-year Acquisition of clear blackish-grey on mantle and scapulars in second-winter plumage, forming obvious dark saddle on most individuals, makes identification straightforward. Wing and tail pattern often little different from first-year, but wing coverts always plainer, paler grey-brown with whitish fringes (all wing coverts often fading to whitish by second summer), and tail often whitish-based at sides (otherwise solidly blackish with thin whitish fringe, fading to pale brown by second summer); head, body and rump whiter, especially by second summer. Bill becoming pale at base, by second summer usually yellowish-based with black tip or subterminal area. Iris acquires adult colour during second year.

Third-year As adult, except: upperwing coverts brown-washed; white tips on outermost primaries smaller or lacking; mirror on 1st primary small or lacking; tail variably marked with dark, usually forming narrow subterminal band or line of spots; and bill often with dark tip, subterminal mark or band.

Adult Differs from Slaty-backed Gull in different wing-tip pattern (has more black above and below: underside of outer primaries black where Slaty-backed grey; usually lacks mirror on 2nd; and lacks white dividing spots on 3rd to 6th primaries); usually slightly narrower (but still broad) white trailing edge to inner wing; and heavier general structure, especially blob-ended bill. Differs from Yellow-footed Gull in pink not yellow legs; paler upperparts (nominate *occidentalis* only); and often faintly grey-streaked head in winter (nominate *occidentalis* only). Bill yellow, paler in winter, with whitish tip and red spot near gonys (spot paler in winter, often very faint orange); orange or reddish gape; iris yellowish-white (especially *wymani*) to dull yellowish-brown (especially nominate *occidentalis*); orbital ring yellow to orange.

Glaucous-winged Gull

Larus glaucescens

(Fig. 66, Photographs 534–541)

Adult summer

The common pale-winged large gull of western North America. In winter, it moves southward from its breeding range and is common on the coast as far south as southern California. Resembles Glaucous Gull, which replaces it as a breeding bird in northwestern Alaska. Glaucous Gull is much less common than Glaucous-winged south of its breeding range in winter, and is rare from southern Canada south to California.

Glaucous-winged can be told from Glaucous Gull at least by the all-black bill on first-years (pale with sharply-demarcated black tip on Glaucous) and on older individuals at least by the pale brown (immatures) or grey (adults) pattern on the wing-tip. This basically straightforward situation, however, is complicated by hybridisation of Glaucous-winged with Western Gull, Herring Gull, and Glaucous Gull in the areas where its breeding range overlaps with theirs. The offspring of these hybridisations are commonest near the breeding areas, but in winter they can be encountered anywhere on the west coast. They can show every intergradation between the parents. Glaucous-winged × Western Gull is the only hybrid regularly encountered south to southern California, and it can be rather common in winter. Glaucous-winged Gull hybrids are discussed at the end of the species description.

Glaucous-winged Gull is slightly smaller than an average Glaucous Gull, with usually obviously smaller bill (which, however, often appears heavy and more 'blob-ended', with depth of bill greater near tip than at base), but otherwise similar in its very heavy appearance. The timing and sequence of moults and the progression of immature plumages are like those of other large gulls (eg Glaucous Gull), with identifiable first-year, second-year, third-year and adult plumages.

MEASUREMENTS (Sample 25) Wing 385–445 mm; tail 161–187 mm; bill 49–64 mm; tarsus 62–76 mm (from Dwight 1925).

First-year Juvenile and first-winter similar to Glaucous Gull, except: bill all-black or with small pale area at base (pale with clear-cut black tip on all first-year Glaucous);

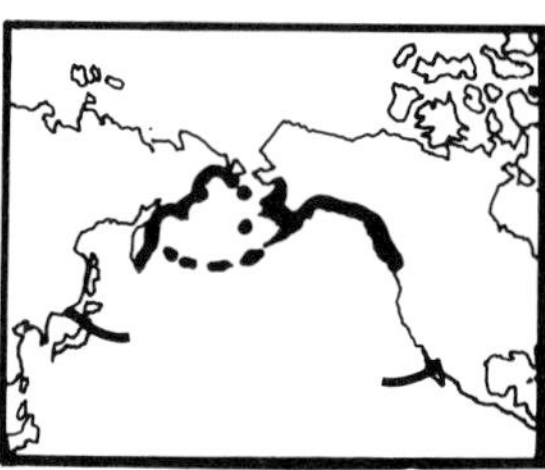

Fig. 65. World distribution of **Glaucous-winged Gull** *Larus glaucescens*, showing approximate breeding range (solid black) and approximate southern limits of winter/non-breeding range (black lines).

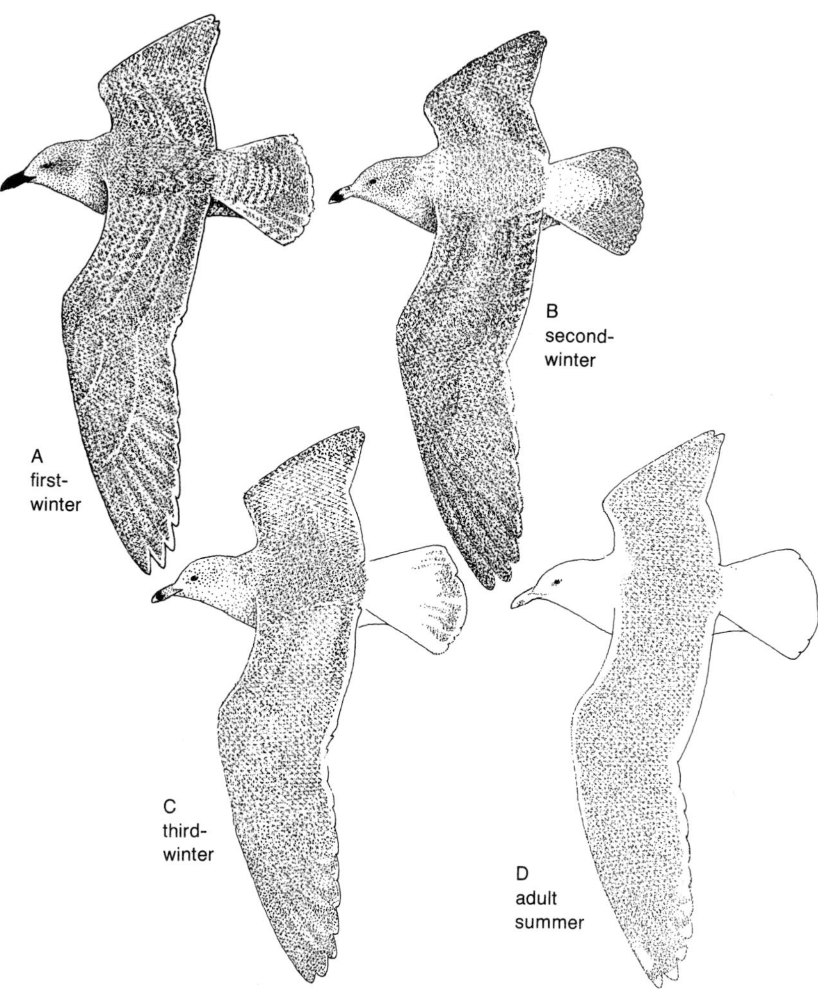

Fig. 66. **Glaucous-winged Gulls** *Larus glaucescens* in flight.

scapulars and wing coverts (except greater coverts) generally pale grey-brown with pattern of pale fringes and bars much like Glaucous Gull, but averaging more uniform; inner greater coverts pale grey-brown, finely marked with pale marbling (obviously barred on many Glaucous); outer greater coverts and tertials mainly uniform grey-brown, more uniform than Glaucous and never obviously barred; primaries and secondaries uniform grey-brown (closed wing-tip matching or slightly darker than general colour of tertials and rest of upperparts (wing-tip obviously whiter than rest of upperparts on Glaucous), with complete pale fringe to each primary giving first-year Thayer's Gull-like pattern when perched, and occasionally subterminal dark arrowhead mark on each inner primary; from below in flight, underwing more uniformly grey-brown, showing much less translucency at wing-tip than Glaucous; tail solidly grey-brown (matching wing-tip colour) with pale fringe and small amount, if any, of pale mottling on outer feathers, contrasting with often coarsely-barred whitish rump (Glaucous typically has paler tail with complex pattern of pale barring or marbling). New mantle and scapulars more uniform, rather dingy grey-brown in first-winter and first-summer plumages. From January onwards, and especially in first-summer plumage, often generally faded and whitish, more similar to faded first-year Glaucous, but bill still mainly or all black without sharply demarcated dark tip, and uniform duskiness of wing-tip and tail usually still evident, although some have very faded, whitish wing-tips.

Second-year Distinctions from Glaucous and general appearance much as for first-year, but even more uniform dingy grey, lacking any obvious pale barrings on wing coverts; clear grey adult coloration on mantle and scapulars (uniform grey saddle in second-summer); and rump white. Bill still mainly black in second winter, and in second summer still always much more extensively dark-tipped than Glaucous Gull. Iris dark (often becoming pale on Glaucous Gull).

Third-year As adult, except: upperwing- and underwing-coverts brown-washed; pattern on primaries less distinct, often pale brownish-grey, and white primary tips smaller; tail marked with varible pattern of pale brown; and usually prominent dark subterminal mark on bill.

Adult Resembles Glaucous Gull, except: grey-patterned primaries (Glaucous lacks any grey pattern on wing-tip, instead having end of each outer primary all-white for third to half of exposed length, shading into very pale grey base) with large, clear-cut white primary tips, and large white mirror on 1st primary (often also small mirror on 2nd, rarely also 3rd); in flight at long range wing-tip appears grey like rest of wing, or with neat, narrow white fringe at tip (Glaucous at long range has extensive, all-white wing-tip); narrower white trailing edge to wing; grey of upperparts and wings variable, from slightly darker than North American subspecies of Herring Gull *L. a. smithsonianus* to as dark as east Siberian subspecies *L. a. vegae* (darkest individuals from south of breeding range, palest from north), thus obviously darker than very pale grey of Glaucous Gull; iris brown to pale brown, eye usually looking dark (always obviously pale on Glaucous); orbital ring typically reddish to purple, in winter paler or yellowish; and bill in winter often has fine zig-zag dark line across mandibles (sometimes only upper mandible) near tip. Grey on wing-tip same or slightly darker grey than rest of upperparts, and usually purer grey, less blue-grey than upperparts. When worn, wing-tip may appear darker than when fresh, or fade to pale brownish-grey: wing-tip still not obviously darker than rest of upperparts, never blackish-grey as on some hybrids.

HYBRIDS Hybridisation of Glaucous-winged Gull with Western Gull, Herring Gull, and Glaucous Gull in western North America adds a great deal of confusion in what is already rather complicated region for gull identification. Hybridisation with Western Gull occurs commonly in relatively small overlap breeding zone in Washington, where hybrids form over half of the Glaucous-winged and Western Gull population in some breeding colonies. These hybrids are migratory like Glaucous-winged, and can be found throughout its winter range, in generally decreasing numbers south to southern California. Hybridisation of Glaucous-winged with Herring Gull occurs less commonly than with Western Gull, mainly around centre of Alaskan south coast; and with Glaucous Gull in western Alaska; hybrid Glaucous-winged × Herring and Glaucous-winged × Glaucous are generally much less common far south of the breeding areas in winter than Glaucous-winged × Western. Glaucous Gull × Herring Gull hybrids also occur in western Alaska, but apparently less commonly than in Iceland (see discussion under 'Identification pitfalls' of Glaucous Gull on p. 144).

Hybrids can show every intergradation of appearance between that of the parent species. It is always worth considering possibility of hybrid parentage as an alternative before making firm identification of any species outside its normal range, and in such cases to check full range of field characters for signs of hybridity. This involves checking for variations outside what is normal for claimed species. Hybridity can show, for example, especially in the following features: bill pattern of first-years (important for identifying first-year Glaucous Gull, which always shows pale, sharply black-tipped bill); bill/head structure and body size (important for telling Thayer's Gull, especially from some Glaucous-winged × Western and Glaucous-winged × Herring Gull hybrids which can show Thayer's-like plumage patterns); tone of grey of adult upperparts coloration; the paler or darker contrast of closed wing-tip with rest of upperparts (important for distinguishing eg pure Western and Glaucous-winged Gulls from their hybrids); degree of contrast of any darkness on tail with rest of upperparts (eg immature Glaucous or Iceland Gull should never have tail markings obviously darker than the rest of the upperparts); or colours of adults' iris and orbital ring (eg adult Glaucous Gull always has pale iris and orbital ring, whereas adult Thayer's Gull shows dark iris and orbital ring). Presence of one or any combination of 'wrong' features of this type, outside the species' normal range of variation, is usually sign of hybridity. Permutation of variations in hybrids is enormous, but for any well-watched individual gull, the process of checking its features for signs of hybridity is usually straightforward.

Red-legged Kittiwake

Rissa brevirostris

(Fig. 67, Photographs 542–544)

A very local species, breeding only on a few islands among the Aleutians and in the Bering Sea, and, apart from extremely rare occurrences farther south, highly pelagic resident in this region all year.

Like Black-legged Kittiwake in structure, except has slightly longer wings on average (with narrower outer wing giving slightly different flight silhouette and action), proportionately slightly shorter tail and shorter legs, and shorter bill which has strongly decurved culmen at tip giving distinctive short, blunt-ended shape. The forehead is short and steep, and the crown flatter, less rounded, than on Black-legged Kittiwake, latter evident in both head-on and profile views. The timing and sequence of moults and the progression of immature plumages are like those of Black-legged Kittiwake, with identifiable first-year and adult plumages, and also (like Black-legged Kittiwake) a proportion are identifiable in second-year plumage.

The legs are scarlet at least from first-summer plumage onwards, so bright that when perched, in some lights, the colour reflects to give a pink hue to the white belly. At least in Europe (and probably elsewhere), variant immature and adult Black-legged Kittiwakes with reddish legs are of regular but very rare occurrence, so identification of Red-legged Kittiwake outside its normal range must embrace the other distinct differences between the two species.

MEASUREMENTS (Sample 12) Wing 290–310 mm; tail 116–132 mm; bill 26–30 mm; tarsus 29–32 mm (from Dwight 1925).

First-year Juvenile very different from Black-legged Kittiwake: completely lacks blackish carpal-bar (thus lacks W pattern of Black-legged); outer primaries and their coverts black; rest of upperwing adult-like grey, but secondaries and inner primaries extensively white, giving rather Sabine's Gull-like pattern; underwing and axillaries white except for grey outer primaries and outer under primary coverts (underwing of Black-legged Kittiwake wholly white, except for black wing-tip); tail white, the only species of gull with all-white tail in juvenile plumage (Black-legged Kittiwake has neatly black-banded tail); black ear-spot like Black-legged Kittiwake, but blackish half-collar on lower hindneck often less well-marked; grey of mantle, scapulars, back and remainder of wing coverts like adult, slightly darker than on Black-legged Kittiwake. First-winter like juvenile, but head grey-washed and half-collar often reduced or lacking. Bill blackish on juvenile, becoming yellow like adult at least by first-summer plumage. Legs brownish on juvenile, becoming scarlet like adult at least by first-summer plumage. When perched, first-summer distinguishable from adult summer by all-black wing-tip, grey-washed head with blackish ear-spot; more extensive white tertial-crescent, and generally less immaculate appearance.

Second-year Proportion probably acquire adult plumage in second-winter, but others ageable as second-year, for example by extensive dark markings among greater primary coverts; black extending strongly up full length of outer webs of outer two or

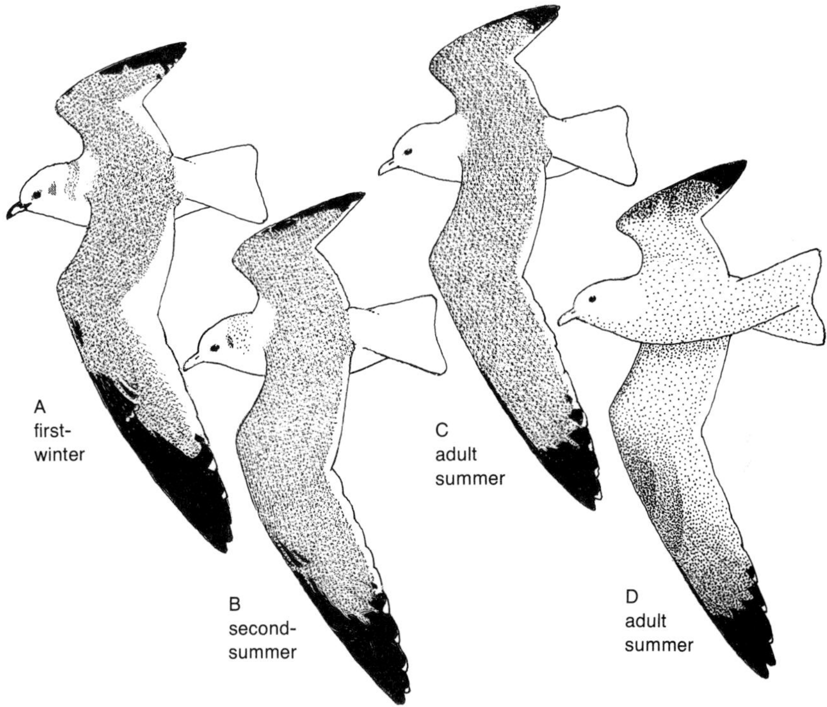

Fig. 67. **Red-legged Kittiwakes** *Rissa brevirostris* in flight.

more primaries (only 1st has full black outer web on adult); and retention of grey wash on head or blackish ear-spot in second-summer plumage (when adult summer white-headed).

Adult Like Black-legged Kittiwake, except: pattern of black on wing-tip similar to Black-legged, but grey of upperwing slightly darker and uniform (lacking shade from grey to whitish on secondaries and before black wing-tip as on Black-legged Kittiwake); white trailing edge to upperwing narrower and more clear-cut; marginal coverts grey (white on Black-legged) thus leading edge of wing dark when viewed head-on; when perched, scapular-crescent more prominent on average; underwing like first-year, except outer underwing more uniformly dull grey, darkest on under primary coverts. In summer, orbital ring, gape and mouth red, bill yellow: in winter, orbital ring and gape duller, bill often greenish-yellow. Legs scarlet. Head white in summer; crown and hindneck grey-washed in winter, with darker grey, often crescentic, ear-spot.

References

BARTH, E. K. 1975. Taxonomy of *Larus argentatus* and *Larus fuscus* in north-western Europe. *Ornis Scand.* 6: 49–63.

BEAUBRUN, P.-C. 1983. Le Goéland d' Audouin sur les côtes du Maroc. *L'Oiseau* 53: 209–226.

DUBOIS, P. 1985. Considérations sur le Goéland d'Armenie *Larus armenicus* en Israël. *Alauda* 53: 226–228.

DWIGHT, J. 1925. The Gulls (Laridae) of the World: their plumages, moults, variations, relationships and distribution. *Bull. Amer. Mus. Nat. Hist.* 52: 63–401.

GARCIA, E. F. J. 1977. Field identification of juvenile Audouin's Gull. *Bull. Gibraltar Ornithological Group* 2: 3–6.

GOSSELIN, M., & David, N. 1975. Field identification of Thayer's Gull *Larus thayeri* in eastern North America. *Amer. Birds* 29: 1059–1066.

HUME, R. A. 1978. Variations in Herring Gulls at a Midland roost. *Brit. Birds* 71: 338–345.

—— 1979. Variations in Herring Gulls. *Brit Birds 72: 390–392.*

LEHMAN, P. 1980. The identification of Thayer's Gull in the field. *Birding* 12: 198–210.

MCGASKIE, G. 1983. Another look at the Western and Yellow-footed Gulls. *Western Birds* 14: 85–107.

MONAGHAN, P., & DUNCAN, N. 1979. Plumage variation of known-age Herring Gulls. *Brit. Birds* 72: 100–103.

NICOLAU-GUILLAUMET, P. 1977. Mise au point et réflexions sur la répartition des Goélands argentés *Larus argentatus* de France. *Alauda* 45: 53–73.

REE, V. 1973. *Larus cirrocephalus*, nueva especie de gaviota para Espana y Europa. *Ardeola* 19: 22–23.

SMITH, K. D. 1972. The winter distribution of *Larus audouinii*. *Bull. BOC* 92: 34–37.

STANLEY, P. I., BROUGH, T., FLETCHER, M. R., HORTON, N., & ROCHARD, J. B. A. 1981. The origins of Herring Gulls wintering inland in south-east England. *Bird Study* 28: 123–132.

VAURIE, C. 1965. *The Birds of the Palearctic Fauna. Non-Passeriformes.* London.

Page index of photographs

1. Juvenile **Black-headed Gull** *L. ridibundus*, England, July 1970 (Richard Vaughan).

2. Juvenile **Black-headed Gull** *L. ridibundus*, England, July 1967 (Richard Vaughan).

3. **Black-headed Gull** *L. ridibundus*, moulting from juvenile to first-winter, England, August 1976 (Pamela Harrison).

4. **Black-headed Gull** *L. ridibundus*, at start of moult from juvenile to first-winter, Wales, August 1979 (R. J. Chandler).

5. **Black-headed Gull** *L. ridibundus*, at start of moult from juvenile to first-winter, Netherlands, July 1980 (Dirk Moerbeek).

6. First-winter **Black-headed Gull** *L. ridibundus*, England, February 1971 (Richard Vaughan).

7. First-winter **Black-headed Gull** *L. ridibundus*, USSR, November 1976 (Pamela Harrison).

8. First-winter **Black-headed Gull** *L. ridibundus*, Denmark, March 1984 (Urban Olsson).

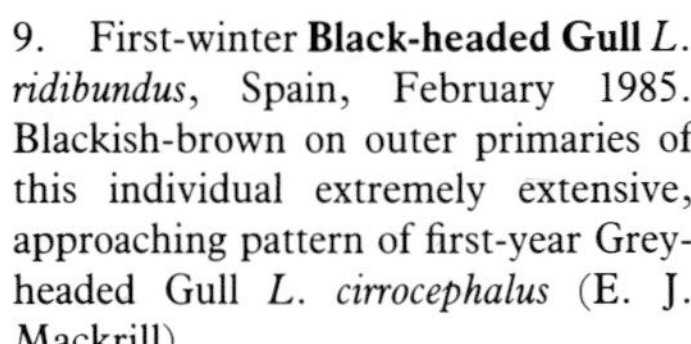

9. First-winter **Black-headed Gull** *L. ridibundus*, Spain, February 1985. Blackish-brown on outer primaries of this individual extremely extensive, approaching pattern of first-year Grey-headed Gull *L. cirrocephalus* (E. J. Mackrill).

10. **Black-headed Gull** *L. ridibundus*, moulting from first-winter to first-summer, England, March 1981 (Peter M. Harris).

11, 12. First-summer **Black-headed Gull** *L. ridibundus*, England, April 1976 (Pamela Harrison).

13. (below) First-summer **Black-headed Gull** *L. ridibundus*, England, May 1981 (Peter M. Harris).

14. **Black-headed Gull** *L. ridibundus*, moulting from first-summer to second-winter, Netherlands, July 1980 (Dirk Moerbeek).

15. Adult **Black-headed Gull** *L. ridibundus*, near end of moult from summer to winter plumage (note outermost primaries still growing), England, October 1980 (Peter M. Harris).

16. Adult winter **Black-headed Gull** *L. ridibundus*, near end of complete autumn moult (outermost primaries not yet fully grown), Wales, August 1985 (R. J. Chandler).

17. Adult winter **Black-headed Gull** *L. ridibundus*, England, February 1981 (R. J. Chandler).

18. Adult winter **Black-headed Gull** *L. ridibundus*, England, October 1970 (Richard Vaughan).

19. Adult winter **Black-headed Gulls** *L. ridibundus*, England, January 1971. Obvious fine black lines on the outer webs of the outermost primaries, as on the upper left and lower right individuals, are probably an indication of second-winter rather than fully adult plumage (Richard Vaughan).

20. Adult winter **Black-headed Gull** *L. ridibundus*, England, January 1985 (E. J. Mackrill).

21. Adult **Black-headed Gull** *L. ridibundus*, moulting from winter to summer plumage, England, March 1976 (R. J. Chandler).

22. Adult summer **Black-headed Gull** *L. ridibundus*, England, February 1977 (R. J. Chandler).

23. Adult summer **Black-headed Gull** *L. ridibundus*, Sweden, June 1981 (Jan Mogren).

24. Adult summer **Black-headed Gull** *L. ridibundus*, Wales, August 1983 (R. J. Chandler).

25. Juvenile **Slender-billed Gull** *L. genei* moulting to first-winter plumage, Spain, July 1985 (E. J. Mackrill).

26. First-winter **Slender-billed Gulls** *L. genei*, Bulgaria, September 1976 (Dr Brigitte Königstedt).

27, 28 First-winter **Slender-billed Gull** *L. genei*, Greece, September 1981 (Paul Doherty).

29. First-winter **Slender-billed Gull** *L. genei*, Turkey, October 1977 (S. C. Madge).

30. Adult winter **Slender-billed Gull** *L. genei*, Iran, February 1971 (Pamela Harrison).

31. Adult winter **Slender-billed Gulls** *L. genei*, with one adult winter Black-headed Gull *L. ridibundus* (right), Iran, February 1971 (Pamela Harrison).

32. Adult summer **Slender-billed Gull** *L. genei*, France, June 1977 (J. G. Prins).

33, 34. Adult summer **Slender-billed Gulls** *L. genei*, USSR, May 1976 (V. D. Siokhin).

35, 36. Adult **Slender-billed Gull** *L. genei* starting complete autumn moult from summer to winter plumage, Spain, July 1985 (E. J. Mackrill).

37. Juvenile **Bonaparte's Gull** *L. philadelphia*, USA, August 1980 (E. J. Mackrill).

38, 39, 40. Juvenile **Bonaparte's Gull** *L. philadelphia* moulting to first-winter, Canada, August 1984 (Urban Olsson).

41. First-winter **Bonaparte's Gulls** *L. philadelphia*, USA, March 1982 (Arnoud B. van den Berg).

42. First-winter **Bonaparte's Gull** *L. philadelphia*, England, April 1981 (David M. Cottridge).

43. **Bonaparte's Gull** *L. philadelphia*, moulting from first-summer to second-winter (note remaining black-banded first-year tail), USA, July 1980 (E. J. Mackrill).

44. Adult winter **Bonaparte's Gull** *L. philadelphia*, Canada, September 1979 (Philip Perry).

45. Adult winter **Bonaparte's Gull** *L. philadelphia*, England, March 1968 (J. B. & S. Bottomley).

46. Adult winter **Bonaparte's Gull** *L. philadelphia*, with adult summer Black-headed Gull *L. ridibundus*, England, March 1968 (J. B. & S. Bottomley).

47. Adult winter **Bonaparte's Gull** *L. philadelphia*, USA, September 1984 (R. J. Chandler).

48, 49. Adult summer **Bonaparte's Gull** *L. philadelphia* commencing moult to winter plumage, Northern Ireland, July 1979, with adult Black-headed Gull *L. ridibundus* (A. McGeehan).

50. Juvenile **Grey-headed Gull** *L. cirrocephalus*, South Africa (Gerry Nicholls).

51. **Grey-headed Gull** *L. cirrocephalus*, near end of moult from juvenile to first-winter, Peru, June 1981 (E. J. Mackrill).

52. First-winter **Grey-headed Gull** *L. cirrocephalus*, Peru, January 1981 (E. J. Mackrill).

53. First-winter **Grey-headed Gull** *L. cirrocephalus*, Botswana, October 1972 (Peter Steyn).

54. Second-winter **Grey-headed Gull** *L. cirrocephalus*, South Africa, February 1974 (J. C. Sinclair)

55. Second-summer **Grey-headed Gull** *L. cirrocephalus*, Kenya, July 1976 (T. Källqvist).

56. Adult winter **Grey-headed Gull** *L. cirrocephalus*, Peru, June 1981 (E. J. Mackrill).

57. Adult summer **Grey-headed Gull** *L. cirrocephalus*, Peru, June 1981 (E. J. Mackrill).

58. Adult summer **Grey-headed Gull** *L. cirrocephalus*, Kenya, July 1976 (T. Källqvist).

59. Adult summer **Grey-headed Gull** *L. cirrocephalus*, South Africa, June 1973 (Gerry Nicholls).

60, 61. Adult **Grey-headed Gulls** *L. cirrocephalus*, moulting from summer to winter plumage, Peru, January 1981 (E. J. Mackrill).

62. **Grey-headed Gulls** *L. cirrocephalus*, including one first-winter (right), South Africa, August 1976 (Gerry Nicholls).

63. Juvenile **Common Gull** *L. canus*, Netherlands, September 1982 (Dirk Moerbeek).

64, 65. Juvenile **Common Gull** *L. canus*, Netherlands, August 1980 (Dirk Moerbeek).

66. First-winter **Common Gull** *L. canus*, England, February 1979 (R. J. Chandler).

67. First-winter **Common Gull** *L. canus*, England, January 1971 (Richard Vaughan).

68. First-winter **Common Gulls** *L. canus*, England, March 1976 (Pamela Harrison).

69, 70. First-winter **Common Gull** *L. canus*, England, February 1980 (Brian Thomas).

71. First-winter **Common Gull** *L. canus*, Scotland, December 1977 (S. R. D. da Prato).

72. First-winter **Common Gull** *L. canus*, Denmark, March 1984. This individual shows well-marked mirror on 1st primary which fading occasionally produces (Urban Olsson).

73. First-summer **Common Gull** *L. canus*, England, April 1985 (R. J. Chandler).

74. First-summer **Common Gull** *L. canus*, England, April 1976 (Pamela Harrison).

75. **Common Gull** *L. canus*, starting moult from first-summer to second-winter, England, June 1980 (E. J. Mackrill).

76. **Common Gull** *L. canus*, moulting from first-summer to second-winter, Netherlands, August 1980 (Dirk Moerbeek).

77. Second-winter (front) and first-winter **Common Gulls** *L. canus*, England, February 1979 (R. J. Chandler).

78, 79. Second-winter **Common Gull** *L. canus*, Republic of Ireland, October 1975 (Richard T. Mills).

80, 81. Second-winter **Common Gull** *L. canus*, England, February 1978 (Paul Doherty).

82. Second-summer **Common Gull** *L. canus*, Sweden, May 1980 (Jan Mogren).

83. Adult winter **Common Gull** *L. canus*, England, December 1974 (Wendy Dickson).

84. Adult winter **Common Gull** *L. canus*, West Germany, December 1982 (Peter Gloe).

85. Adult winter **Common Gull** *L. canus*, England, January 1985 (E. J. Mackrill).

86. Adult winter **Common Gull** *L. canus*, Denmark, March 1984 (Urban Olsson).

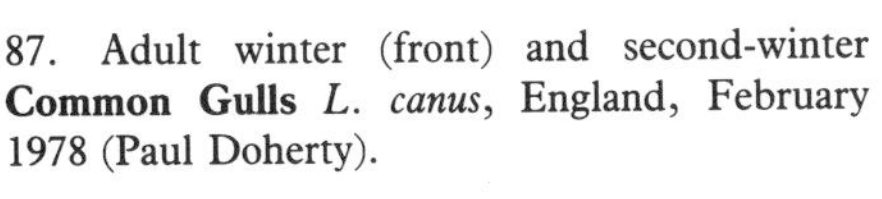

87. Adult winter (front) and second-winter **Common Gulls** *L. canus*, England, February 1978 (Paul Doherty).

88. Adult summer **Common Gull** *L. canus*, Norway, July 1956 (John Barlee).

89. Adult summer **Common Gull** *L. canus*, Scotland, June 1976 (Pamela Harrison).

90. First-winter **Common Gull** *L. c. brachyrhynchus* (Mew Gull), USA, November 1984 (David W. Sonneborn).

91. First-winter **Common Gull** *L. c. brachyrhynchus* (Mew Gull), USA, December 1984 (Louis R. Bevier).

92. Second-winter **Common Gull** *L. c. brachyrhynchus* (Mew Gull), USA, January 1985 (Louis R. Bevier).

93. Second-winter **Common Gull** *L. c. brachyrhynchus* (Mew Gull), USA, August 1984. Prominent dark tail markings are a regular feature on second-years of this subspecies, unlike nominate *canus* (Urban Olsson).

94. Adult summer **Common Gull** *L. c. brachyrhynchus* (Mew Gull), USA, June 1985 (Jon L. Dunn).

95. Adult winter **Common Gull** *L. c. brachyrhynchus* (Mew Gull), USA, January 1983 (Killian Mullarney).

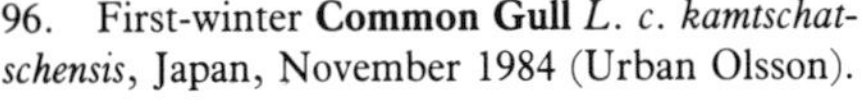

96. First-winter **Common Gull** *L. c. kamtschatschensis*, Japan, November 1984 (Urban Olsson).

97. Second-writer **Common Gull** *L. c. kamtschatschensis*, Japan, November 1984. Note extensive dark markings on underwing coverts, which may be a regular feature of second-years of the large Siberian subspecies, but which are probably never shown by nominate *canus* (Urban Olsson).

98. Juvenile **Mediterranean Gull** *L. melanocephalus*, Greece, July 1982 (J. G. Prins).

99, 100. Juvenile **Mediterranean Gull** *L. melanocephalus* moulting to first-winter, Netherlands, August 1982 (F. H. Jansen).

101. First-winter **Mediterranean Gull** *L. melanocephalus*, England, December 1978 (R. J. Chandler).

102, 103. First-winter **Mediterranean Gulls** *L. melanocephalus*, Spain, February 1985 (E. J. Mackrill).

104. First-winter **Mediterranean Gull** *L. melanocephalus*, England, January 1979 (Alistair Forsyth).

105. First-winter **Mediterranean Gull** *L. melanocephalus*, England, December 1963 (R. H. Charlwood).

106. First-winter **Mediterranean Gull** *L. melanocephalus*, (second from right) with adult winter Black-headed Gulls *L. ridibundus*, England, October 1978 (R. J. Chandler).

107. Two first-winter (left), two adult winter (right) and one second-winter (flying) **Mediterranean Gulls** *L. melanocephalus*, Portugal, February 1983 (Peter M. Harris).

108. Second-winter **Mediterranean Gull** *L. melanocephalus*, England, December 1982 (James Smith).

109, 110. Second-winter **Mediterranean Gulls** *L. melanocephalus*, Spain, winter 1984/85 (E. J. Mackrill).

111. Second-winter **Mediterranean Gull** *L. melanocephalus* moulting to second-summer, Spain, March 1985 (E. J. Mackrill).

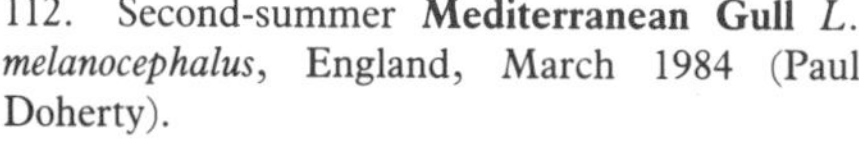

112. Second-summer **Mediterranean Gull** *L. melanocephalus*, England, March 1984 (Paul Doherty).

113. Adult winter **Mediterranean Gull** *L. melanocephalus*, England, December 1980 (Paul Doherty).

114. Adult winter **Mediterranean Gull** *L. melanocephalus*, Spain, December 1984 (E. J. Mackrill).

115. Adult winter **Mediterranean Gull** *L. melanocephalus*, Spain, February 1985 (E. J. Mackrill).

116. Adult **Mediterranean Gull** *L. melanocephalus* near end of moult from winter to summer plumage, England, February 1978 (R. J. Chandler).

117, 118. Adult **Mediterranean Gulls** *L. melanocephalus* near end of moult to summer plumage, Spain, March 1985 (E. J. Mackrill).

119. Adult summer **Mediterranean Gulls** *L. melanocephalus*, Greece, May 1968. A comparison with Photo 116 demonstrates how the apparent extent of the hood on all hooded gulls can be affected by the posture of the individual: the more hunched the posture, the less extensive the hood (Wolfgang Makatsch).

120. Juvenile **Ring-billed Gull** *L. delawarensis*, Canada, September 1984 (R. J. Chandler).

122. First-winter **Ring-billed Gull** *L. delawarensis*, USA, September 1985 (R. J. Chandler).

121. Juvenile **Ring-billed Gull** *L. delawarensis*, moulting to first-winter, USA, August 1984 (Urban Olsson).

123, 124, 125 (lower right). **Ring-billed Gulls** *L. delawarensis* near end of moult from juvenile to first-winter, USA, August 1980 (E. J. Mackrill).

126. **Ring-billed Gull** *L. delawarensis* near end of moult from juvenile to first-winter (note the few remaining dark-centred, juvenile scapulars), Canada, September 1979 (Philip Perry).

127. First-winter **Ring-billed Gull** *L. delawarensis*, USA, December 1975 (Robert Barber).

128. First-winter **Ring-billed Gull** *L. delawarensis*, USA, March 1982 (Arnoud B. van den Berg).

129. First-winter **Ring-billed Gull** *L. delawarensis*, Canada, August 1984 (Urban Olsson).

130, 131. First winter **Ring-billed Gulls** *L. delawarensis*, USA, October 1980 (E. J. Mackrill).

133. First-summer **Ring-billed Gull** *L. delawarensis*, USA, March 1982 (Arnoud B. van den Berg).

132. First-winter **Ring-billed Gull** *L. delawarensis*, USA, February 1974 (Davis Finch).

134. First-summer **Ring-billed Gull** *L. delawarensis*, England, May 1981. The missing innermost one or two primaries indicates the start of the moult to second-winter, which apparently takes place on average a month earlier than on Common Gull *L. canus* (Peter M. Harris).

135. First-summer **Ring-billed Gull** *L. delawarensis*, USA, May 1982, showing extreme wear and fading on wing coverts as discussed on p. 18 (Hubert Huneker).

136. Second-winter **Ring-billed Gull** *L. delawarensis*, USA, February 1982 (Arnoud B. van den Berg).

137. Second-winter **Ring-billed Gull** *L. delawarensis*, USA, September 1985 (R. J. Chandler).

138. Second-winter **Ring-billed Gull** *L. delawarensis*, England, February 1979 (W. R. Hirst).

139. Second-winter **Ring-billed Gull** *L. delawarensis*, USA, March 1976 (Roger Higson).

140. Second-summer **Ring-billed Gull** *L. delawarensis*, Canada, June 1977 (John W. Chardine).

141. Adult winter **Ring-billed Gull** *L. delawarensis*, USA, January 1983 (Arnoud B. van den Berg).

142. Adult winter **Ring-billed Gull** *L. delawarensis*, USA, March 1976 (Roger Higson).

143. Adult summer **Ring-billed Gulls** *L. delawarensis*, Canada, June 1977 (John W. Chardine).

144. Adult summer **Ring-billed Gull** *L. delawarensis*, USA, March 1982 (Arnoud B. van den Berg).

145. Adult summer **Ring-billed Gulls** *L. delawarensis*, USA, March 1968 (P. Devillers).

146. Juvenile **Laughing Gull** *L. atricilla*, USA, October 1980 (E. J. Mackrill).

147. Juvenile **Laughing Gull** *L. atricilla*, USA, September 1985 (R. J. Chandler).

148. Juvenile **Laughing Gull** *L. atricilla*, USA, August 1980 (Urban Olsson).

149. **Laughing Gull** *L. atricilla* moulting from juvenile to first-winter, USA, September 1985 (R. J. Chandler).

150. First-winter **Laughing Gull** *L. atricilla*, USA, October 1978 (J. B. & S. Bottomley).

151. First-winter **Laughing Gull** *L. atricilla*, USA, October 1980 (E. J. Mackrill).

152. First-winter **Laughing Gull** *L. atricilla*, England, Febrary 1984 (Paul Doherty).

153. First-winter **Laughing Gull** *L. atricilla*, England, April 1969 (J. B. & S. Bottomley).

154. First-winter **Laughing Gull** *L. atricilla*, Peru, February 1979 (E. J. Mackrill).

155. First-summer **Laughing Gull** *L. atricilla*, USA, April 1980 (S. R. D. da Prato).

156. First-summer **Laughing Gull** *L. atricilla*, USA, May 1982, showing extreme wear and fading on wing coverts as discussed on p. 18 (Hubert Huneker).

157. Second-winter **Laughing Gull** *L. atricilla*, USA, April 1980 (E. J. Mackrill).

158. **Laughing Gull** *L. atricilla* near end of moult from first-summer to second-winter, Scotland, October 1978 (Donald A. Smith).

159. Second-winter **Laughing Gull** *L. atricilla*, USA, April 1980 (E. J. Mackrill).

160. First-winter, second-winter and adult winter **Laughing Gulls** *L. atricilla*, USA, October 1978 (J. B. & S. Bottomley).

161. Adult **Laughing Gull** *L. atricilla* moulting from summer to winter plumage (one new, white-tipped primary is visible, the remainder are old), USA, October 1978 (J. B. & S. Bottomley).

162. Adult **Laughing Gull** *L. atricilla* moulting from summer to winter plumage (outermost primaries only partially grown), USA, October 1980 (E. J. Mackrill).

163. Adult summer **Laughing Gull** *L. atricilla*, USA, July 1977 (Alan Brady).

164. Adult **Laughing Gull** *L. atricilla* moulting from winter to summer plumage, USA, February 1982 (Arnoud B. van den Berg).

165. Adult summer **Laughing Gull** *L. atricilla*, USA, July 1980 (E. J. Mackrill).

166. Adult summer **Laughing Gull** *L. atricilla*, USA, July 1980 (E. J. Mackrill).

167. Adult summer **Laughing Gull** *L. atricilla*, USA, summer 1978 (E. J. Mackrill).

168. Adult summer **Laughing Gull** *L. atricilla*, USA, February 1982 (Arnoud B. van den Berg).

169. **Franklin's Gull** *L. pipixcan* near end of moult from juvenile to first-winter, Canada, September 1979 (Philip Perry).

171. First-winter **Franklin's Gull** *L. pipixcan*, Galapagos, December 1976 (Norman van Swelm).

170. **Franklin's Gull** *L. pipixcan* near end of moult from juvenile to first-winter, Canada, August 1984 (Urban Olsson).

172. First-winter **Franklin's Gulls** *L. pipixcan*, Peru, November 1980 (Arnoud B. van den Berg).

173, 174, 175. First-winter **Franklin's Gulls** *L. pipixcan*, Peru, November 1980 (E. J. Mackrill).

176. **Franklin's Gull** *L. pipixcan* showing (in this and in Photos 177 to 184) the progression of the complete spring moult from first-winter to first summer, Peru, April 1981 (E. J. Mackrill).

177 to 184. (above and next page) **Franklin's Gulls** *L. pipixcan* showing (in these and with Photo 176) the progression of the complete spring moult from first-winter to first-summer. 177. Peru, March 1980 (Piet Meeth); 178, 179. Peru, April 1981 (E. J. Mackrill); 180. Peru, March 1981 (E. J. Mackrill); 181, 182, 183. Peru, April 1981 (E. J. Mackrill); 184. Peru, April 1981 (moult to first-summer completed) (E. J. Mackrill).

182, 183, 184. See caption on previous page.

185. First-summer **Franklin's Gull** *L. pipixcan*, Chile, May 1980 (Arnoud B. van den Berg).

186. **Franklin's Gull** *L. pipixcan* near end of complete autumn moult (outer primaries not yet fully grown) from first-summer to second-winter (age indicated by large extent of black on wing-tip and small white primary tips), North Dakota, USA, August 1980 (E. J. Mackrill).

187. Second-winter **Franklin's Gull** *L. pipixcan*, Peru, October 1980 (E. J. Mackrill).

188. Second-winter or adult winter **Franklin's Gull** *L. pipixcan*, Peru, November 1980. The intermediate wing-tip pattern renders firm age-diagnosis inadvisable (E. J. Mackrill).

189. Second-winter **Franklin's Gull** *L. pipixcan*, England, February 1978 (M. Parker).

190. **Franklin's Gull** *L. pipixcan* moulting from second-winter to second-summer, Peru, April 1981 (E. J. Mackrill).

191. Second-summer **Franklin's Gull** *L. pipixcan*, Peru, April 1981 (E. J. Mackrill).

192. Adult winter **Franklin's Gull** *L. pipixcan*, Peru, December 1975 (Piet Meeth).

193. Adult **Franklin's Gull** *L. pipixcan* in complete spring moult from winter to summer plumage, Peru, March 1980 (Piet Meeth).

194, 195, 196. Adult summer **Franklin's Gulls** *L. pipixcan*, Peru, April 1981 (E. J. Mackrill).

197, 198. Juvenile **Audouin's Gull** *L. audouinii*, Greece, August 1976 (Richard Vaughan).

199, 200, 201, 202. Juvenile **Audouin's Gulls** *L. audouinii*, Spain, July 1984 (E. J. Mackrill).

203, 204. First-summer **Herring Gull** *L. a. michahellis* (not Audouin's Gull as previously captioned), Spain, April 1977 (Donald A. Smith)

205, 206. Second-summer **Audouin's Gull** *L. audouinii*, Spain, May 1984 (D. Oelkers).

207. Second-summer **Audouin's Gull** *L. audouinii*, Spain, April 1977 (Donald A. Smith).

208. Second-summer **Audouin's Gull** *L. audouinii*, at start of moult to third-winter, Spain, July 1984 (E. J. Mackrill).

209, 210. Third-summer **Audouin's Gulls** *L. audouinii*, Spain, June 1984 (E. J. Mackrill).

211. Adult summer **Audouin's Gull** *L. audouinii*, Spain, June 1984 (E. J. Mackrill).

212. Adult summer **Audouin's Gull** *L. audouinii*, Morocco, April 1984 (E. de Juana).

213. Adult summer **Audouin's Gull** *L. audouinii*, Greece, May 1966 (Ilse Makatsch).

214, 215. Adult summer **Audouin's Gull** *L. audouinii*, Spain, April 1980 (R. J. Chandler).

216, 217, 218. Adult summer **Audouin's Gulls** *L. audouinii*, Spain, June 1984 (E. J. Mackrill).

219. Juvenile **Herring Gull** *L. argentatus*, Wales, August 1980 (R. J. Chandler).

220. Juvenile **Herring Gull** *L. argentatus*, Wales, August 1985 (R. J. Chandler).

221. First-winter **Herring Gull** *L. argentatus*, England, October 1983 (Paul Doherty).

222. First-winter **Herring Gull** *L. argentatus*, Sweden, January 1984 (Jan Mogren).

223. First-winter **Herring Gull** *L. argentatus*, Denmark, October 1983 (Urban Olsson).

224. First-summer **Herring Gull** *L. argentatus*, England, May 1979 (R. J. Chandler).

225. First-summer **Herring Gull** *L. argentatus*, England, May 1979. The missing innermost primaries indicate the start of the moult to second-winter (R. J. Chandler).

226. Second-winter **Herring Gull** *L. argentatus*, England, November 1983 (Paul Doherty).

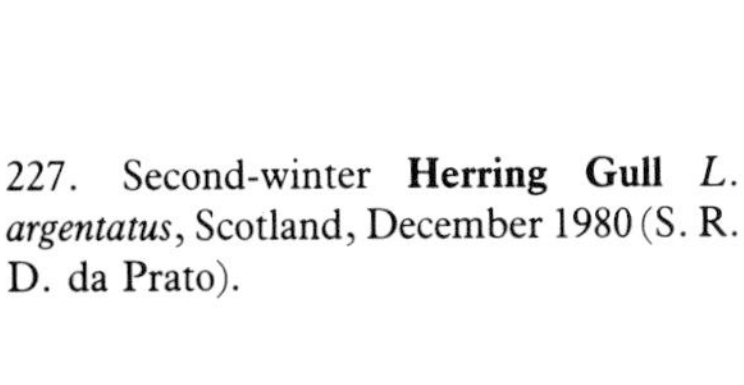

227. Second-winter **Herring Gull** *L. argentatus*, Scotland, December 1980 (S. R. D. da Prato).

228. Second-winter **Herring Gull** *L. argentatus*, England, March 1966 (Richard Vaughan).

229. Second-summer **Herring Gull** *L. argentatus*, Wales, April 1977 (R. J. Chandler).

230. Second-summer **Herring Gull** *L. argentatus*, England, May 1983 (Paul Doherty).

231. Second-summer **Herring Gull** *L. argentatus*, Wales, April 1979 (R. J. Chandler).

232. **Herring Gull** *L. argentatus* moulting from second-summer to third-winter, England, June 1981 (Peter M. Harris).

233. Third-winter **Herring Gull** *L. argentatus*, Scotland, April 1983 (Paul Doherty).

234. Third-winter **Herring Gull** *L. argentatus*, England, January 1979 (R. J. Chandler).

235. Third-summer **Herring Gull** *L. argentatus*, England, June 1983 (E. J. Mackrill).

236. Third-summer **Herring Gull** *L. argentatus*, Wales, April 1979 (R. J. Chandler).

237. **Herring Gull** *L. argentatus* moulting from third-summer to adult winter, England, June 1983 (E. J. Mackrill).

238. Third-summer type (left) and adult summer **Herring Gulls** *L. argentatus*, England, May 1976 (Pamela Harrison).

239. Adult summer **Herring Gull** *L. argentatus*, Wales, April 1979. Restricted dark markings on the greater primary coverts may be shown by individuals at any age, and are not necessarily a sign of immaturity (R. J. Chandler).

240. Adult winter **Herring Gulls** *L. argentatus*, England, December 1970 (Richard Vaughan).

241. Adult summer **Herring Gulls** *L. argentatus*, England, May 1976. Mainly with large species, it is often possible to distinguish between the sexes when a pair is standing together: here, the slightly larger general size and larger bill of the individual at the rear indicates that it is the male (Pamela Harrison).

242. Adult summer **Herring Gull** *L. argentatus*, England, June 1983 (E. J. Mackrill).

243. Adult summer and one second-summer (right) **Herring Gulls** *L. argentatus*, England, April 1968 (John Barlee).

244. Juvenile **Herring Gull** *L. a. smithsonianus*, USA, November 1983 (Tom Wurster).

245. First-winter **Herring Gull** *L. a. smithsonianus*, USA, September 1985 (R. J. Chandler).

246. First-winter **Herring Gull**, probably *L. a. argentatus*, Sweden, September 1979. Note apparently whiter head, more white on wing coverts and tertials, and pale-fringed primary-tips, indicating nominate *argentatus* (Jan Mogren).

247. Adult summer **Herring Gull** *L. a. argentatus*, Sweden, April 1980. Note darker grey upperparts and greater extent of white on outer primaries (especially all-white tip to 1st primary and obvious white divide between black and grey on 4th and 5th) unlike typical *argenteus* (Jan Mogren).

248. First-winter gull *Larus*, England, December 1983. This, and the first-winters in 249 and 250, are considered by the author to be extreme 'pale' examples of first-winter Herring Gull *L. a. argentatus*. In all three, note (compared with *argenteus*) greater extent of white among barring of upperparts, wing coverts, tertials and tail, and pale-fringed primary-tips. It is suggested that such individuals may develop into adults with reduced black on wing-tips, like that in photo 251. It is also possible that they are hybrid Herring Gull × Glaucous Gull *L. hyperboreus* (Paul Doherty).

249. First-winter gull *Larus*, England, February 1984. See caption to 248 (D. M. Turner).

250. First-winter gull *Larus*, Sweden, February 1982. See caption to 248 (Carl H. Christiansson).

251. Adult winter **Herring Gull** *L. a. argentatus*, England, January 1984. Such extreme examples, in which black on wing-tip is greatly reduced and is much less than on *argenteus*, are not infrequent. They are slightly darker grey on the upperparts than *argenteus*, eliminating the possibility that they are hybrid Herring Gull × Glaucous Gull *L. hyperboreus* (Paul Doherty).

252. First-winter **Herring Gull**, probably *L. a. heuglini*, Kenya, January 1980. Note large size compared with accompanying Lesser Black-backed Gull *L. f. fuscus*, and heavy structure, whitish head, and all-black bill recalling first-winter Great Black-backed Gull *L. marinus* (Jan Mulder).

253. Adult winter **Herring Gull**, probably *L. a. heuglini*, Kenya, November 1984. This individual's primary moult is half complete (Paul Doherty).

254. Adult **Herring Gull**, probably *L. a. taimyrensis*, Kenya, January 1980. Note paler upperparts than probable *L. a. heuglini* in photo 253 (Jan Mulder).

255. **Herring Gulls** *L. a. vegae* with three adult Black-tailed Gulls *L. crassirostris*, Japan, winter (Takao Baba).

256, 257. Adult winter **Herring Gulls** *L. a. vegae*, Japan, winter (Takao Baba).

258. Adult summer **Herring Gulls** *L. argentatus atlantis*, Madeira, March 1980 (Arnoud B. van den Berg).

259. Juvenile **Herring Gull** *L. a. michahellis*, Spain, June 1985 (Rafael Vidal Quintana).

260. First-winter **Herring Gull** *L. a. michahellis*, Greece, September 1981 (Paul Doherty).

261. First-winter **Herring Gull** *L. a. michahellis*, Spain, December 1984 (E. J. Mackrill).

262. First-summer **Herring Gull** *L. a. michahellis*, Spain, April 1980 (R. J. Chandler).

263. First-winter (left), two second-winter (right) and adult winter **Herring Gulls** *L. a. michahellis*, Spain, December 1984 (E. J. Mackrill).

264. Second-winter (right) and third-winter **Herring Gulls** *L. a. michahellis*, with adult winter Lesser Black-backed Gull *L. fuscus*, probably *intermedius* (centre), Spain, December 1984 (E. J. Mackrill).

265. Second-winter **Herring Gull** *L. a. michahellis*, Spain, December 1984 (E. J. Mackrill).

266. Third-winter **Herring Gull** *L. a. michahellis*, Spain, December 1984 (E. J. Mackrill).

267. Adult winter **Herring Gulls** *L. a. michahellis* (right) with adult winter *L. a. argenteus*, Netherlands, October 1982 (Arnoud B. van den Berg).

268. Adult winter **Herring Gull** *L. a. michahellis* (right) with adult winter Lesser Black-backed Gull *L. fuscus*, probably *graellsii*, Netherlands, October 1982 (Arnoud B. van den Berg).

269. Adult winter **Herring Gull** *L. a. michahellis*, (right) with adult winter Lesser Black-backed Gull *L. fuscus*, probably *intermedius*, Spain, December 1984 (E. J. Mackrill).

270. Adult winter **Herring Gull** *L. a. michahellis*, Spain, December 1984 (E. J. Mackrill).

271. Adult summer **Herring Gull** *L. a. michahellis*, Spain, April 1980 (R. J. Chandler).

272, 273. Juvenile **Herring Gull** *L. a. mongolicus*, Mongolia, August 1979 (Alan Kitson).

274, 275. Adult summer **Herring Gulls** *L. a. armenicus*, Israel, March 1984 (Urban Olsson).

276. Juvenile **Herring Gull** *L. argentatus* (left) and juvenile **Lesser Black-backed Gull** *L. fuscus*, Wales, August 1985 (R. J. Chandler).

277. Juvenile **Lesser Black-backed Gull** *L. fuscus*, Sweden, August 1984 (Urban Olsson).

278. Juvenile **Lesser Black-backed Gull** *L. fuscus*, England, August 1976 (Pamela Harrison).

280. First-winter **Lesser Black-backed Gull** *L. fuscus*, Denmark, October 1983 (Urban Olsson).

279. Juvenile **Lesser Black-backed Gull** *L. f. fuscus*, Sweden, September 1976 (Stellan Hedgren).

281. First-winter **Lesser Black-backed Gull** *L. fuscus*, Denmark, October 1983 (Urban Olsson).

282. Second-winter **Lesser Black-backed Gull** *L. fuscus* (*L. f. graellsii* on paleness of grey mantle) near end of moult from first-summer, England, August 1976 (Pamela Harrison).

283. Second-summer **Lesser Black-backed Gull** *L. fuscus*, West Germany, June 1981 (Peter Gloe).

284. (right) Second-summer **Lesser Black-backed Gull** *L. f. graellsii* starting moult to third-winter, England, June 1981 (Peter M. Harris).

285. Adult winter **Lesser Black-backed Gull** *L. fuscus*, probably *intermedius*, Spain, December 1984 (E. J. Mackrill).

286. Adult summer **Lesser Black-backed Gull** *L. f. graellsii*, England, May 1970 (Richard Vaughan).

287. Adult summer **Lesser Black-backed Gull** *L. f. graellsii*, Spain, March 1985 (E. J. Mackrill).

288. Adult summer **Lesser Black-backed Gull** *L. fuscus*, Norway, July 1956 (John Barlee).

289. Adult summer **Lesser Black-backed Gull** *L. f. intermedius*, Norway, June 1976 (H. B. Skjelstad).

290, 291, 292, 293. Adult summer **Lesser Black-backed Gull** *L. f. fuscus*, Sweden, June 1981 (R. J. Chandler).

294. Juvenile **Great Black-backed Gull** *L. marinus*, England, November 1983 (Paul Doherty).

295. Juvenile **Great Black-backed Gull** *L. marinus* (left) with third-winter type (right) and two first-winter Herring Gulls *L. argentatus*, England, October 1976 (Pamela Harrison).

296. Juvenile **Great Black-backed Gull** *L. marinus*, Scotland, January 1981 (S. R. D. da Prato).

297. First-winter **Great Black-backed Gull** *L. marinus*, Sweden, September 1979 (Jan Mogren).

298. First-winter **Great Black-backed Gull** *L. marinus*, England, January 1983 (Paul Doherty).

299. First-summer **Great Black-backed Gull** *L. marinus*, England, May 1979 (R. J. Chandler).

300. **Great Black-backed Gull** *L. marinus* moulting from first-summer to second-winter, West Germany, July 1982 (Peter Gloe).

301. Second-winter **Great Black-backed Gull** *L. marinus*, England, November 1983 (Paul Doherty).

302. Second-summer **Great Black-backed Gull** *L. marinus*, England, May 1980 (R. J. Chandler).

303. Second-summer **Great Black-backed Gull** *L. marinus*, West Germany, July 1982 (Peter Gloe).

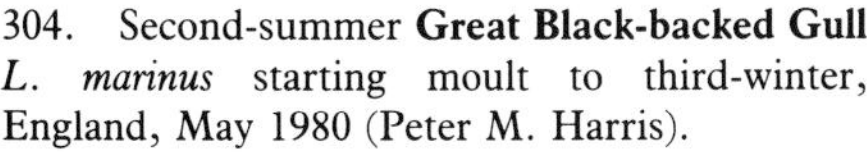

304. Second-summer **Great Black-backed Gull** *L. marinus* starting moult to third-winter, England, May 1980 (Peter M. Harris).

305. Third-summer **Great Black-backed Gull** *L. marinus* with first-winter Black-headed Gull *L. ridibundus* (left) and two adults moulting from winter to summer plumage, England, February 1969 (Richard Vaughan).

306, 307. Third-summer **Great Black-backed Gulls** *L. marinus*, England, May 1979. One has lost the innermost primary, indicating the start of moult to adult winter/fourth-winter (R. J. Chandler).

308. Adult summer **Great Black-backed Gull** *L. marinus*, Netherlands, January 1984 (Arnoud B. van den Berg).

309. Adult summer **Great Black-backed Gulls** *L. marinus* with first-summer Herring Gull *L. argentatus*, England, May 1976 (Pamela Harrison).

310. Adult **Great Black-backed Gull** *L. marinus* at start of complete moult from summer to winter plumage, Sweden, June 1980 (Jan Mogren).

311. Adult **Great Black-backed Gull** *L. marinus* moulting from summer to winter plumage, England, August 1977 (R. J. Chandler).

312. Juvenile **Great Black-headed Gull** *L. ichthyaetus*, Mongolia, August 1979 (Alan Kitson).

313. First-winter **Great Black-headed Gull** *L. ichthyaetus*, Kenya, January 1984 (Jan Mulder).

314, 315. First-winter **Great Black-headed Gulls** *L. ichthyaetus*, Israel, March 1984 (Urban Olsson).

316. First-summer **Great Black-headed Gull** *L. ichthyaetus* starting moult to second-winter, USSR, May 1978 (E. N. Panov).

317. First-summer **Great Black-headed Gull** *L. ichthyaetus*, USSR, April 1974 (V. A. Zubakin).

318, 319. Second-winter **Great Black-headed Gull** *L. ichthyaetus* near end of moult from first-summer, captive, National Zoological Gardens, Abu Dhabi, December 1976 (Jeffery Boswall).

320. Second-winter **Great Black-headed Gull** *L. ichthyaetus*, India, March 1978 (T. Shiota).

321. Second-winter **Great Black-headed Gull** *L. ichthyaetus*, Kenya, January 1984 (Jan Mulder).

322, 323. Third-summer **Great Black-headed Gulls** *L. ichthyaetus*, Mongolia, May 1977 (Alan Kitson).

324. Adult summer **Great Black-headed Gulls** *L. ichthyaetus*, USSR, May 1974 (V. A. Zubakin).

325. Adult summer **Great Black-headed Gull** *L. ichthyaetus*, USSR, May 1974 (V. A. Zubakin).

326. Adult summer **Great Black-headed Gulls** *L. ichthyaetus*, USSR, May 1978 (E. N. Panov).

327. Adult summer **Great Black-headed Gulls** *L. ichthyaetus*, USSR, May (E. A. Bragin).

328. **Little Gull** *L. minutus* starting moult from juvenile to first-winter, England, September 1970 (Richard Vaughan).

329, 330, 331. **Little Gulls** *L. minutus* moulting from juvenile to first-winter, Denmark, October 1983 (Urban Olsson).

332. First-summer **Little Gull** *L. minutus*, England, July 1983 (Paul Doherty).

333. **Little Gull** *L. minutus* moulting from first-summer to second-winter, England, July 1983 (Paul Doherty).

334. **Little Gull** *L. minutus* moulting from first-summer to second-winter, England, September 1980 (Philip Perry).

335. **Little Gull** *L. minutus* near end of moult from first-summer to second-winter (note remaining black-tipped, first-year tail feather, and that not all second-years have obvious black on the wing-tip), England, September 1970 (Richard Vaughan).

336. Second-winter **Little Gull** *L. minutus*, England, September 1980 (Philip Perry).

337. Second-winter **Little Gull** *L. minutus*, West Germany, August 1979. Few second-years have such obvious dark marks on the tertials (Peter Gloe).

338. **Little Gull** *L. minutus*, England, April 1982. The whiteness of the underwing coverts and lack of extensive black on the head indicate second-winter or -summer plumage, despite lack of black markings on outer primaries (Peter M. Harris).

339. **Little Gull** *L. minutus* moulting from second-winter to second-summer, West Germany, May 1980 (Peter Gloe).

340. Second-summer **Little Gull** *L. minutus*, England, July 1983 (Paul Doherty).

341. Second-summer **Little Gull** *L. minutus*, West Germany, May 1979 (Peter Gloe).

342. Second-summer **Little Gull** *L. minutus*, Poland, June 1980 (J. De Ridder).

343. Adult summer **Little Gull** *L. minutus*, Denmark, May 1958 (J. B. & S. Bottomley).

344. Adult summer **Little Gull** *L. minutus*, Poland, June 1980 (J. De Ridder).

345. First-winter **Ross's Gull** *R. rosea*, Japan, January 1974 (S. Mori).

346. First-winter **Ross's Gull** *R. rosea*, Republic of Ireland, February 1985 (J. Wilson).

347. First-summer **Ross's Gull** *R. rosea*, England, July 1974 (J. B. & S. Bottomley).

348. **Ross's Gull** *R. rosea*, Sweden, May 1981. Lack of neck ring suggests that this may be second-summer (Urban Olsson).

349. Adult winter **Ross's Gull** *R. rosea*, Scotland, January 1975 (Dennis Coutts).

350. Adult summer **Ross's Gull** *R. rosea*, USSR, June 1978 (V. A. Zubakin).

352. Adult summer **Ross's Gull** *R. rosea*, USSR, June 1972 (P. Tomkovitch).

351. Adult summer **Ross's Gull** *R. rosea*, USSR, July 1971 (A. A. Kistchinski).

353. Adult summer **Ross's Gull** *R. rosea*, USSR, summer (Dr A. J. Kondratiev).

354. Adult summer **Ross's Gull** *R. rosea*, England, May 1984 (Steve Young).

355. Adult winter **Ross's Gull** *R. rosea*, England February 1983 (Phil Vines).

356, 357, 358. Juvenile **Sabine's Gull** *L. sabini*, Sweden, October 1969 (Bent Bengtsson).

359. First-winter **Sabine's Gull** *L. sabini*, Ivory Coast, February 1983 (E. J. Mackrill).

360. First-winter **Sabine's Gull** *L. sabini* moulting to first-summer, El Salvador, March 1980 (Piet Meeth).

361. **Sabine's Gull** *L. sabini* moulting from first-winter to first-summer, Australia, March 1982 (G. R. Shannon).

362, 363. First-summer **Sabine's Gull** *L. sabini*, Denmark, August 1982 (Knud Pederson).

364, 365. First-summer **Sabine's Gull** *L. sabini*, England, September 1974 (Keith Atkin).

366. Adult winter **Sabine's Gull** *L. sabini*, South Africa, February 1978 (J. C. Sinclair).

367. Adult **Sabine's Gull** *L. sabini* moulting from winter to summer plumage, El Salvador, March 1980 (Piet Meeth).

368. Adult **Sabine's Gull** *L. sabini* moulting from winter to summer plumage, South Africa, February 1979 (J. C. Sinclair).

369, 370. Adult summer **Sabine's Gulls** *L. sabini*, Canada, June 1976 (Brian Hawkes).

371. Adult summer **Sabine's Gull** *L. sabini*, Canada, June 1985 (H. Darrow).

372. Juvenile **Kittiwake** *R. tridactyla*, England, August 1976 (Keith Atkin).

373. Juvenile **Kittiwake** *R. tridactyla*, Norway, August 1975 (Sverker Hahn).

374. Juvenile **Kittiwake** *R. tridactyla*, Wales, August 1979 (R. J. Chandler).

375. First-winter **Kittiwake** *R. tridactyla*, Scotland, February 1981 (S. R. D. da Prato).

376. First-winter **Kittiwake** *R. tridactyla*, England, January 1983 (Paul Doherty).

377. First-winter **Kittiwake** *R. tridactyla*, Spain, December 1984 (E. J. Mackrill).

378. First-summer **Kittiwake** *R. tridactyla*, England, May 1980 (R. J. Chandler).

379, 380. First-summer **Kittiwake** *R. tridactyla*, England, June 1981 (Peter M. Harris).

381. First-summer **Kittiwake** *R. tridactyla*, England, May 1979. The extreme wear and fading of some first-summer individuals is well shown. (R. J. Chandler).

382. Another much worn and faded first-summer **Kittiwake** *R. tridactyla*, England, June 1985 (Steve Young).

383. **Kittiwake** *R. tridactyla* moulting from first-summer to second-winter, England, June 1983 (E. J. Mackrill).

384. Second-winter **Kittiwake** *R. tridactyla*, Scotland, January 1978 (Donald A. Smith).

386. Second-winter **Kittiwake** *R. tridactyla*, England, March 1984 (Steve Young).

385. Second-summer **Kittiwake** *R. tridactyla*, England, May 1980 (R. J. Chandler).

387. Adult winter **Kittiwake** *R. tridactyla*, Denmark, October 1983 (Urban Olsson).

388. Adult winter **Kittiwake** *R. tridactyla*, mid-Atlantic, winter 1969 (E. L. Marchant).

389. Adult summer **Kittiwake** *R. tridactyla*, England, May 1976 (Pamela Harrison).

390. Adult summer **Kittiwake** *R. tridactyla*, England, May 1979 (R. J. Chandler).

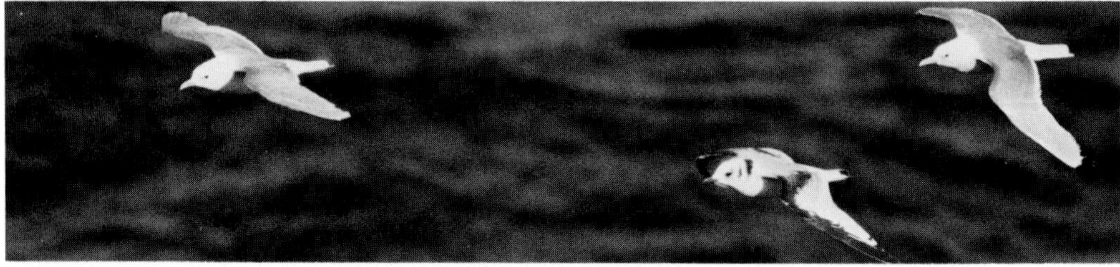

391. Two adult and one juvenile **Kittiwakes** *R. tridactyla*, Scotland, August 1984 (R. J. Chandler).

392, 393. First-winter **Ivory Gull** *P. eburnea*, Northern Ireland, December 1978 (A. McGeehan).

394. First-winter **Ivory Gull** *P. eburnea*, England, December 1979 (S. R. D. da Prato).

395, 396. First-winter **Ivory Gull** *P. eburnea*, England, January 1980 (Jeff Pick).

397. First-summer **Ivory Gull** *P. eburnea*, Sweden, April 1971 (Stellan Hedgren).

398. Adult winter **Ivory Gull** *P. eburnea*, Scotland, December 1980 (Bobby Tulloch).

399. First-winter **Glaucous Gull** *L. hyperboreus*, England, January 1978 (Jeff Pick).

400. First-winter **Glaucous Gull** *L. hyperboreus*, England, February 1984 (Paul Doherty).

401. First-winter **Glaucous Gull** *L. hyperboreus*, Republic of Ireland, December 1980 (A. McGeehan).

402. First-winter **Glaucous Gull** *L. hyperboreus*, Finland, January 1977 (J. Haapala).

403. First-winter **Glaucous Gull** *L. hyperboreus*, Denmark, March 1984 (Urban Olsson).

404. First-summer **Glaucous Gull** *L. hyperboreus*, England, February 1972 (J. B. & S. Bottomley).

405. First-summer **Glaucous Gull** *L. hyperboreus*, with worn and faded wings and tail typical of this age, England, May 1980 (R. J. Chandler).

406. **Glaucous Gull** *L. hyperboreus* moulting from first-summer to second-winter, Scotland, July 1976 (Donald A. Smith).

407. Second-winter **Glaucous Gull** *L. hyperboreus*, England, March 1982 (Paul Doherty).

408. Second-winter **Glaucous Gull** *L. hyperboreus*, England, February 1982 (Paul Doherty).

409, 410. Third-winter **Glaucous Gull** *L. hyperboreus*, England, March 1983 (Paul Doherty).

411. Fourth-winter **Glaucous Gull** *L. hyperboreus*, England, February 1984 (Paul Doherty).

412. Fourth-winter **Glaucous Gull** *L. hyperboreus*, England, November 1983 (Paul Doherty).

413. Second-summer (left) and first-summer **Glaucous Gulls** *L. hyperboreus*, Iceland, June 1979 (R. N. Hobbs).

414 (and 415). **Glaucous Gull** *L. hyperboreus* starting moult from second-summer to third-winter, Norway, April 1976 (H. B. Skjelstad).

415 (and 414). **Glaucous Gull** *L. hyperboreus* starting moult from second-summer to third-winter, Norway, April 1976 (H. B. Skjelstad).

416, 417. Third-winter **Glaucous Gull** *L. hyperboreus* (the same individual as in Photos 414 and 415), Norway, October 1976 (H. B. Skjelstad).

418. Third-summer **Glaucous Gull** *L. hyperboreus*, Iceland, June 1974 (Jeffery Boswall).

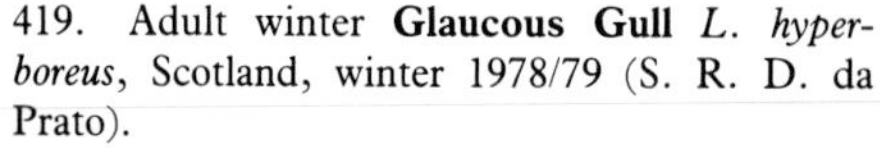

419. Adult winter **Glaucous Gull** *L. hyperboreus*, Scotland, winter 1978/79 (S. R. D. da Prato).

420. **Glaucous Gull** *L. hyperboreus*, probably fourth-summer (patchiness of grey upperparts and wing-coverts indicates that this individual is not fully mature), England March 1974 (J. B. & S. Bottomley).

421. Adult summer **Glaucous Gull** *L. hyperboreus*, Iceland, June 1979 (R. N. Hobbs).

422. Adult winter **Glaucous Gull** *L. hyperboreus*, England, winter (P. J. Greenhalf).

423. First-winter **Iceland Gull** *L. glaucoides*, Scotland, January 1981 (S. R. D. da Prato).

424. (centre) First-winter **Iceland Gull** *L. glaucoides*, England, January 1983 (Paul Doherty).

425. (bottom) First-winter **Iceland Gull** *L. glaucoides*, Denmark, March 1984. An exceptionally coarsely-marked individual (Urban Olsson).

427. First-winter **Iceland Gull** *L. glaucoides*, Netherlands, January 1984 (Arnoud B. van den Berg).

426. First-winter **Iceland Gull** *L. glaucoides*, England, January 1983 (Paul Doherty).

428. First-winter **Iceland Gull** *L. glaucoides*, Scotland, April 1983 (Paul Doherty).

429. **Iceland Gull** *L. glaucoides* moulting from first-summer to second-winter, England, September 1974. This individual's moult seems exceptionally late (resulting in extremely worn and faded tail feathers, primaries, greater coverts and lower scapulars), perhaps the result of some physical abnormality. (J. B. & S. Bottomley).

430, 431, 432, 433. Second-winter **Iceland Gull** *L. glaucoides* Denmark, January to April 1983 (Knud Pedersen).

434. **Third summer Iceland Gull** *L. glaucoides*, Netherlands, February 1981. The extensive clear grey on the upperparts and lesser and median coverts, and the uniform (rather than barred) pale brown areas on the otherwise whitish wings and tail indicate third-year plumage. (Dirk Moerbeek).

435. **Iceland Gull** *L. glaucoides*—details as Photo 434 (J. De Ridder).

436. **Iceland Gull** *L. glaucoides*—details as Photo 434 (Edward van IJzendoorn).

437. Adult summer **Iceland Gull** *L. glaucoides*, Scotland, March 1977 (S. R. D. & S. da Prato).

438. Adult summer **Iceland Gull** *L. glaucoides*, Denmark, March 1983 (Erik Christopherson).

439. Adult winter **Kumlien's Iceland Gull** *L. g. kumlieni*, Canada, January 1983 (Stuart Tingley).

440, 441. Juvenile **Sooty Gulls** *L. hemprichii*, Kenya, January 1977 (J. F. Reynolds).

442. Three first-winter (right) and one adult or second-winter (left) **Sooty Gulls** *L. hemprichii*, Kenya, winter 1977 (P. L. Britton).

443. First-winter (right) and second-winter **Sooty Gulls** *L. hemprichii*, Kenya, January 1978 (Norman van Swelm).

444, 445. **Sooty Gulls** *L. hemprichii*, moulting from first-summer to second-winter (note remaining, faded, first-year wing-coverts and pointed outer primaries), Yemen, April 1979 (R. F. Porter).

446. **Sooty Gull** *L. hemprichii* near end of moult from first-summer to second-winter, Yemen, April 1979 (R. F. Porter).

447. Second-year (left) and adult moulting from summer to winter **Sooty Gulls** *L. hemprichii*, Yemen, April 1979 (R. F. Porter).

448. Second-year **Sooty Gull** *L. hemprichii* (note trace of age-diagnostic partial tail-band), Oman, October 1976 (M. D. Gallagher).

449. Second-summer **Sooty Gull** *L. hemprichii*, Oman, July 1977 (M. D. Gallagher).

450. Adult **Sooty Gull** *L. hemprichii* near end of moult from summer to winter plumage, Kenya, January 1978 (Norman van Swelm).

451. Adult summer **Sooty Gulls** *L. hemprichii*, Oman, July 1977 (M. D. Gallagher).

452. Adult **Sooty Gull** *L. hemprichii*, Oman, October 1976 (M. D. Gallagher).

453. Adult summer **Sooty Gull** *L. hemprichii*, south Yemen, July 1985 (Arnoud B. van den Berg).

454. Two first-summer (centre) and adult summer **White-eyed Gulls** *L. leucophthalmus*, Egypt, March 1980 (Jan Visser).

455. **White-eyed Gull** *L. leucophthalmus* moulting from first-summer to second-winter, Egypt, September 1980 (Wim C. Mullié).

456, 457. **White-eyed Gull** *L. leucophthalmus* moulting from first-summer to second-winter, Egypt, July 1985 (Arnoud B. van den Berg).

459. Second-summer **White-eyed Gull** *L. leucophthalmus*, Egypt, June 1984 (Arnoud B. van den Berg).

458. Second-summer **White-eyed Gull** *L. leucophthalmus*, Yemen, April 1980. The bill on this individual is wholly blackish, and the greater coverts and coverts of outer wing brownish. The broad, blackish secondary bar, and relatively narrow white trailing edge and small white tips on inner primaries indicate second-year rather than fully adult plumage (compare Photo 464) (S. C. Madge).

460. Three second-summer or adult summer **White-eyed Gulls** *L. leucophthalmus* moulting to winter plumage, and two Sooty Gulls *L. hemprichii* (foreground and right), Yemen, April 1979 (R. F. Porter).

461. Adult summer **White-eyed Gull** *L. leucophthalmus* (left) and two adult summer Sooty Gulls *L. hemprichii*, Yemen, April 1979 (R. F. Porter).

462. Adult summer **White-eyed Gull** *L. leucophthalmus*, Egypt, June 1984 (Arnoud B. van den Berg).

463, 464. Adult summer **White-eyed Gulls** *L. leucophthalmus*, Israel (now Egypt), April 1980 (S. D. G. Cook).

465. Adult summer **White-eyed Gull** *L. leucophthalmus*, Egypt, July 1985 (Arnoud B. van den Berg).

466. Juvenile **Heermann's Gull** *L. heermanni*, USA, September 1983 (Richard E. Webster).

467. First-winter **Heermann's Gull** *L. heermanni*, USA, January 1980 (Richard E. Webster).

468. First-winter (left) and adult winter **Heermann's Gulls** *L. heermanni*, USA, March 1982 (Arnoud B. van den Berg).

469. Second-winter **Heermann's Gull** *L. heermanni*, USA, September 1984 (R. J. Chandler).

470. Second-winter **Heermann's Gull** *L. heermanni*, USA, September 1984 (Richard E. Webster).

471. Second-winter **Heermann's Gull** *L. heermanni*, USA, August 1982 (Richard E. Webster).

472. Second-winter (right) and adult winter **Heermann's Gulls** *L. heermanni*, USA, September 1984 (R. J. Chandler).

473. Adult winter **Heermann's Gull** *L. heermanni*, USA, September 1984 (R. J. Chandler).

474. Adult **Heermann's Gull** *L. heermanni* near end of complete moult to winter plumage, USA, September 1984 (Richard E. Webster).

475. Adult summer **Heermann's Gull** *L. heermanni*, USA, February 1984 (Richard E. Webster).

476. First-winter **California Gull** *L. californicus*, USA, January 1981 (Richard E. Webster).

477, 478. First-winter **California Gull** *L. californicus*, USA, December 1984 (Louis R. Bevier).

479. First-summer **California Gull** *L. californicus*, USA, March 1985 (Richard E. Webster).

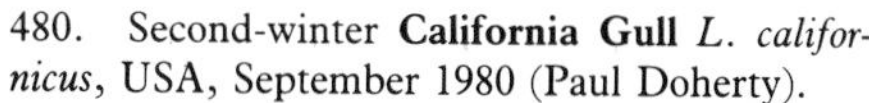

480. Second-winter **California Gull** *L. californicus*, USA, September 1980 (Paul Doherty).

481. Second-winter (right) and adult summer **California Gull** *L. californicus*, USA, March 1982 (Arnoud B. van den Berg).

482. Second-winter **California Gull** *L. californicus*, USA, September 1984 (R. J. Chandler).

483. Third-winter **California Gull** *L. californicus*, USA, March 1982 (Arnoud B. van den Berg).

484. Adult winter **California Gull** *L. californicus* near end of complete moult (outer primaries not yet fully grown), USA, September 1984 (R. J. Chandler).

485. Adult winter **California Gull** *L. californicus*, USA, January 1983 (Arnoud B. van den Berg).

486. Adult winter **California Gull** *L. californicus*, USA, December 1982 (Richard E. Webster).

487. Adult summer **California Gull** *L. californicus*, USA, February 1982 (Richard E. Webster).

488, 489. First-winter **Thayer's Gull** *L. thayeri*, USA, November 1983 (Tom Wurster).

490. First-winter **Thayer's Gull** *L. thayeri*, USA, February 1984 (Richard E. Webster).

491, 492. First-winter **Thayer's Gull** *L. thayeri*, USA, February 1977 (Alan Brady).

493. Adult summer **Thayer's Gull** *L. thayeri* (front) with Herring Gulls *L. argentatus*, Canada, May 1985 (Phil Ranson).

494. Adult summer **Thayer's Gull** *L. thayeri*, Canada, July 1983 (Dustin Huntington).

495. **Slaty-backed Gull** *L. schistisagus* moulting from juvenile to first-winter, Japan, November 1984 (Urban Olsson).

496, 497. Juvenile **Slaty-backed Gull** *L. schistisagus*, Japan, November 1984 (Urban Olsson).

498, 499. First-winter **Slaty-backed Gull** *L. schistisagus*, Japan, November 1984 (Urban Olsson).

500. First-summer **Slaty-backed Gull** *L. schistisagus*, USA, May 1980 (R. H. Day).

501, 502, 503. Second-winter **Slaty-backed Gull** *L. schistisagus*, Japan, November 1984 (Urban Olsson).

504. Second-summer **Slaty-backed Gull** *L. schistisagus*, USA, May 1980 (R. H. Day).

505, 506. Third-winter **Slaty-backed Gulls** *L. schistisagus*, Japan, November 1984 (Urban Olsson).

507, 508. Adult winter **Slaty-backed Gulls** *L. schistisagus*, Japan, November 1984 (Urban Olsson).

509, 510. Adult winter **Slaty-backed Gulls** *L. schistisagus*, Japan, November 1984. Individual viewed from below is nearing end of complete moult, with two outer primaries not yet fully grown (Urban Olsson).

511, 512, 513. Juvenile **Yellow-footed Gulls** *L. livens*, Mexico, August 1984 (Richard E. Webster).

514. Juvenile **Yellow-footed Gull** *L. livens*, USA, July 1982 (Richard E. Webster).

515. First-summer **Yellow-footed Gull** *L. livens*, USA, March 1984 (Richard E. Webster).

516. **Yellow-footed Gull** *L. livens* at start of complete moult from first-summer to second-winter, Mexico, April 1984 (Richard E. Webster).

517. **Yellow-footed Gull** *L. livens* near end of complete moult from first-summer to second-winter (outer two primaries, innermost secondaries, and outer tail feathers not yet fully grown), Mexico, August 1984 (Richard E. Webster).

518. Second-winter **Yellow-footed Gull** *L. livens*, USA, December 1982 (Richard E. Webster).

519. Second-summer **Yellow-footed Gull** *L. livens*, Mexico, December 1983 (Richard E. Webster).

520. Adult summer **Yellow-footed Gull** *L. livens*, Mexico, December 1983 (Richard E. Webster).

521, 522. Juvenile **Western Gulls** *L. occidentalis*, USA, September 1984 (R. J. Chandler).

523. First-winter **Western Gull** *L. occidentalis*, USA, January 1980 (Richard E. Webster).

524. First-winter **Western Gull** *L. occidentalis*, USA, December 1984 (Louis R. Bevier).

525. First-winter **Western Gull** *L. occidentalis*, USA, October 1982 (Richard E. Webster).

526. Second-winter **Western Gull** *L. occidentalis*, USA, January 1980 (Richard E. Webster).

527. Second-winter **Western Gull** *L. occidentalis*, USA, January 1984 (Richard E. Webster).

528. Second-winter **Western Gull** *L. occidentalis*, USA, January 1983 (Killian Mullarney).

529. Second-summer **Western Gull** *L. occidentalis*, USA, March 1982 (Arnoud B. van den Berg).

530. Third-winter **Western Gull** *L. occidentalis*, USA, January 1984 (Richard E. Webster).

531. Adult **Western Gull** *L. occidentalis*, USA, January 1983 (Arnoud B. van den Berg).

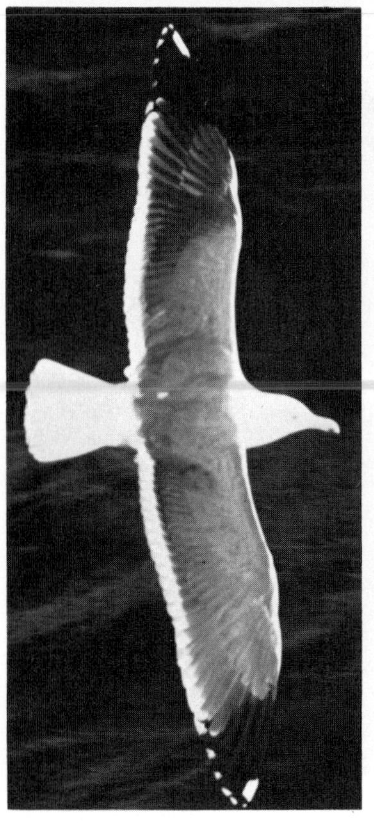

532. Adult **Western Gull** *L. occidentalis*, USA, January 1984 (Richard E. Webster).

533. Adult **Western Gull** *L. occidentalis*, USA, July 1981 (Richard E. Webster).

534, 535, 536. First-winter **Glaucous-winged Gulls** *L. glaucescens*, Japan, November 1984 (Urban Olsson).

537. Second-winter **Glaucous-winged Gull** *L. glaucescens*, Japan, November 1984 (Urban Olsson).

538. Third-winter **Glaucous-winged Gull** *L. glaucescens*, Japan, November 1984 (Urban Olsson).

539. Adult winter **Glaucous-winged Gull** *L. glaucescens*, Japan, November 1984 (Urban Olsson).

540. Adult **Glaucous-winged Gull** *L. glaucescens* moulting from summer to winter plumage, USA, September 1984 (R. J. Chandler).

541. Adult summer **Glaucous-winged Gull** *L. glaucescens*, USA, July 1979 (R. H. Day).

542. Adult summer **Red-legged Kittiwake** *R. brevirostris*, USA, July 1981 (R. H. Day).

543, 544. Adult summer **Red-legged Kittiwakes** *R. brevirostris*, USA, August 1980 (R. H. Day).